GEORGE III
AND THE HISTORIANS

GEORGE III AND THE HISTORIANS

By

HERBERT BUTTERFIELD

*Master of Peterhouse and
Professor of Modern History in the
University of Cambridge*

COLLINS
ST JAMES'S PLACE, LONDON
1957

CONTENTS

5

CONTENTS

PREFACE

THE REFLECTIONS and enquiries which, at intervals, have been more or less consciously directed to the production of the present work, have been stimulated by two problems and moved by two purposes. In the first place, our generation has come into a state of considerable confusion in regard to the reign of George III, where the Whig historians at one time and the Namier school at another time have been particularly importunate in their demands upon us. The history of England at this period has been distorted, now by partisanship, now by theories concerning the nature of historical scholarship or scientific method. And it would seem that the massiveness of the evidence, the complication of the issues and the disorder in the literature itself, have made many readers and students only too afraid to come to their own conclusions about the narrative or the problems involved. I wonder whether it is possible to take both the historical student and the general reader a little farther than usual into the workshop of the historian, examining (so far as the reign of George III is concerned) the sources of myths and errors, the kind of inferences that are made from the evidence, and the various forms of thinking which insert themselves into the procedures of the historian—not excluding those considerations and assumptions of which the practitioners of the craft are too often perhaps unconscious. Only in this way can we hope to recover our bearings in this historical field, and prevent ourselves from being the slaves of mere authority—the slaves, sometimes, of an authority that we do not understand.

Secondly, in spite of all the things we say about the victory of the scientific method and the superiority of the twentieth century over its predecessors, it is possible that in these days the reading of history has become less critical than it once was, the reviewing of books less scientific, and the faith in accepted "authorities" more unthinking. The existence of a wider reading-public and the development of a more popular taste for history hold the promise of unspeakable good, but these things have not been quite without their dangers. The fact that historians nowadays confine themselves more definitely to their restricted field means that fewer people can assess the value of work in regions not their own, so that it is only perhaps from a narrower area that effective criticism can usually emerge. The tendency to look for a historian who will serve as an "authority" is one which seems to have increased during my lifetime, though history is a realm in which trust is the enemy of truth, and all critical standards are in peril if one is required to believe Ranke because Ranke is a reliable man. I am not sure that the professionalising of history has not resulted in the unconscious development of authoritarian prejudices among the professionals themselves; and it could happen that by 1984, if readers are not their own critics, a whole field of study might become the monopoly of a group and a party, all reviewing one another and standing shoulder to shoulder in order to stifle the discrepant idea, the new intellectual system, or the warning voice of the sceptic. There have been times when the presentation of masses of footnotes would seem to have been sufficient to delude the critic in respect of the genuinely scientific character of a piece of work. And even today there has come to be such an inclination to take notice only of the last word that has been said about a given subject that the last word may be a return to something which was said long ago, and men may still remain unaware of the fact.

In the present volume, therefore, I have attempted three things which in a sense have always been separate in my mind, but which for some time now have come to be so closely connected that they blend into a single theme. First of all I have tried to beat the drum for the awakening of criticism; because, though we all have a formal knowledge of the necessity for criticism, it seems to be the case that we easily fall into routine. Alternatively, there will be blind spots in our thinking, dead patches in our consciousness, regions of insensitivity in which our critical faculties seem to suffer suspension. Some people think that they are being critical when they are merely revolting against an author's general views, his political partisanship, for example, though in reality the critical endeavour has to penetrate into the structure of the historical narrative itself. Granted that we all possessed a formal knowledge of the critical attitude which is required for the handling of historical evidence, it would always remain true that knowledge in itself is never enough to save us from sin. We can learn some things in a way from books, while holding the knowledge as external, as part of our luggage—never really bringing the matter home to ourselves. Perhaps it is useful that somebody should always be sounding the alarm-bell, to awaken us out of mere habit, and to jolt us out of that state of what I should call "suspended criticism" into which it is easy for any of us to lapse.

As a student of the history of historiography, I have long been interested not merely in the kaleidoscope of changing views on the subject of George III, but also in the causes of the changes, and, indeed, in the whole curve of development which scholarship has taken. I have tried to discover now the man responsible for the initiation of a new idea or attitude, now the location of the source of a myth or an error, now the forces and factors which helped to determine the next turn that would be given to the study of George III. When our ideas on some large historical theme are in a state of disorder we may find it useful to make ourselves

9

acquainted with the history of the historiography of that particular subject. I have dealt with this up to the time of the emergence
of the Namier school, that is to say, up to the period after the
First World War.

When the books of Professor Namier first appeared, their importance was recognised but they did not pass without criticism.
On the one hand it was argued at times that some of their more
general results were less novel than they were sometimes claimed
to be, while on the other hand it was asserted that in some of their
novel aspects they had not in fact established a convincing case.
It can always be said that the apostles of older ideas tend to put up
a blind and tough resistance to the emergence of the new; but
it can also be said that the passage of a generation is an effective
factor in the case, and the new generation may grow up in the
new system without ever quite examining the reasons for the
change. After the period of initial reviewing has passed it is not
always the case that methodical criticism is brought to bear on
a new system of ideas, and though Professor Toynbee's work has
been seriously examined in many countries, I am not clear that
the work of the Namier school has gone through such an examination. That work is so imposing and important that it certainly merits a more serious and continuous discussion than is
possible for a reviewer at the moment when a new book appears.
And the Namier school is a formidable one, because, apart from
the massiveness of its researches, it represents the most powerfully
organised squadron in our historical world at the present time,
the disciples relaying the ideas of the master with closer fidelity
than I remember to have been the case in any other branch of
historical study since it became a serious form of scholarship.
Since it is possible for a school to become so formidable an orthodoxy as to check the free play of criticism, and since it is not
impossible for massive researches to be accompanied by mistaken
thinking or mistaken ideas about the nature of history, I have tried

to provide some materials for the establishment of a critical approach, and have set out my own reservations, while attempting at the same time to show where the school stands in the history of scholarship. What I wish most of all to secure is that, on certain topics, we should at least not close our minds too soon.

Peterhouse, Cambridge   *H. Butterfield*
    6 August 1957

BOOK ONE
THE HISTORIAN AND HIS EVIDENCE

THE HISTORIAN AND HIS EVIDENCE

It is sometimes asserted by apologists that those who study history are trained to be on guard against the polemical misuse of evidence. Even when they have forgotten all the curriculum history they ever learned, it is supposed that such students will be more discriminating readers of newspapers, less gullible victims of propaganda, than other people. It is always possible, however, that the reading of history, especially when conducted for examination-purposes—that is to say when the work of memorising or the process of mere recapitulation has any part in the affair—will have the effect of making students more the slaves of the printed word than they were before. And I have known students who, far from cherishing their intellectual independence, have been anxious to learn who their examiner was going to be, so that they could be sure of the kind of answer it would be profitable for them to produce. Some of the worst examples of teaching tyranny I have ever known have occurred not in elementary work but in documentary studies of Special Periods or at the stage of actual research, where serious situations have occurred because a pupil refused to be enslaved to a teacher. In my own university this danger is mitigated (though it can never be entirely removed) by the rule that the teacher of a research student shall not also be the examiner.

The human mind easily slips into repose under the wing of some authority; and, for example, we bow readily before the natural scientist, whose experiments we should certainly be unable to check for ourselves. We can at least know, however, whether the supposed discoveries of the scientist do in fact help to cure a

15

disease or produce a new fabric or provide us with a more powerful explosive; while in history we have no such way of making
sure whether the established authorities are seriously misleading
us. Here, then, is a field of study in which it is particularly in-
cumbent on the reader to keep all his critical faculties awake. For
this reason it may be useful if we remind ourselves of what lies
behind any page of a modern history-book, and what mental
operations are involved in the use of sources.

It is easy for us to realise that, when he is dealing with ancient
history, the research student has to do more than the usual amount
of detective-work on every square inch of the evidence. In my
young days I remember the excitement caused by the discovery
in England of a broken Roman tile with the letters U.E.L.L.A.
scrawled across it. It was suggested that the completed word must
have been "Puella," and that a bricklayer in an idle moment had
written "my gal" on the first thing that came to hand. At first
there was an idea that Britain must have been more deeply
Romanised than many people had imagined if even a bricklayer
found it natural to do such a casual piece of writing in Latin. I
gathered, however, that the clue was insufficient to decide the
issue; for I remember hearing it put as a counter-argument that
the bricklayer might have been imported from Gaul. Let us note
in any case that history can never be written by the mere tran-
scribing of evidence; that a single piece of evidence does not
present us with its own interpretation but needs other evidence
—needs sometimes much knowledge of the general historical context—before its meaning can be elicited. The student, in fact, treats
his evidence rather in the way that a detective treats a clue.

When one hears undergraduates talk about "doing their documents"—which is a common mode of speech in universities—one
is bound to feel dubious about the kinds of procedure which some
of them seem to have in mind. In particular one seems to detect
at times the tendency to believe things because they are in the

documents, just as there is a tendency to imagine that a vast volume of selected documents provides a purified form of history —a kind not vitiated by the intervention of any particular historian. The first thing that the student has to learn when he is initiated into the technique of the professional historian is not to believe a thing merely because it is in the documents, and not for a moment to imagine that the documents are there simply to be believed.

The documents clearly showed that in Anglo-Saxon England the king would call together assemblies of the whole people. Until the end of the eighteenth century there were writers who went on arguing therefore that in the time of the Anglo-Saxons there had existed a parliament, and that not merely the representatives of the commons but actually every commoner in the country had the right to attend its meetings. It took the world a long time to learn that documents must not be interpreted too literally when they speak of "the whole people"; just as it took them a long time to learn that the "free-men" whose liberties were guaranteed in *Magna Carta* might not necessarily be exactly the class of people which the same term was used to designate in later centuries. In regard to the Middle Ages, one of the earliest principles of criticism which I remember meeting was one that was formulated in seventeenth-century England—the thesis that one must take account of the changes which take place over long periods in language, in verbal usage and even in the ordinary meaning of familiar words. In fact an extraordinary amount of historical effort has long been devoted to the recovery of the different meanings, the subtly different connotations, possessed in former times by words that are still in common use. There are men who have spent years in the study of the history of a very few words, and much of our understanding of the past—much of our interpretation of historical documents or ancient writings—may depend on our awareness and our sensitiveness in regard to this matter.

There is a further critical principle which was not entirely over-looked in seventeenth-century England; and this, too, was bound to have particular importance for the students of the Middle Ages. Many kinds of historical document can be properly interpreted only if we pay due regard to the form of the society from which they emanated and to which they have particular reference. In the history of the historiography of *Magna Carta* this point has been of very considerable significance; and we must not imagine that the ordinary modern reader of *Magna Carta* is going to understand the document properly merely by looking at the words. In many respects it would rather be true to say that we bring all the history that we know—and especially all our knowledge of English society in the early thirteenth century—in order to interpret *Magna Carta*, and only after this has been done can we extract from it the additional information that it may supply. For this reason one must not be regarded as hunting for paradox if one asserts that it is often necessary to know a great deal of history before one is equipped for the interpreting of historical documents. John Wesley, when he went to America, imagined that if the Bible could be put before the unspoiled Red Indians, they would have a direct apprehension of its meaning—they would attain a clearer version of the truth than was possible for minds that had been warped by successive generations of commentators. We must never imagine—though some people do seem to imagine—that such a procedure as this would be prudent or proper in the case of historical documents. In fact one can have brilliant historians who are far from being central in their scholarship, and who miss the target because they insist on reading only the original sources. They despise too much the achievement of the secondary authorities, and they lose important things which a long tradition of scholarship has established and which are available for their assistance.

Even in the field of modern history these principles are by no means inapplicable; and those who wish to interpret the documents of a certain age must read a great many of them, and must have a great intimacy with the age itself, if they are to avoid serious error. There is some advantage in discussing modern documents more specifically, however; for many of the points that emerge have their validity in the present-day world—they provide important maxims for students of even contemporary affairs.

First and foremost, it is important to note how precarious our history would be if it rested merely on ordinary human testimony. It is well known that, when there has been an accident in the street, those who were present will exhibit extraordinary divergencies if each is examined individually and gives his own separate account of what took place. The observers see different things, or they notice different things, or they jump to some rapid conclusion from one particular aspect of the affair that happened to catch their eye. They may be imprecise even in the way in which they call to mind the thing that they actually saw, and sometimes they will re-fabricate it unconsciously as they try to make the affair more logical for themselves. Alternatively, they will mix their observations with their afterthoughts or entangle them in their memory with images that their imagination has played upon. Often, in fact, it happens that men are really altering or manufacturing the narrative when they think that they are only trying to remember. It is dangerous even to trust a trained historian, for one of these, whom I personally knew, could not re-tell a story at the dinner-table without adding something of his own to round it off. There was another who, whenever a good story was told to him, was sure to be repeating it before the end of the day as a thing which had happened to himself. In history it is dangerous even to trust the saints, for, precisely because they are so innocent, they may easily be imposed upon, so that they fail to see how one must criticise and verify a report that one is passing on from somebody else. When we ourselves are actually involved in the episode that we are trying to reproduce, our whole narrative can easily be deflected by an additional element of unconscious wishful thinking. And sometimes it requires more than ordinary honesty—it requires a trained mind and a refined state of the intellect—to enable one to escape from aberrations like these, that is to say, from what might be called involuntary distortion. Let us be clear that all these causes of deviation and derangement can be discovered before ever one begins to raise the question of the witness who for some reason or other is deliberately dishonest.

From all this it follows that anything which is of the nature of mere reporting is liable to be full of pitfalls for the historian; and certain forms of evidence which many people seem to regard as being, so to speak, unanswerable—the testimony of eye-witnesses, for example, and the first-hand narratives of people who have participated in some important episode—constitute in fact a comparatively low grade amongst the various types of historical evidence. Personal memoirs, therefore, which so often have the further disadvantage of having been written some time after the events with which they deal, must be placed at a very low level indeed; for they are not only darkened by the further lapse of time —they are almost inevitably distorted by all the things that have happened in the interval. In the case of memoirs, we are confronted with the kind of narrative which is still more definitely the product of reconstruction in retrospect. When Lord Grey brought out his memoirs after the First World War, his account of the events of the early 1900's was written very largely in the light of what he knew to have happened later—in July 1914. Even a more dishonest memoir-writer may be more useful to the historian if we can catch him out in memoirs written before 1914—before he could have known that he might have to defend himself against the charge of having had part in the origins of the war, and before he could have known the kind of points on which future historians would particularly want to test him. For it is bound to be the rarest thing in the world to find a writer of memoirs who is not in some sense or other trying to justify himself.

I have heard it argued that memoirs are only to be relied upon where their author gives something away which he does not realise himself to be giving away. This is a useful point to have in mind when dealing with all kinds of "reporting"; and certainly we must be on the alert when the writer of memoirs is attempting to persuade us of anything. Some people have argued that memoirs are useful only when they receive corroboration from other sources; but there are pitfalls even here. The historiography of George III's reign received a considerable set-back at one period owing to the publication of sets of memoirs and correspondence which often confirmed one another because they came from men of similar party-views. In the past it was sometimes natural for the opposition evidence to appear before the internal evidence—the actual papers of the government itself—had become available for the historian. Some have said that a memoir-writer is to be trusted only when he is giving evidence against himself; but even this has turned out to be an unsafe criterion. It has occasionally happened that men have not been so wicked as they like to pretend that they have been; and even Bismarck provides some examples of this, for when he wrote his memoirs he tried to exaggerate his part in the making of Germany, or, rather, he came to delude himself concerning the degree of mastery that he had had over events—a fallacy which it is difficult to avoid when one is reconstructing one's life retrospectively. And the result was that he sometimes painted himself as more Machiavellian than he really had been—more responsible for engineering the war of 1870, for example, than we can now see to have been the case. Catherine de' Medici, after carrying out the massacre of St. Bartholomew, found the Huguenots her bitter enemies and had no choice but to throw herself into the arms of the Catholics. She found herself at the mercy of the Catholic party in fact; and in particular she had to court Philip II of Spain, to whom, for some time previously, she had been giving serious offence. In order to win such people over to her side, she now pretended to have been planning the massacre of St. Bartholomew for years—pretended that, in her flirtations with the Huguenots, she had in reality been deluding them, so that she might destroy them the more thoroughly at the finish. Her own statements on this subject—though they did not deceive the Spaniards—provided serious difficulties for the historians who studied the episode in the nineteenth century. We now know that in fact she decided on the massacre very suddenly and only be-because she found herself in a desperate situation. But modern students did not easily reconcile themselves to the fact that Catherine de' Medici was so untruthful that we must not believe her too readily even when she is giving evidence against herself.

Amongst the tests to which we can subject a man's memoirs, there is one which is apt to be very revealing, though it is often possible only at a later date. It is the comparison of the narrative which was written in retrospect with the correspondence of the same author at the time when the events were actually taking place. Results of a most interesting kind can be achieved if Horace Walpole's famous *Memoirs of the Reign of George III* are compared with the letters written by Walpole in the early years of that reign. Some of the correspondence, which was printed at an early date, was used to defend George III, while the *Memoirs* themselves became perhaps the principal basis for the hostile "Whig" inter-pretation of his reign. Walpole even wrote the first draft of the *Memoirs* from a point of view rather more friendly to the King; but the conflict against the American colonies made him the bitter enemy of George III, and he made his new attitude retrospective, projecting his hostility back into his description of the beginning of the reign. In particular he altered the innuendo of the work—the general interpretation of the motives and intentions of the King. We cannot simply say that Walpole's earliest views were the correct ones, especially as he confesses that events which took place in later years caused him to revise his ideas about the opening stages of the story. We can only say that at some points his evidence is that of a contemporary witness, while at other points it is more like the account which a later historian would produce, and in both cases the narrations will require the appropriate kind of criticism. When the *Memoirs* are compared not merely with Walpole's own letters, but with all the other correspondence—all the other evidence—for any particular period, it becomes clear that they are in fact more accurate, and indeed more fair, in one part than in another, while within a given period they will be more precise and reliable—or Walpole will be more qualified to give evidence—in one aspect of political life, and less qualified in other phases of the history. Only when a set of *Memoirs* has been related to all the other available evidence in this way, and the structure of the work laid bare (as well as the intentions and the bias of the author), can we make a scientific use of such literature, and employ it to increase our knowledge of the relevant period. And it will be clear that each set of *Memoirs* requires a separate critical apparatus, almost a separate science, for its proper comprehension. Those who deal with Lord Grey's *Twenty-Five Years*, for example, need to discover a different set of tests, a different body of rules, a different kind of sieve, a different way of construing things—they have to learn in a painfully slow way the kind of handling which will ultimately enable them to extract from the work evidence that is both new and true. And if we merely adopt the easy policy which satisfies the uncritical, dividing memoirs into "honest" and "dishonest," "reliable" and "unreliable"—which in fact generally results in the decision that the authors on "our side" need no historical criticism—we are not only making a mistake; we are putting the clock back at least a hundred years, so far as the science of the historian is concerned. Nor is it very satisfactory when, without the apparatus of scientific criticism—and sometimes without possessing as yet even the means of making the required tests—we are content to allow our knowledge of very recent history to be based largely on memoirs and memoir-material.

For a time in the nineteenth century the historical writing on the subject of George III, like the historical writing on the subject of the French Revolution, rested to a considerable degree on memoir-material, subject to the kind of deficiencies that have been described. We today would regard this as typical of a primitive stage in the development of the historiography of a given subject; and we reach a significant moment in the rise of a more scientific kind of history when memoirs cease to be merely "good" or "bad" and are endowed with an elaborate critical apparatus. We realise today that it is one thing to compile a description of a Napoleonic battle from the reports of eye-witnesses, each of whom in fact will generally have had very little idea of what was happening in the confusion. It is history of a higher grade altogether when from the French Ministry of War we recover in vast masses the actual orders given at every stage in the battle by Napoleon to his Marshals, and by the Marshals to their subordinates, and so forth. These written orders are sometimes minutely timed, and the men who received them help to complete the story that they have to tell; for these men would send back reports on their doings and whereabouts, on their execution of the orders received, and on the difficulties that they happened to be in.

In any case, an actual written order is not a report. Once the command is in our hands, it is a thing that cannot lie to us. Here is a veritable act, a feat of human volition, an actual historical event, which stands before our eyes. In this sense an instruction from the British Foreign Secretary to the British Ambassador in Vienna—since it constitutes a command—is a more unanswerable piece of evidence than the Ambassador's reply, which merely reports on the way in which the order has been carried out. If an ambassador has had an interview with the Foreign Minister of the country in which he resides, it may certainly happen that, when he writes to his home government about it, he will pretend that in the course of the conversation he has been more clever than he really was—he will report himself as having said some of the things which he would have said if he had thought of them in time. Even he, however, cannot expect to go very far in untruthfulness when he is writing to his own superiors; he cannot, for example, pretend that he has succeeded in a piece of negotiation if he has failed—he can hardly dare to make claims that might soon appear demonstrably false. He writes under conditions which make it only too likely that certain kinds of untruth will be quickly exposed. This form of document, therefore—even though it has the character of a "report"—has considerable significance for the historian. A woman will be more likely to tell her true age if she knows that her statement stands a fair chance of being checked by reference to a birth-certificate. The most extreme untruths occur when a man knows that he can lie with impunity—and this explains why we tend to be sceptical when even our friends begin to recount to us their dreams. Students a hundred years ago found that their work stood on a different footing when they were able to study the papers of a government office—papers not written with an eye to the future historian, often not expected ever to meet the eye of the outsider—the very instruments by means of which business had been carried on—papers preserved only because men of business do have to refer on occasion to the transactions of former years. If the office in question happens to be a Foreign Office, the opening of its archives means that now, at last, one can really discover how a country's foreign policy has been conducted. That is why, from the 1830's, when government archives were increasingly used, and more particularly from the 1860's when they were more unreservedly opened to the play of scholarship, there occurred a radical transformation of the basic conditions of historical study, and one chapter after another of European history was absolutely revolutionised.

It is important to note, however, that even official documents have a way of presenting pitfalls to the historian. Some men who made devastating exposures of memoirs have been open to the reproach that they used diplomatic dispatches as though these needed no historical criticism. Government offices themselves resort to ruse on occasion; and in a country in which some documents on foreign policy will have to be placed before parliament at a fairly early date, there have been times when an ostensible dispatch has been released to the public, while the real truth has been reserved for a more private form of communication. It is bound to make a difference to the actual writing of dispatches if the author of these expects that they will be produced before parliament or published to the world within a limited time. In this as in other fields it is important, furthermore, that one should not be too naïve, too literal, in one's interpretation of the documents. If one finds an Italian Foreign Minister insisting to the German Ambassador that his country means to be friendly to Germany, one has to be careful not to translate the man's utterances into a rigid formula of policy. The Italian Foreign Minister may indeed be flattering the ambassadors of all the other countries in a similar way; and perhaps he would be more likely to make protestations about his desire for friendly relations with Germany if he was on the point of doing something which he knew would give offence to that country.

It is possible to have authentic historical sources but to be using them for not quite the right purposes. In the nineteenth century, for example, the diplomatic papers, which were available before many other kinds of document, were treated as authoritative in fields in which their value in reality was only limited. In the absence of better material, historians used diplomatic dispatches for their accounts of the internal affairs of the country in which the ambassador resided. The dispatches of the Brandenburg envoy in London at one time added something to the knowledge of what went on in the English parliament in the sixteenth century. The accounts which Venetian ambassadors wrote for their government were taken as authoritative for the economic condition of this country in Tudor times. This meant that history was still being based on what was a less reliable kind of reporting; and England would be depicted as seen through the eyes of a foreign ambassador resident in London. Nowadays we should have much more appropriate material (often office-material, too) for the study of a country's internal history. But, curiously enough, when the first-class sources have been used as a basis, the diplomatic reports may still have a useful supplementary service to perform.

At first, moreover, the diplomatic archives were only partially opened; and sometimes only selections from the papers were made available to scholars. Under such circumstances as these it may happen that a flood of new materials may even carry historians further away from the truth than they were before. There was a curious and sinister intrigue against Frederick the Great of Prussia on the eve of the Seven Years' War; and the partial opening of the archives proved unfortunate, for in the new documents which were produced there was no evidence of such a thing. Those who wished to deny the existence of the conspiracy were now able to claim that their case was proved. In reality, the intrigue in question belonged to the most secret depths of the secret diplomacy of the time; and it was natural that most of the foreign offices and ambassadors received not the slightest hint of what was afoot. Diplomats had even written to their governments that all was quiet in the capital in which they resided, when in reality the most sensational things were happening almost under their very noses. When the archives were more fully opened, however, and the innermost secrets of one or two courts had been brought to light, that particular intrigue was exposed beyond any doubt, though the centre of it was not quite in the place that had been suspected.

Even when diplomatic documents were used for their proper purpose—the study of foreign policy—and even when they were available in their completeness, they were not without further pitfalls for the student. It transpired for example that if one studied the foreign policy of the age of Louis XIV or the Napoleonic era purely through the papers of the British Foreign Office, one could simply be locking oneself more and more tightly in the British Foreign Office view of Louis XIV and Napoleon. Indeed, if one were to write a history of the Bank of England purely from the records in the Bank of England itself, it is not clear how one could escape the danger of seeing many things too much from the Bank of England's point of view. It may happen that, when England and France are in dispute with one another, the French government will take some course of action which the British Foreign Office will regard as shockingly wicked. Yet if one examines the papers in the French Foreign Ministry, and if one uses great endeavour to see the point of view of that Ministry, one may realise that there was reason in the action—there was an explanation which one would never have discovered in any other way. At the end of the enquiry, therefore, the French may appear in a more creditable light than one had imagined to be possible. From this there emerges a truth which is too often overlooked at the present day: namely, that the papers of a foreign office are the crucial sources for the policy and conduct of that office itself; but they are less reliable sources for the policy of any other country's foreign office—concerning French and German policy the British archives will generally give rather what I have called "reporting". When after the First World War certain revolutionised countries, like Germany and Russia, began to publish their diplomatic papers, other countries, like France and Britain, followed suit, knowing that one's secrets and even one's sins look better as revealed in one's own archives than as seen in the documents of other countries. And it is a common trick of writers, especially of contemporary history, to take advantage of the carelessness and haste of uncritical readers—making a plentiful parade of British documents to expose German policy, but showing reticence in regard to those matters for which the British documents are really authoritative: namely the policy and the workings of the British Foreign Office itself.

It will be realised, therefore, that the historian who is concerned with Anglo-French relations in a given period, will produce too partial a story if he confines his researches to British diplomatic documents. If a British ambassador has an interview with the Foreign Minister in Paris, there may be surprising divergencies in the reports that the two men produce, for if ten thousand words have been spoken and they are abridged in a report of eight hundred words there is tremendous scope for selectivity. It is often possible, however, to combine two such reports and arrive at a story which has greater breadth than either of the separate summaries—a story which, moreover, enables us to account for the discrepancies between the individual narrations. When this kind of procedure has been followed, inch by inch, over the whole length of the period under consideration, it becomes possible to have a narrative of Anglo-French relations which quite supersedes either the British or the French point of view. The resulting narrative will in fact transcend anything which either of the foreign offices singly could have been aware of at the time.

Above all, when a Foreign Minister gives an instruction to an ambassador in a foreign capital, the document which he produces will be an authoritative record of the command that he is giving to his subordinate. Indeed, once we possess the manuscript it is an actual order that we hold in our hands; but the document may not be equally authoritative for the motives and purposes that induced the home government to issue the instruction. If the dispatch does give some record of reasons and motives these on occasion are apt to be the ostensible ones—the considerations that are to be presented to the foreign government concerned or to the outside world in general. Sometimes it has only been in a more private kind of communication—sometimes it might only be in the most intimate correspondence between a Foreign Secretary and his Prime Minister, for example—that the real aims and intentions of a diplomatic move (and therefore the real policy of the government) have been revealed. A minister who was intending to manœuvre an unfriendly power into a corner, with the object of provoking it to take the initiative in the resort to war, would not necessarily expose his *arrière-pensée* in a formal diplomatic document. And sometimes the most secret of secrets will be something which was never put on to paper at all.

One conclusion, however, is inescapable; and historical writing during the last century has repeatedly demonstrated its importance. Of all the documents which can be used for the history of foreign affairs, the ones which we call "policy-making" documents are the most momentous for the study of a country's diplomacy. Because the policy-making documents are so often more private— much less formal than the correspondence with ambassadors abroad, for example—they tend to be more elusive, and sometimes the real clue will only appear in a personal letter or a casual note. After going through all the official dispatches—following the diplomatic moves in detail and observing the conduct of an embassy day by day—it is important for the student of nineteenth-century diplomacy to consult a more intimate class of document, including the private papers of the men concerned. At the last stage of the enquiry, the real clue may lie in the more personal communications; and some scrap of paper not in the Foreign Office at all may acquire a pivotal importance, so that it affects our interpretation of all the rest of the evidence. And that is one of the reasons why the technical historian can never be content with mere selections, and can never feel that his work is done.

When Charles II of Spain died early in November 1700, leaving a will which designated the grandson of Louis XIV as his successor, England and Holland forced William III to recognise the Bourbon candidate as king, and it has always been assumed that only some further acts of wilfulness on the part of the French monarch induced the maritime powers to go to war on the issue of the Spanish Succession. It is questionable, however, whether anything which Louis XIV could have done would have prevented William III from going to war with him, especially as the Austrian Habsburgs had resolved to fight him in any case and William had it in his power to conduct an imposing propaganda campaign in England. It is interesting to note, therefore, that though parliament was initially against him, and the weight of English opinion seemed to prefer Charles II's will to the alternative—namely, the Partition Treaty—William III was confident from the first that he would be able to have his war with France. Writing to Heinsius in Holland as early as 16 November he gave away his real design, and showed that, in spite of appearances, he meant to gain his objective. "I shall draw this people along by prudent action and in gradual stages", he said, "without their realising what is happening." A few words of self-revelation in this style have an effect on our interpretation of the entry of England into the Spanish Succession War, and at least must awaken a peculiar kind of alertness in us, as we study the rest of the evidence.

In July 1807 the Tsar Alexander of Russia met, on a raft at Tilsit, the Emperor Napoleon, who had just defeated his troops at Friedland. From that moment we find that the sentimentalist Tsar deserted his recent allies—England in particular—and joined hands with the power that had been his enemy. It was supposed that, like many other people, he had fallen a victim to the charm and the seductive projects of Napoleon. He became the object of bitter reproaches because he deserted the Prussians, who had been his particular protégés, and who now had to suffer the consequences of their own defeat at Jena in the previous October as well as the joint defeat at Friedland. It is only from one or two small policy-making documents that we learn, firstly, how it was Alexander himself who went to the meeting at Tilsit in the hope of seducing Napoleon into an alliance; and, secondly, how it had been the Prussians who had initiated the policy of deserting England and had inspired Alexander with the project that led to their own discomfiture.

Great interest was aroused in this country some years ago by an episode which perhaps will appropriately illustrate the way in which the historian has to pursue his evidence and the way in which a point narrated in half a sentence or relegated to a footnote may have behind it a tremendous amount of detective-work. The problem arose out of that famous occasion when the German Chancellor was talking to the British Ambassador at the outbreak of the war of 1914, and spoke of England's guarantee of Belgian neutrality as though a great deal of fuss was being made about "a scrap of paper". This caused much sensation in England at the beginning of the war, because it was very convenient for the propagandists; but as people began to reflect on the affair in tranquillity they began to wonder in what language the German Chancellor had been speaking when he made the remark. By the time the serious enquiry had been set on foot, however, both the German Chancellor and the British Ambassador were dead. The Ambassador had not told his friends at the British embassy which language had been used, but there was an Englishman in Berlin who said that he had been told that the Chancellor, Bethmann-Hollweg, had made the remark in German. The case was not clear, however, because there was also evidence that the Chancellor spoke in English during the conversation. It transpired, in fact, that the Chancellor preferred to speak in English when he was interviewing the British Ambassador, for, happily, our foreign friends do like to exercise themselves in our language when they are conversing with us. Moreover, it appeared that the Ambassador had revealed to one person that the German Chancellor had not used the very derogatory phrase "a scrap of paper", but the milder term, "a piece of paper" (or its German equivalent)—the Ambassador having gingered up the language a little (in the way that diplomats and even non-diplomats are apt to do) in his dispatch to the Foreign Office. So the enquiry was pushed forward, and the British Foreign Office (which sometimes shows a most disinterested zeal for the discovery of the truth about such things) gave every assistance to the enquiry, if it did not in fact initiate the investigation itself. The men who had been at the embassy in Berlin at the beginning of August 1914 were by this time scattered in various quarters of the globe; but they, as well as the family of the Ambassador, were approached and an interesting verdict was reached. It was held that though the conversation in question would have been opened, as usual, in English, the German Chancellor would be bound to break into his native language when he became really excited, as, of course, he did on this occasion. He would be all the more likely to do so, since the British Ambassador was not in any way deficient in his knowledge of German. And the conclusion was reached that Bethmann-Hollweg made the remark in German, and gave the German equivalent for a "piece" rather than a "scrap" of paper—the Ambassador making the phrase more picturesque by a translation which might well have come most naturally to his mind. In fact there is possibly a reason why the term which he used was one that would come readily to the mind of the Ambassador at the moment. At his house there had recently been a private production of a play by Sardou, translated into English under the title *A Scrap of Paper*; and he himself had had a part in the production. Here is the kind of point which, if contemporaries do not settle it, may be too elusive for future historians to establish. But it is difficult to produce a water-tight demonstration; and, even if contemporaries are fairly clear about the matter, the future historian will still harbour a doubt, unless he finds actual literary evidence that clinches the matter.

All of us will be able to realise on the one hand how easy it is for a man to cheat his biographer, and, on the other hand, how little the people around us at the present day can know or understand of our profounder internal life. A man like Martin Luther must have taken some of his fondest secrets with him to the grave; and certainly the historian must often be defeated—must expect to be defeated—on those issues of private feeling and ultimate motive which are a mystery even to intimate contemporary friends, and which so often lie between a man and his Maker. We have seen that the absence of one single scrap of secret evidence may rob us of the most important aspect of the truth—the clue to the interpretation of a whole correspondence. For this reason it is necessary that we should hold our history in a flexible manner, always realising that there may be a piece of pivotal evidence undiscovered as yet; that generations of research students are still going to bring new things to light or alter our views; and that some evidence may be for ever lost to us precisely because it was too important to be allowed to survive on paper.

It is still true that in regard to the vast universe of things which it is relevant and useful for us to know, history can reach a greater assurance than many people realise. On the question of the origins of the war of 1914, for example, we today know far more than any single government or foreign office had the slightest chance of knowing when the events were actually occurring. It is even rather a delicate matter to try to destroy official evidence—at least evidence of certain types; for a man cannot always be sure that other people will destroy the collateral evidence, and that all record of a transaction will in fact be blotted out. If I were clever enough to destroy a collection of evidence in the British Foreign Office I could not be sure that the people in Brussels would not be foolish enough to allow some traces of the episode to be found in their archives. In fact, therefore, certain limits are set to the possibility of deceiving the historian, and the future may discover something like a mathematical formula for those limits.

We may not know the most private secrets of Martin Luther, but, in the realm of those more communicable things which it is relevant and significant for us to know, we are unspeakably better informed than any of the man's own contemporaries could be. The last intimacies of thought and motive are likely to be out of our reach; but we know far more about Luther than he himself could have summoned into his memory or brought up into his consciousness on any given occasion. History can come to a closer discussion of statesmanship or poetic inspiration than any states-man or poet who may have set out to describe the things he felt to have been happening in his mind. Indeed, the things that the statesman or the poet may have told us about the matter are available for the historian, but are only a part of the material that the research student can use. History can tell us more about scientific development or the processes of scientific discovery than the scientist himself has managed to recapture when he has been doing his best to tell us what actually seemed to him to have occurred. Once again, what the scientist felt to be happening is only a section of the available evidence, and it is not always im-possible to show that he has been wrong in his self-examination. There are blanks; and we shall probably never know, for example, just what it was that happened when the Tsar Alexander met Napoleon on the raft at Tilsit. In some respects the deficiencies may become greater as time proceeds—we cannot reconstruct a modern battle on the basis of written orders in the way that we can reconstruct a Napoleonic one; and, where written orders fail us, an elaborate historical criticism is needed to check the oral evidence and the retrospective accounts of high military officers. Our politicians now know that the historians are on their track, so that they prepare for them in advance—they write with the public in mind or they leave crucial things unrecorded. For older periods the historian has been somewhat at the mercy of chance, which has decided whether certain kinds of evidence shall survive or be destroyed; though official records, preserved for business purposes, have often come down to us, and have sometimes had the special value which attaches to documents written by men who never imagined that the historians would be wanting to make use of them. If the men of the present day, holding a certain narrative shape in their minds, were to select what documents should be handed down to the future, they might be imposing their own construction of the story upon posterity and robbing the historian of the power to revise their verdicts. And the same is true when a selection of documents is published, even though the selection may be a very voluminous one. Yesterday's historians who were at the mercy of chance might be in no worse case than tomorrow's historians, if these latter are going to be at the mercy of our choice. All this is what we must expect in history. And it means that all is well provided we realise the limitations and know just what it is that we don't know.

BOOK TWO

GEORGE III
AND HIS INTERPRETERS

Introduction

So MUCH has been said in recent decades about the earlier historians of George III—and so much of this has been to their detriment—that in fairness to them we ought to do more than merely glance at them obliquely; we ought to set out to gain a clearer idea of what they actually wrote. If we survey the history of the historiography of this whole subject, learning not merely the attitude of the year 1900 to George III, but the attitude also of 1860 and 1800, for example, we can give our knowledge something like a new dimension, rescuing it somewhat from time and fashion, and coming as close as we are likely to come to the vision that is *sub specie æternitatis*. Following the various historians in succession, we can see the subject as a developing theme; we can find how errors arose; and we can discover how in different periods new historical outlooks are liable to emerge. George III can be disengaged more effectually from the impressionism of any particular observer, the caprice of any particular historian, or the prejudices of any particular period. By examining the history of the historiography, we can acquire even a better appreciation of the state of scholarship at the present day. We can distinguish what is really original in the work of more recent writers. And we can discern more easily what requires to be done next.

The results of such a study would compile themselves into a measureless amorphous mass if the topic itself did not have an essential core, or if it could not be resolved into a hard piece of subject-matter, amenable to analytical treatment. Fortunately, in the case of George III, there exists a problem which is precise and strategic, and upon which the whole issue can be focused—a problem upon which much of the controversy has been concentrated ever since the serious historical reconstruction of the subject began. On the question of the King's intentions at the moment of his accession has depended to a considerable degree the attitude of the historian to the reign of George III in general. The interpretation of the alleged new system of the court between 1760 and 1763 seems to decide whether the historian of the reign starts off on the right foot or the wrong. The essential issues of the epoch seem to marshal themselves before us as the stage is being set for the very first act in the drama. If, then, we compare the way in which the historians of George III's reign have treated the initial problem, the opening moves of the game, we shall have a chance of arriving at results which will be precise enough to repay analysis.

It is important that the assertions that are to be made about bygone historians should be supported by actual quotation. It is necessary also that we should pay attention not only to the detail of the narrative but also to the overall views of the authors with whom this study will be concerned. The extracts which are reproduced from these writers must be fairly long sometimes, especially as it will be necessary on occasion to present a man's thought in its continuity. Those who are not interested in the close analysis or careful comparison of the quoted texts may find it useful to read the successive authors, if only as one might read an anthology of historical writings on the subject of George III.

CHAPTER ONE

THE EARLY SOURCES

---

1. Sources friendly to the Court

THE STARTING-POINT for historical interpretation must lie in the ideas of the people who were living while the events in question were taking place. Their way of envisaging their struggles and formulating the issues of the time provides the historian with his initial framework. This version may continue to be reproduced for a long period; yet it may actually have been devised to serve as a weapon in the conflict which the historian is trying to narrate. It is possible even that the victors in a struggle will want to double their success by dictating for some time afterwards the way in which the story shall be told. The day may come, however, when the historian, embracing both of the parties, or comprehending the issue at a higher altitude, will resurrect the forgotten aspects of the case, or see that all men were somewhat the victims of events—all of them struggling amid currents which they could not quite measure or understand. In such cases the history may have to be re-stratified and the narrative thoroughly re-cast.

But, whatever new structure the story may require, the ideas of the men who were living at the time will be somehow comprised in the final version of the narrative. The ideas that men have about the events in which their life is involved are to be regarded as a dimension of the events themselves. The things that men think they are fighting about are an ingredient in the very conflict in which they are engaged.

The earliest decisive source for the opening years of the reign of George III—and the one most commonly quoted by historians at least down to almost the middle of the nineteenth century—was the evidence of Bubb Dodington. This man had been connected with the Earl of Bute in the days of Frederick, Prince of Wales, and apparently enjoyed close relations with him after George III's accession, being raised to the peerage as Lord Melcombe in 1761. His *Diary*, published in 1783, threw some light on the views of the men who had been associated with Prince Frederick. It gave glimpses of George III in his younger days, though it failed to answer certain critical questions concerning the boy's political education in the years after the death of his father. It showed that Bute and Dodington did in fact differ in opinion about certain matters in the years 1760–61. Behind the occasional minor differences, however, there seemed to be a deeper community of ideas, and these were taken for granted by Dodington—they are the assumed basis for the discussions that took place. Historians were ready to accept the *Diary*, therefore, as evidence for the ideas that had been current in the neighbourhood of Bute.

Dodington wrote as a man who, from the very beginning of the new reign, took it for granted that a change in the system of government was in contemplation at court. It appeared that Bute was at least prepared to converse with his friend on the basis of the assumption that the object was to get rid of the Duke of Newcastle and the elder Pitt, the leaders of the existing government. The *Diary* itself, and the reports of conversations which it contained, carry the suggestion that, though circumstances might impose a temporary alliance, the interests of George III and Bute were clearly separate from those of the leading ministers. In view of later historical controversies it is significant to note that Bute and Dodington discuss the general election that is to take place in 1761; and here we find them wondering whether men who have entered the House of Commons as the dependents of Newcastle will be likely to remain true to Newcastle or to follow George III, supposing at a later date there is a breach between the minister and the King. In February 1761 the answer to the question appears to have been agreed upon; and we learn that "the new Parliament would be the King's, let who will chuse it". It was reckoned, in fact, that the King was not likely to suffer in the future, even if Newcastle were allowed to manage the election now.

The most important part of the evidence of Dodington, however, was to be supplied a little later, in 1802, when the historian Adolphus reproduced some points from the correspondence which this politician had been conducting in the same period with Bute. Within a month of George III's accession we find Dodington writing:

> During the last two reigns, a set of undertakers have farmed the power of the crown at a price certain; and under colour of making themselves responsible for the whole, have taken the sole direction of the royal interest and influence into their own hands, and applied it to their own creatures, without consulting the crown, or leaving any room for the royal nomination or direction. This should be prevented before any pretence of promise can be made. [Adolphus, *History*, Vol. I, pp. 27-8.]

Less than a month later Dodington writes to Bute again:

> Remember, my noble and generous friend, that to recover monarchy from the inveterate usurpation of oligarchy is a point too arduous and important to be achieved without much difficulty, and some degree of danger. [*Ibid.*, p. 547.]

It was on this evidence first of all that historians, at an early stage in the story, based the most significant of the interpretations of George III in the early years of his reign. According to this view, the new King, from the time of his accession, contemplated a change not merely of personnel but also in the system of government. He set out to vindicate monarchical authority against the corrupt, oligarchical Whigs.

This view of the intentions of the court from the year 1760 found confirmation in printed sources which had been available for a long time. During the period of his ascendancy, the Earl of Bute had been pilloried as a royal "favourite", and the opposition press had produced not only essays on favouritism in general but also studies of sinister examples of it which had appeared in history. They had exploited the analogies to be found in the case of Edward III and Mortimer, as well as in the reign of Richard II, and in the France that had been so unfortunate under Madame de Pompadour. They had made much of the parallels in the reign of Queen Anne, when favouritism had also brought the Tories to power, and then had led to a treaty with France like the one which Bute himself was responsible for making—a treaty that could be alleged to have robbed Britain of the fruits of victory. Perhaps it was for the purpose of meeting wild slanders and crude charges of favouritism that the friends of the court set out to present to the public a reasoned case.

The *Gentleman's Magazine*, which reprinted passages from current periodicals, and which the historians of the reign began to use at an early date, provided (e.g. in 1762) considerable examples of the propaganda which was now produced. It quoted in particular the *Auditor*, which it described as Bute's own paper, and which had been founded in June 1762 for the purpose of counteracting the influence of the famous *North Briton*. The declared aim of the paper was "to administer an antidote to the poison of sedition" and "to applaud the methods of government, when they are founded in policy and wisdom". And the *Auditor* itself formulates that idea of the initial policy of George III which governed the early historiography of the subject, and which prevailed throughout the first half of the nineteenth century. The third issue of the paper was insistent about the point that "the executive part of government is lodged in the crown, together with the fiduciary power from the laws to make war or peace".

44

Furthermore, said this periodical, the Crown had the power "to name statesmen", and "the present Minister [Bute] is appointed by the crown". It was in its seventh issue, however, that the *Auditor* stated the larger case which, apart from being a familiar one at the time, was to influence so powerfully the historiography of George III.

> His late majesty King *George I*, when he came to the crown of *Great Britain*, was wholly unacquainted with our laws, manners and language; and therefore naturally fell into the hands of such as were able to seize the helm, to whose direction he resigned himself implicitly, reserving to himself little more than the name [i.e. of king].
>
> Thus a ministerial system was established by the nature of things at the accession of his late Majesty King *George II*, who, though he had lived a competent time in *Britain*, would not presume to judge for himself, but remained like his father, a royal ward to his state guardians, till his present majesty ascended the throne, who, having spent his youth in acquiring the knowledge of our laws, customs, and manners, was enabled to see, hear, and think for himself.

The *Auditor* then argued that the Duke of Newcastle, who "had been used to make [i.e. accustomed to making] a cypher of his king", had refused to continue at the head of the ministry, now that "he could make a cypher of him no longer". The Duke, in fact, had become recalcitrant because he no longer "disposed of all the good things in the land". Concerning the main body of what were called "the Whigs"—the party identified with the Duke—we learn in the twelfth issue of the paper:

> There is a species of men in this country who consider themselves possessed of an hereditary right to the favours of government. One man's father perjured himself upon such an occasion in the service of the ministry, another got drunk at such an election, and a third refused a particular toast at an assize meeting; hence the title of their sons upon the treasury list for preferment. But, by the late revolution at court, the corruption of their ancestors is no longer a recommendation of these gentlemen.

Not only do we meet the claim, then, that a new system is being established, but the apostles of the régime of Bute go so far as to talk of "the late revolution at court". They identify the long rule of the Whigs with the practice of political corruption, and seek to acquire capital by attacking the palpable abuses. A new order is to be established, however, and now, says the seventh number of the *Auditor*, the King

> is endeavouring to eradicate the deep system of ministerial power which has too long prevailed, and to fulfil the executive trust vested in him by the laws himself; neither referring his government wholly to his ministers, nor suffering them to be entirely nominal, but using them as *ministers*, that is, as proper instruments in his own hand, to assist in their proper departments in the administration of his government.

The view that George III intended to revise the system of government (if only by restoring it to its earlier, healthier state) was not the invention of his enemies, therefore, or the slander of Whig historians—it was the interpretation put forward by the friends of the court. The picture given by the propagandists of that party after the elevation of Bute agrees with the statements which we have seen issuing from the circle around the Favourite at the very beginning of the reign. The assertion that the new reign was to imply a new system was not a hostile imputation in any case, nor was it taken to be such in the early 1760's. And later, when it first appears in the more serious kind of historiography, this thesis is still being used essentially for the purpose of explaining and defending George III. Not merely for a further half-century after that, but throughout the history of historical writing on this period, the role of this particular interpretation has been to provide a justification for the King and the court.

It will easily be understood that the nineteenth-century historians made considerable use of the *Annual Register*, which had begun to appear in 1758. The utility and the availability of this work are attested by the fact that the issues for the early years of George III's reign had reached their sixth, seventh or eighth editions by the year 1805. The attitude adopted in these volumes towards the controversies of those early years is all the more interesting if—as appears to be generally accepted—they can be regarded as evidence for the ideas of Edmund Burke at that time. In the midst of the conflicts, the Annual Register set out to maintain a neutral position, attempted to summarise the arguments on both sides, and kept at least the appearance of moderation and impartiality. After weighing the pros and cons, however, it decided on successive occasions in favour of the King. And certainly its narratives cannot be dismissed as the evidence of a hostile witness.

On the resignation of the elder Pitt in 1761, the Annual Register (1761, p. 44) commended the policy of the King and declared that "the popular cause was worse sustained, and the ministerial better". It favoured the abandonment of the Seven Years' War, since "every end we could rationally propose to ourselves in carrying it on was answered". It admitted that there were defects in the treaty concluded by Bute, but it did not identify itself with those who cried out against the terms of the settlement. In fact, it pointed out that the peace was "altogether agreeable to the system which many now in opposition had always pursued". The attitude of certain men in the circle of Bute to the régime that was associated with the Duke of Newcastle, and the language used concerning this régime in the writings issued on behalf of the court party, have already been noted, and might have been interpreted as the peculiarities of a particular clique. Their significance is broadened when we see that even the Annual Register adopts very much the same point of view. It describes the Duke of Newcastle as one who "by the obligations which . . . he was enabled to confer . . . had attached a great number to his fortunes, and formed an interest in the parliament and the nation, which it was extremely difficult to overturn, or even shake". Newcastle had never had the opportunity, the narrative continues, to cultivate his own interest with the present king, before the accession of the latter to the throne in 1760. Bute had done much to earn the confidence of George III; he not only "obtained" but actually "deserved" the priority in the new reign.

> Another noble person had been in an employment near [George's] person; and having formed his mind with much attention and success to those virtues which adorn his station, deserved and obtained a very uncommon share of his confidence. [1762, p. 46.]

We are not listening to a malignant witness for the prosecution, then, when we read in the *Annual Register* (1762, p. 47) that the new reign involved a change in the system of government, and that the spokesmen for the court had been proclaiming the change from the very start.

> From the beginning of this reign it had been professed, with the general applause of all good men, to abolish those odious party distinctions [i.e. between Whig and Tory] and to extend the royal favour and protection equally to all his majesty's subjects.

The same work, in the issue for 1763 (p. 39), describes the supporters of Bute as arguing in the following manner:

> What was the end, for which they contended? Undoubtedly that the constitutional dignity of the crown should be restored; that the King and kingdom should no longer be governed, or rather insulted, by a cabal; and that his majesty should, as the law intended, chuse and retain his own ministers, unless some legal disqualification prevented their appointment, or some well proved delinquency furnished a reason to remove them from his service.

The *Annual Register* makes it clear that views of this kind were very much in the air at the time; and the fact that such was the state of opinion—the mere fact that such were considered to be the useful ideas to present to the public as even an ostensible political programme—has very real significance, however in-accurate all this might be as a diagnosis of the existing situation. Even evidence for the existence of a controversy over the prin-ciple of oligarchy can be found in some of the further remarks contained in this volume of the *Annual Register*. The opposition are described as hostile to the new ministers of George III because these latter have "no solid ground of power in themselves"—they could not make an independent stand against the Crown. Government was in the hands of men who were bound to behave as dependents, bound to "act as the passive instruments of [Bute]". Furthermore, though it might have to be admitted (as it was formally admitted in George II's reign) that the King had the "right" to choose his own ministers, the *Annual Register* is a witness to the fact that a constitutional issue was beginning to emerge—one to which we must not deny existence merely be-cause we think that it ought not to have been raised. Indeed, the future development of the constitution gave a retrospective justi-fication to those who raised it, whatever private motives they may have had for doing this. The opposition, we are told (1763, p. 41),

> contended that the spirit of the constitution required, that the crown should be directed . . . by public motives, and not by private liking and friendship. . . . Nothing but the very popular use of the pre-rogative can be sufficient to reconcile the nation to the extent of it.

When the *Annual Register* signifies its own decision on this par-ticular issue, however (pp. 41–2), it appears that once again its author leans to the side of the King:

> Whether these ideas . . . be consistent with the preservation of any degree of monarchical authority in the commonwealth, the reader is left to judge. It is, indeed, not altogether easy to determine whether the limitations on the executive power ought or ought not to be extended further, by any other sort of popular controul than the

laws themselves have carried them. . . . It seems repugnant to the genius of every stable government . . . to direct its actions by so uncertain, variable, and capricious a standard, as that of popular opinion.

In the Preface to the volume for 1763, the *Annual Register* described its policy of "neutrality" in regard to the "domestic dissentions" of the time. The work might be regarded as an attempt to provide what we should call contemporary history, and in this sense it stands apart from the political propaganda of the period. At the very least it gives us evidence for a contemporary opinion, and it illustrates what was considered to be a relevant way of presenting the issue to the public. But, if anything, it is biassed in favour of the monarchy, and in 1761 it supported David Hume's allegedly Tory interpretation of the seventeenth-century constitutional conflict—the view that the Stuarts had erred "not so much in extending the prerogative" as in failing to see how "the opinions and fashion of the age" had required a slackening of the reins. The same volume (p. 44) describes the conduct of George III at the time of Pitt's resignation as "grounded upon the firmest principles of integrity and honour, which must raise the highest veneration for his royal character not only among his subjects but amongst all nations". With all its monarchical inclinations, the *Annual Register* does not take its stand on a rigid interpretation of royal rights or a static view of the British form of government, but allows for a certain give-and-take and recognises that a constitutional issue has been raised by the régime of Bute. It even confesses that the decision between the opposing points of view is a difficult one.

2. The Opposition Evidence

FROM THE beginning of the nineteenth century, the more serious students of George III's reign made use of the evidence of Bubb Dodington and such versions of the court party's case as have been described above. In the meantime, however, the crude attack on Bute as the mere "Favourite" had never ceased; and it was still to be prolonged in a vulgar literature which ran for a considerable period in a parallel stream. The writers in question directed their hostility against Bute's own person, often exonerating the young George III, who could be regarded as having risen superior to the temptations around him. They often gathered much of their material from a pamphlet produced a few years after the downfall of Bute himself—the *History of the Late Minority*, which had been written in 1765 to support the party around the elder Pitt. Our attention is drawn, therefore, to a type of source which still remains to be considered—the propaganda of George III's opponents, who produced less flattering interpretations of the early years of the reign.

The *History of the Late Minority* calls attention to the abuses which had emerged in the early 1760's, and says that "if no such man as the Earl of Bute had been in existence when the late King died, not one of those evils would have happened". The work takes a popular line and the attack that it makes is a personal one. It argues that favouritism was the characteristic of the new reign, and that the resulting system enabled Bute to drive the elder Pitt out of office. By invading every department and corrupting subordinate servants, Bute had then made it impossible for the Duke of Newcastle to continue in the ministry. Bute "stormed all the public offices; turned out every dependent, relation, and friend of the Duke of Newcastle", and "barred up all the avenues to the Royal closet". He created peers, multiplied the Lords of the Bed-chamber, established new posts of emolument, and then used all these sources of patronage for the corruption of members of parliament.

To the gratification of his ambitious views, is to be attributed all the divisions and distractions into which this unhappy kingdom has been plunged, since his present Majesty's accession to the crown. . . . Scarce was the ink dry which had marked his name upon the council book, when, although no minister himself, yet he assumed a magis-terial air of authority, and began to give law in the court. . . . He also engaged himself deeply with his artful coadjutors in forming his faction. He made certain of meeting with the cordial affection of . . . the Jacobites; and . . . he was as certain of having the support of that other infatuated set of men, called Tories; these, with a great part of the Scots . . . formed his troop. . . . The slavish and arbitrary doctrines, which they had imbibed with their milk, they hoped to see soon established as the laws of the land. [1766 ed. pp. 10–27.]

In the *History of the Late Minority*, however, there are also references to a more pretentious political programme which, again, is associated with the opening years of George III's reign. The plans and purposes themselves, and also the assumptions underlying them, are curiously reminiscent of the things which we have already seen in the letters and the propaganda of the supporters of Bute. We are told that factions and connexions were to be destroyed, that the policy of proscription—that is to say, the exclusion of the Tories—was to be abandoned, and that there was to be an enquiry into the abuses connected with the holders of office. Furthermore, "the true use and design of parlia-ment" were to be restored; and the constitution was now to be brought back to its former "purity". In the *History of the Late Minority*, however, and elsewhere in the opposition literature of the time, these ideals, though they were imputed to George III, were also traced back to their alleged origin. They were regarded as constituting the programme of the party around George III's father, Frederick, Prince of Wales.

It was perhaps natural that the main body of the Whigs who had held power for so long, and who now felt menaced by the rise of Bute, should connect the proclaimed policies of the new régime with the opposition which both they and George II had had to meet in the previous reign. It was true that the court of the Prince of Wales, in days when the heir to the throne was the natural leader of opposition to the government, had adopted a programme very similar to the one that was being associated with the new régime, the one that was being proclaimed by the supporters of Bute. There, too, the cry had been against corruption and proscription, against jobbery and party, and against the oligarchical pretentions of the ruling Whigs. Before George III had ever come to the throne there had also been public scandal and controversy over the allegation that he was being educated in the arbitrary principles of the Stuart dynasty and the Jacobite faction. The men who had been in power up to 1760 would find it to their interest to connect the new régime with the dubious education of the King, or with the still earlier period when the court of his father, Frederick, had been in bad odour. Perhaps they would have been ready to make a correlation of this sort whether there had been genuine grounds for it or not.

The *History of the Late Minority* has a limited role in the development of the historiography of George III's reign. Its influence was important chiefly in the more popular attacks on Bute, and the student of the work would naturally infer that this was likely to be the case. In spite of the allegations repeatedly made by writers of our own generation, Burke's *Thoughts on the Cause of the Present Discontents* has also been curiously limited in its influence on historical scholarship. Its effect was not apparent for a long time, and it would seem that Burke's elaborate intellectual constructions easily lent themselves to historical criticism. They were too deliberately contrived, and too deeply coloured by the author's imagination to convince the serious historians of a generation which knew the late King or remembered the closing decades of his reign. Even the Whig historians in the latter part of the nineteenth century were sometimes cautious in their use of this work. Even Lecky had doubts; and such doubts related to the very points which our own contemporaries have attacked.

The *Thoughts on the Cause of the Present Discontents* arose out of the great controversies of 1769–70, when John Wilkes had stirred up considerable political feeling in the country at large. The refusal to allow his re-election to the House of Commons, after his expulsion, had given the parliamentary opposition a wonderful pretext for attack. That part of the opposition which was connected with the Earl of Chatham, Lord Temple and George Grenville hoped at this time to achieve a combination with the other part, where the Marquis of Rockingham, instead of the Duke of Newcastle, now held the leadership. Burke wrote his treatise in defence of the interests of the Rockingham group, and it was part of his purpose to justify that very principle of political party or political "connexion" which seemed threatened by the new reign, and which was derided in the propaganda of the court. The fact that he saw the necessity for defending this particular principle is perhaps a further testimony to the policy of the ruling party—further evidence that here was a point which the men around George III had chosen to attack. At the same time, Burke was trying to mark out the line which divided the Rockinghamites from the friends and allies of Chatham; and it served his purpose to emphasise the distinction between his teaching and that of the *History of the Late Minority*, the work which supported Chatham. The contrast between these two publications is certainly evident in their attitude to the role of Bute himself; for Burke takes a line which is absolutely the opposite to that of the *History*. Concerning the new system which he imputes to the reign of George III, he says, "We should have been tried with it, if the Earl of Bute had never existed" (*Works* II (1803), p. 258).

According to Burke, "a new project was devised by a certain set of intriguing men, totally different from the system of administration which had prevailed since the accession of the House of Brunswick". He, too, had heard that the plan had arisen in the first place in the circle around Frederick, the Prince of Wales. The purpose of the whole enterprise was: "*to secure to the court the unlimited and uncontroulled use of its own vast influence, under the sole direction of its own private favour*". In order to achieve their objective the directors of the design had decided "*to draw a line which should separate the court from the ministry*".

> Two systems of administration were to be formed; one which should be in the real secret and confidence; the other merely ostensible to perform the official and executory duties of the government.

Under the real advisers, who were out of reach of parliamentary attack, "*a party . . . was to be formed in favour of the court against the ministry*". And the whole resulting system, according to Burke, "is commonly called in the technical language of the court, *double cabinet*" (*ibid*. II, 231–3, 256).

Many of the ingredients of this system are mirrored—or a suggestion of them appears—in the correspondence and the published propaganda of the men around the court. Burke's imagination has been at work upon the materials, however, and his systematising mind has produced an elaborate piece of artifice which might hardly have been recognisable to the very people he was attacking. It might be argued on his behalf that what he really described was the system which in his view would be bound to emerge in the long run if Dodington and the *Auditor* had their way, and if a king were to arrive who would resolutely use the enlarged opportunity for the establishment of his personal power. It seems certain, however, that Burke, though he claimed to be reproducing the plans envisaged by the court party at the beginning of the reign, used evidence from the more recent conduct of the King—from the latter half of the 1760's—and ran this new material into his picture of George III's original design. In the historiography of this whole subject there has always been the danger that the actions and expressions of George III in 1770 might be abstracted and used to authorise statements about his ideas and purposes in 1760, without regard to the changed context in which they occurred. It is curious all the same, that, at a crucial point in the argument, Burke claims to be quoting the language of the court, and it would seem that he was laying himself open to easy exposure if he were wildly wrong in such an assertion. The words he uses are worth repeating: concerning the alleged new system of government he says that it was "commonly called in the language of the court, *double cabinet*". We cannot say that Burke had never heard this terminology used by the supporters of Bute; but some of these may have gone further in their language than they were authorised to do, so that they are not necessarily to be taken very seriously.

Burke clearly does reproduce, however, some of the assertions of the court party, and both his quotations and the form of the treatise, which is in a sense the defence of aristocratic power, may be taken to confirm the other evidence on this subject. He derides what he alleges to be the slogans of the court—such things as the "abolition of party", the "casting out of corruption", and the "resistance to aristocratic power". The leaders of the new régime, he says, would in any case have to find a way of inducing parliament to acquiesce in their projects. They were to do this by the dissolution of "all connexions and dependencies", so that "*no concert, order, or effect, might appear in any future opposition*". In fact, "party was to be totally done away", and by the same means "corruption was to be cast down from court". Using knowledge that he can only have acquired later in the 1760's, Burke discusses at some length the alleged attempts to dissolve those party-allegiances and political alliances which had given such solidarity to the Whig connexion. He at least affects not to criticise the King personally, and it seems to be his object to attack rather the men around the court. These men, he says, "now beheld an opportunity of drawing to themselves, by the aggrandisement of a court faction, a degree of power which they could never hope to derive from natural influence or honourable service." He writes at one point:

> One of the principal topicks which was then, and has been since, much employed by that political school, is an affected terrour of the growth of an aristocratick power, prejudicial to the rights of the crown, and the balance of the constitution. [p. 244]

Elsewhere, he summarises the arguments of his enemies as follows:

> The time was come, to restore royalty to its original splendour. *Mettre le Roy hors de page*, became a sort of watchword. And it was constantly in the mouths of all the runners of the court, that nothing could preserve the balance of the constitution from being overturned by the rabble, or by a fraction of the nobility, but to free the sovereign effectually from that ministerial tyranny under which the royal dignity had been oppressed in the person of his majesty's grandfather. [p. 242]

We have seen already the independent evidence on which some of these statements rest. Yet, if Burke wrote the narratives in the *Annual Register* in the early 1760's, his views had undergone a great change by 1770—a change which, of course, we must not necessarily regard as having been insincere.

It will be seen that in many respects the two hostile treatises, the *History of the Late Minority* and the *Thoughts on the Cause of the Present Discontents*, mirror the propaganda of the court party itself and report the slogans of the men who were in the circle of Bute. The former pamphlet, however, concentrates attention on the problem of Favouritism and the personal ambition of Bute; while the latter puts the emphasis on the growth of royal influence and the alleged policy of the "double cabinet".

57

3. George III and the "Patriot" Ideal

THE ENEMIES of the court in the early years of George III's reign repeatedly directed their attack against both the name and the programme of the so-called "Patriot" party. They were not simply inventing the connexion between the new régime and the old "Patriot" party, however—they were returning the ball that had been served them in the first place by the supporters of Bute. It is clear that these latter—or some of their spokesmen— thought it a matter of pride to connect themselves with the "Patriot" ideal. The fifth issue of the *Auditor* contains an idealised portrait of what is described as a "Patriot Prince"; and this organ of the Bute faction does not allow the reader to overlook the fact that the portrait is intended to refer to George III, both as Prince of Wales and as King.

The "Patriot" ideals continued to exist in any case; and they could exist independent of any special regard for George III or any desire to flatter the court. This is illustrated in the work of the first historian whom we need to mention, a writer who comes a little before the birth of the serious historiography of the period. William Belsham, whose *Memoirs of the Reign of George III* appeared in 1795, was a dissenter and showed a particular concern for the fate of the dissenting interest. On the one hand, he was a bitter opponent of those Whigs who had the predominance in England in the middle of the eighteenth century, and he hated most of all their bellicose foreign policy—hated the Seven Years' War, for example. On the other hand, he showed a special animosity against Bute and against the whole programme of the government in the early years of the reign of George III. He took care to screen the King himself from the effects of his criticism, and he used the evidence of Dodington to show that the associates of Bute contemplated a change in the system of government. But, though he so disliked the Whigs and so opposed the war in which they were engaged, he was clearly unfriendly to the kind of change that he saw taking place in the early years of the reign. He reserved his eulogies for the programme of the older "Patriot" party, though he had a reservation to make in respect of the attitude which that party had adopted towards religious dissent.

He liked the idea of an attack on the Whig policy of "engrossing . . . the executive offices of the State". He approved of the protest that was made against both the system of corruption and the policy of proscription. He applauded the extension of royal favour "to all who had not by culpable misconduct forfeited their claim to it, without any distinction of party". But to Belsham this programme had nothing to do with the early years of George III's reign. It was identified only with the ideals of Frederick, Prince of Wales. The early death of Frederick had been the great disaster; for, in the period that followed it, the education of the young Prince George, he said, had been conducted on different principles altogether. Belsham's complaint was that George III had simply fallen into the hands of Tories with "strong monarchical prepossessions"—men with "high and arbitrary" maxims of government. In other words, he had deserted the "Patriot" ideal.

*   *   *

In political history the things that men actually do may matter very much, but the things that they think they are doing or imagine themselves to be doing are part of the story; they have to be included in a description of their policy. It would be conceivable that, in the years 1760–63, both the friends and the enemies of the court should have wrangled over what each of them regarded as "a change of system", while the present-day historian, looking for tangible results and specific alterations, might feel that concrete and measurable changes did not really occur. The nineteenth-century historians, lacking any microscopic knowledge of the mechanics of government before and after 1760, might still have diagnosed "a change of system" because from that date the men on both sides so often talked on the assumption of "a change of system". It would be enough for them that there was a change in the proclaimed ideas of the court, and it would hardly occur to them that these should be dismissed as nothing more than an alteration of language. We ought not to be too materialistic in our attitude to this question, and we must not assume too mechanically that the nineteenth-century historians would be wrong even in such a case as this. If a monarch is merely pretending to make a change of régime—if his agents merely pretend to proclaim a new order without bringing about corresponding alterations in the concrete world or even intending anything very much—even in this extreme case the purely theoretical change may still have important political repercussions. The resolve to carry on old policies but to conduct them under a new flag or with different slogans may itself be tantamount to a change of system. Policies, in fact, are not to be interpreted apart from the ideas and intentions which give them so much of their meaning.

When the serious historiography of George III's reign was being established, those writers who could not justify the new reign on the theory of a change of system did not know how to justify it at all. They regarded the new court and its policies as merely deplorable, even if they directed their attack rather against the Favourite than against the King.

CHAPTER TWO

THE RISE
OF A SERIOUS HISTORIOGRAPHY

---

1. The Founding of the Main Tradition

THE FIRST serious attempt to produce what we should call a "historical" reconstruction of the early years of George III's reign was that of John Adolphus, who, in 1802, published a *History of England* running from 1760 to 1783. Adolphus himself is of special interest to the student because he doubles his importance in historical scholarship by the production of an equally significant history of the French Revolution. In all this, he stands in a central position; for he both started and typifies a moderate English interpretation of political events—a conservative but comprehending kind of historiography, which enabled this country to play a characteristic part in the development of French Revolutionary studies. In reality he was a Tory, and later in life he expressed his "admiration" at the fact that always—in things both great and small—his opinions had agreed with those of Lord Eldon. When Eldon died it was suggested that he was the most suitable person who could be found to write the man's biography. (See *Recollections of John Adolphus* (1871), p. 266.) It would not be incorrect to say that he produced the classical Tory defence of George III.

His interest in the earlier years of George III's reign may be described as having been a genuinely historical one, and he seems to have set about his task without any conscious polemical intent. He had no desire to construct a melodramatic narrative, with heroes and villains sharply contrasted, and he confessed in his *History* (Preface, p. vii):

> I have generally found in the state of party connexions, and the legitimate objects of honourable ambition, sufficient means of accounting for the actions of men either possessed of, or struggling for power, without feigning, as a cause of their conduct, an excess of mental depravity or political turpitude.

Authors, he said, "imagine, for the personages of their narratives, a consistent uniformity of intention and conduct, which truth never has been able to pourtray". In reality, "the historian feels with sensible regret, the necessity of recording the aberrations of the most elevated minds"; and "that work must be a romance, not a history, which fails to shew that individuals, whose general views have been directed to the welfare of their country, have been in occasional acts, rash, vain, factious, arbitrary or absurd". In general, he was not predisposed to impute to individuals "base designs against either Liberty or Government". It was not his intention in any case to write the kind of history which provides fuel for present controversies.

If there were not evidence of his fidelity to his ideals in the part of his book with which we are concerned—and concrete proof that he could convince even political opponents of his fairness— these principles might be regarded as suspiciously convenient for a writer who meant to shield George III and Bute from the melo-dramatic charges that were made against them. Adolphus made it clear that his sympathies were not with the left wing and that it was not in his inclination to support a policy of what he laconically described as "crude reforms". He stresses his regard for the con-stitution of his country, but adds: "I have treated that constitution not as a project but an establishment"—by which he apparently means that he is attached to it as it already stands, and does not interpret it (as some of the reformers do) in terms of what he might be wanting it to become. In the preface to his work (p. ix), he gives an overall judgment upon the reign of George III which sufficiently indicates the state of his sympathies:

> I can without hesitation declare my opinion, that in the period on which I have written, the throne has been filled by a monarch who has sought the love of his subjects through the means of public spirit and private virtue; and who has tempered a noble desire to preserve from degradation the authority he inherits, with a firm and just regard to the constitution and liberties which conducted him to the throne. . . . Far from thinking that the aims of successive administrations have been . . . to overthrow the liberties and constitution of the country; I am persuaded that liberty has been better understood, and more effectually and practically promoted during this period, than in any which preceded; and that the affairs of government have been always honestly though sometimes imprudently, and in the conspicuous instance of the American war, unsuccessfully administered.

Adolphus finds the anti-Whig interpretation of history ready-made—finds it existing not merely in 1763 or 1762 but before George III had been on the throne many weeks. Apart from Bubb Dodington's *Diary*, he uses new evidence of his own—correspondence (already quoted above) between Dodington and Bute in 1760, and also private information about Bute himself. He puts a case which is already familiar to us, and which is based on the assertions of the court party—assertions anterior to the complaints of Newcastle and his associates. Imputing to George III a determination to change the system of government, he approves such a design and (pp. 14–15) sets out to explain the necessity for it.

> The two last monarchs being foreigners, and opposed by a native prince who had numerous adherents . . . confided a large portion of their power to a few distinguished families, in order to secure possession of the crown. These families, strengthened by union and exclusive influence, became not only independent of, but, in many respects, superior to the throne. . . . But the new King . . . was enabled to emancipate himself from the restraint to which his ancestors had submitted. The Earl of Bute formed the plan of breaking the

phalanx which constituted and supported the ministry, and of securing the independence of the crown, by a moderate exertion of the constitutional prerogative. This plan . . . was well conceived, and necessary; but . . . Bute was not a proper person to carry it into effect. He was not connected, either by blood or by familiar intercourse, with the leading families in England: he was not versed in the arts of popularity, or used to the struggles of parliamentary opposition; and his manners were cold, reserved and unconciliating. Prejudices were easily exerted against him as a native of Scotland.

Adolphus's version of this chapter of English history received curious confirmation from George III himself; and though this may not have been given in terms that covered every aspect of the story—though, also, the testimony of George himself (particularly at an interval of over forty years after the events in question) could hardly be decisive for the historian—it would have been a little strange for the King to speak as he did about the work if he had been aware of a serious structural inaccuracy in the narrative. The publication of George Rose's *Diaries and Correspondence* in 1860 revealed (Vol. II, pp. 188–9) the fact that George III had read Adolphus. Speaking in 1804 of "his accession, and of the first measures taken after it", he had expressed "a good deal of surprise at the accuracy with which some of them were related" in the book, "as far at least as respected himself". The *History of England* was in fact well received in the country at the time, and was highly praised for its industry and impartiality. The *Critical Review* (1803, p. 431) disagreed with Adolphus on one matter—it persisted in thinking that Bute had possessed an indirect influence at court long after his retirement from political office. It accepted, however, the judgment that the beginning of George III's reign saw

the destruction of the oligarchical system which surrounded the throne—a system which, in every view, must have been beheld with an indignant eye by the son, since from it his parents had suffered so severely.

In the *Edinburgh Review* (Vol. I, p. 323) a Whig critic, who admitted that he had read the work with a predisposition to find fault, paid particular tribute to the care and fidelity of the author, even allowing him "the praise of perfect impartiality". Adolphus, he said, "is inclined to place Lord Bute's character in a higher point of view than we are disposed to do, [but] he is by no means blind to his defects."

We agree with our author in rejecting the vulgar and rancorous abuse which has been bestowed upon Lord Bute. As to the secret and mysterious influence which he was supposed to retain for a long period after his resignation, Mr. Adolphus observes, that, with the exception of the ministerial changes which took place soon after his resignation, no report was ever less consonant to truth; and he adds on the authority of private information which in this instance we are inclined to believe—"It was his constant and repeated complaint to his intimate friends that he was neglected by his Sovereign. . . ."

*　　　　*　　　　*

The year after Adolphus had produced his book saw another thoughtful and industrious attempt to analyse British politics during the period of Bute's ascendancy. Robert Bisset, who had already written a life of Edmund Burke, published in 1803 his *History of the Reign of George III*. As he claimed to be moving into a field that had not already been occupied, it would appear that he had been engaged on the task, and had at least begun the writing of the book, before the publication of Adolphus's work. He made use of periodicals and state papers, as well as certain documents which had been communicated to him privately; and he tells us that he had made a point of consulting men who were conversant with the various technical fields that his *History* attempted to cover. Whereas a number of later historians seem clearly to have been affected by Adolphus in their formulation of the arguments on behalf of George III, or the case against the party of the Duke of Newcastle, Bisset's version shows signs of having

E　　　　　65

been developed in an independent manner. His explanation of George III and his notion of Whig oligarchy are so nearly the same, however, that we must wonder whether, in their fundamentals, they did not spring from a tradition that had been kept in currency until the opening of the nineteenth century.

Bisset starts (p. 260) from the view that George II's "preference of one party of his British subjects, during a great part of his reign, though neither very liberal nor very wise, was the natural consequence of the circumstances in which he was placed, operating on his limited capacity". Bisset attached considerable importance to the role of the elder Pitt in the years just before 1760, when he was leading the country in the Seven Years' War. The ascendancy of Pitt represented a stage in the production of a new system and helped to mediate the transition to the régime of George III. It revealed to the world the fact that "connexion with a certain confederacy was not necessary to the highest ministerial ability", and that the corruption established by Walpole was "not necessary to superior genius, magnanimity and energy". Bisset clearly held that in 1760 the time was ripe for a change of system, and as he wrote of this period he clearly sympathised with the aims of George III. He thought that the elder Pitt was correct in his desire for immediate war with Spain in 1761, but wrong in resigning after his colleagues had overruled him. He described Newcastle as nursing the hope that the resignation of Pitt would enable him to be the master of the government, and said that the Duke wrongly "attached the qualifications of a statesman, to descent from certain families, or connexion with a certain confederacy". George III, on the other hand, he said (p. 306), "evidently meant to choose his servants WITHOUT RESPECT TO THEIR PARTY CONNECTIONS, according to his estimation of their fitness for the offices of state". The whole view is not very different from that of Adolphus but tends to diminish the suddenness of the change and to emphasise the similarity or the con-

tinuity between George III and the elder Pitt. It finds the ante-
cedents of George III in the ministerial career of Pitt rather than
in the court of Frederick, Prince of Wales; though in a sense the
reference carries us back to "Patriot" ideals in either case.

In the young King, however, Bisset informs us, "a sound and
acute understanding was not furnished with the actual experience
and discernment into characters, which a more enlarged intercourse with mankind, in such a mind, must have produced". Also,
he relates (p. 308),

> the change of policy in the present king, who would not employ men
> merely because they were whigs, and belonged to ... great families,
> was misconstrued or misrepresented, as a predilection for principles,
> contrary to those which had supported his family. The minister
> [Bute] was represented as the abettor of arbitrary power; as holding
> an office through the partiality of his master's affection, to which
> he was not entitled by his abilities, nor fitted by his principles.

Bisset's verdict on this question was as follows: "In examining
the real facts, the historian finds no document to support this
charge of arbitrary principles." In conclusion, he says: "Candour
must allow, that the comprehensive principle on which his
majesty resolved to govern, was liberal and meritorious, though
patriotism may regret that he was not more fortunate in his first
choice [i.e. that of Bute]."

*   *   *

Whatever doubts there might be concerning the plans and
purposes of George III, there can be no controversy over the
question of the existence of bitter animosity against Bute in the
early years of the reign. That animosity continued for decades,
and, as we have already noted, it was prolonged in a popular kind
of historical literature. Even those historians who were more
balanced in their judgments and more friendly to George III
tended to be critical in their treatment of the "Favourite".
Belsham's *Memoirs* in 1795 had not been moderate or sympathetic,

and indeed they had been particularly hostile to Bute. They described him as a man who had sought "to engross the monopoly of power" and had given "clear proof of his intention to establish a plan of despotism at home". Belsham also adopted the view, long assiduously propagated by enemies of the court, that, after his resignation, Bute had continued to hold "the reality of ministerial power" behind the scenes.

Adolphus in 1802, however, was saved by his fidelity and moderation, his care in the use of Dodington's *Diary*, and his private information and manuscript sources, which appear to have come from the family or the friends of Bute. He escaped the popular errors and extravagances, and in this side of his work proved more reliable than many of the writers of the nineteenth century. He accepted the view that George III had derived "his principal knowledge of the constitution from Bute"; but he noted that the latter was well acquainted with the theoretical side of the constitution, and had procured part of Blackstone's *Commentaries* for the instruction of the Prince while the work was in manuscript. So far as the resignation of Pitt was concerned, Bute, says Adolphus, did not regard its occurrence in 1761 as "favourable to the King's affairs". So far as the resignation of Newcastle was concerned, Bute, when he was notified of its imminence, told the Duke that it might retard the conclusion of peace. Adolphus denies that Bute had any intention of hurrying the country into a disgraceful peace with France. He says that the election of 1761 had been delayed in order to enable Bute to strengthen his interest against that of Newcastle, but that Bute "took no measures to counteract those ministers, who were resolved to secure parliamentary adherents by means of government interest, but intirely independent of the crown". What Adolphus thoroughly condemns is the penalisation of so many people connected with the parliamentary opposition at the time of the crucial conflict over the peace treaty with France. Under Bute, he says (p. 128), the pernicious precedent was introduced, of removing every dependent of government, even to the lowest clerks in the public offices, to introduce others of his own nomination.

He removed this passage, however, from the second edition of his work in 1840.

Volume IX of Coote's *History of England*, which deals with the early years of George III's reign, appeared in 1802, and is bitterly hostile to Bute. Its account of those years is an example of the kind of historical narrative which primarily follows the pattern set in 1766 by the *History of the Late Minority*. Bisset, in 1803, follows a more reasonable course, as one might expect, and sees Bute as "a man of talents somewhat exceeding mediocrity".

> If we estimate his conduct from facts . . . we can by no means find just grounds for the odium which he incurred. . . . It was apprehended that the project of the minister was to govern by what his opponents called a system of mere court favouritism. The supposed operation of this plan was exhibited with great force . . . by speakers in parliament and political writers. . . . If we examine his particular nominations, we shall find that he neither exalted the friends of liberty nor despotism, but *his own friends*.

*   *   *

A Cambridge professor, William Smyth, attempted in about the year 1810 to produce an answer to Adolphus; and this is to be found in one of his *Lectures on Modern History* (see especially pp. 330–48). The chapter refers to George III as being still alive and in about the fiftieth year of his reign, though it appears that in 1823 a further passage was added to the text. Smyth's work has had no discoverable influence, for his Whiggism was rooted in the *ancien régime*, and even his form of the Whig interpretation of history was likely to have little relevance for his successors. Here, as in his study of the French Revolution, he was to a considerable degree under the influence of Burke. His theme was really the defence of aristocracy, and particularly the Whig aristocracy of the eighteenth century.

If Adolphus argued that the Whig oligarchy had held George III's predecessors in leading-strings, Smyth complained that on the contrary the aristocrats had been too complacent, too unwilling to check George I in the conclusion of his expensive treaties, for example. Even Sir Robert Walpole, he said, had shown "too great anxiety for the favour of the sovereign"; and though his observations were no doubt prompted by his jealous Whiggism, Smyth did anticipate the modern view that the early Hanoverian kings were not mere puppets in the hands of the oligarchy after all. In his view there were only two occasions on which the minister had thwarted the wishes of the monarch—the time when Carteret had been driven from office and the time when the elder Pitt had been forced into the ministry against the will of George II. Even in the latter case the elder Pitt, after becoming a minister, had very quickly gone over to "the German system of policy"—in other words, had become too much the servant of the King.

Smyth described "the constitution of these kingdoms" as having been "always in its letter a strong arbitrary monarchy"; but he asserted that there was "a vital principle" by which it was "heretofore in its practice rendered a benign limited monarchy, and to all essential purposes a free government". In his view:

> The king is not to be a cipher in the state; he is to select his ministers and servants from the public men which the country supplies; but it is *the proper exercise of this discretionary power* that is the question before us . . . and as it would be one extreme to leave him no exercise of his judgment, or no powers of choice, on the one hand; so is it, on the other hand, *another* extreme to lay down, and have it avowed as a system, that the government shall always be carried on by those whom he or the court think proper to denominate his friends.

According to Smyth, "the great desideratum" was an aristocracy "with popular feelings". But this was not to be found in
ancient Rome or modern Venice; it was not to be seen amongst
the remnants of feudalism in France or in contemporary Germany.
And how could such a thing be created?

> Now I must confess it appears to me, that we were furnished very
> tolerably with what we could desire, when we had the aristocracy of
> England such as it existed during the reigns of George I and George II.

Smyth's criticism of Adolphus and his complaint against the régime of Bute was based on his view of the role of the ruling class.

> It was the very end and aim of this new system to destroy this
> very aristocracy, at least that part of this aristocracy with which we
> are at present concerned; that part more particularly distinguished
> for its more popular principles, receiving confidence alike from the
> favour of the sovereign, and the approbation and gratitude of the
> people. . . .
> According to the new system, the king was to be as independent
> of his aristocracy, and not as intermingled as possible in all their
> interests and sympathies; to be rescued from the necessity of sharing
> his consequence with any order, or any individuals of that order.
> He was to rule by men who looked only to the throne, not by the
> Whig families who had some respect for themselves, as well as
> reverence for the monarch; and who looked also to the people. He
> was to choose his ministers, and that entirely as his own partialities
> directed him; that is, "favourites", under the title of friends, were
> to be preferred as fit objects of his confidence. . . . But this was not
> all. Great efforts were to be made to accomplish this destruction of
> the political influence and popular feelings of the Whig families; a
> miserable system of intrigue was to be entered upon. The least
> honourable men of each knot and division of the aristocracy were
> to be brought over to the court party, the better to destroy all con-
> fidence and union among those who remained. . . . And these
> new converts, these deserters and stragglers from their family and
> party attachments, from the notions of their ancestors, from the
> popular sympathies by which they had hitherto been so honourably

distinguished, these were the men who were to be associated as friends and familiars to the bosom of their sovereign.

In 1823 Smyth writes that "the new system has gone far to destroy the Whig families and their influence". And, he adds,

A fearful void, an arena that may very easily be covered with tumult and bloodshed, is immediately disclosed when the monarch is set on one side, and the people on the other, and an aristocracy with popular feelings is withdrawn from between them.

By 1843, when Smyth's lectures were published, this aristocratic Whiggism was already out of date.

*   *   *

We can gain an impression of the state of the historiography of this whole subject in 1813 from Volume XV of the *Parliamentary History* which appeared in that year and carried the debates of the two Houses over the early part of George III's reign. The somewhat lengthy historical notes appended to this part of the work are taken chiefly from Belsham, Adolphus and Bisset, and from the *History of the Late Minority*.

2. Early Developments

IT WOULD be wrong, then, to imagine that George III is one of those historical personages who from the very start have been particularly unfortunate in the way they have been commemorated. It is not the supporters of this monarch who have the right to complain that historiography set off on the wrong foot, or that the Whigs, stealing a march on everybody else, poisoned the springs of scholarship. The reign of Adolphus lasted for half a century, and his influence endured much longer still. Few interpretations of history have held the field for so long a period—or have dominated scholarship in so consistent a manner—as the one put forward by this writer. Scarcely a serious historian—not even Macaulay or Lecky—failed to incorporate into his work the evidence and the arguments which Adolphus offered and the general lines of his reconstruction. And in spite of the period of Whig historiography—when, even again, few writers failed to begin their narrative with an account of the Whig ascendancy and the case for the assertion of the monarchical principle—the prevailing framework of story was still governed by the ideas of Adolphus until the emergence of the Namier school. If it can be argued that Adolphus in 1802 somewhat overstated his case—that in fact George III was less radical in his purposes than perhaps he even felt himself to be or his enemies chose to assert—this view in itself (this emphasis on the analogy with Pitt, which appears again in writers like Lord Mahon and the Rev. William Hunt at a later time) was incorporated in the subtly different defence of the King put forward by Robert Bisset in 1803.

Even Sir George Otto Trevelyan at the end of the nineteenth century recognised the extraordinary affection felt for George III in the later decades of his reign—an affection which may have had some influence on the historians who dealt with his early years at a time when he was still alive. George III died in 1820, however, and it is arguable that after this date the students of his reign would deal with his personality more freely.

His death was followed by the publication in that year of Edward Holt's *Public and Domestic Life of George III*. In 1821 appeared Robert Huish's *Memoirs*, which in many places showed even a verbal dependence on the work of Holt. Both of them (but particularly Huish) showed an unmeasured hostility to Bute, though they were entirely favourable to the King himself. Both tell us that Bute was responsible for giving the young George III "predilections more befitting a despot of the Stuart line, than a successor of William III". Huish (p. 261) gives figures to demonstrate the increased use of secret-service money between 1758 and 1762. Both writers revive a charge that had been made in the middle of the eighteenth century; they say that a work by the Jesuit writer, the Père d'Orléans, on *The Revolution of the House of Stuart*, had been used to pervert the mind of the young Prince George. According to Dodington's *Diary*, the Prince's mother had denied this charge in 1753, though she had admitted that another of her sons, Prince Edward, had been involved in "a little dispute" over "le Père Perefix's history of Henry IV". In 1753, Prince George's sub-governor, Stone, had been accused of conduct which unfitted him for his educational task, but the case against him had failed. Dodington's *Diary*, however, reported George's mother, the Princess Dowager, as saying that her husband had regarded Stone as a Jacobite, and that she herself agreed with this view. Dodington's published *Diary*, therefore, had the effect of leaving the whole problem in an unsatisfactory state. Huish maintained that, apart from the work of the Père d'Orléans, Ramsay's *Travels of Cyrus* and Filmer's *Patriarcha* had been put before Prince George for the purpose of leading him astray. Up to this point there is no hint that Bolingbroke's *Patriot*

King was responsible for the despotic views which that Prince was accused of holding; and Horace Walpole's *Memoirs*, which assert the influence of Bolingbroke, were still unpublished and unknown. In any case, both Holt and Huish are clear that George III, by a native rectitude of understanding, foiled all the attempts that had been made to pervert his mind. They take the line that he was not more tenacious of his just prerogative than it was a king's duty to be for the sake of the country as a whole.

Huish favoured George III in his opposition to the Whig oligarchy that had hitherto dominated the country; though he used Burke's *Thoughts on the Cause of the Present Discontents* in an unexpected way, namely as the key to the malignant activities of Bute and his faction. He adds (p. 82) that it was the Earl of Bath who had given Bute the idea of a "double cabinet" of the kind that Burke had described in this treatise. The correspondence of Alderman Beckford, he says, would confirm the fact that the Earl of Bath had given the advice "that official men ought never to be trusted with information of any measure until it was given them to execute".

The question of the education of George III and the problem of Bute were brought to the notice of the world again in 1821 and 1822 by the publication of two important sets of political memoirs. First there appeared the narrative of the years 1754–8 by the Earl of Waldegrave, who had been the Governor of George, Prince of Wales. Then, according to the *Quarterly Review* (Vol. XXV, p. 414), the handsome payment which the publisher had made for the manuscript of this work, "awakened out of the dust of the family scrutoirs" Horace Walpole's *Memoirs of the Reign of George II*. These were purchased by John Murray, "at a magnificent price"; and John Wilson Croker, who was in a position to know, says that the sum was two thousand pounds. The two publications drew attention to the rise of Bute, and both of them—Horace Walpole in one of his most unpleasant passages—touched on the ancient rumours concerning the Princess Dowager's intimacy with the man. Huish had referred to the rumours for the purpose of illustrating the fortitude of George III in the face of slander; but an account of the new memoirs in the *Edinburgh Review* for 1822 showed that these works had provided material for the revival of malicious innuendoes. Allusions to these stories, says this article, "will be found in the private correspondence of all the distinguished politicians of the time. They may have been false, but they appear to have been universally believed".

Waldegrave's memoirs, partly because they gave the impression of studious fairness and came from so close an observer, provided a stronger case than had existed before for an unfavourable view of the personality of the youthful George, as well as raising doubts about his education. Concerning the Prince, Waldegrave had reported: "I found his Royal Highness uncommonly full of princely prejudices, contracted in the nursery, and improved by the society of bedchamber women and pages of the backstairs." He described the youth as "strictly honest" but wanting "that frank and open behaviour which makes honesty appear amiable". His religion was "free from all hypocrisy, but not of the more charitable sort". The Prince did "not want resolution, but it is mixed with too much obstinacy". There was "a kind of unhappiness in his temper. . . . Whenever he is displeased . . . he becomes sullen and silent and retires to his closet." Against his governors and preceptors "the mother and the nursery always prevailed", says Waldegrave. In George's twenty-first year, however, "there has indeed been some alteration: the authority of the nursery has declined, and the Earl of Bute, by the assistance of his mother, has now the entire confidence". This portrait of the youthful George was to be very important to the historians—and some of its phrases were echoed and re-echoed—throughout the nineteenth century.

At this point in the story we see the beginning of an important historical controversy and the opening of a new chapter in the story of historical writing on the subject of George III. John Wilson Croker now comes forward in the defence of that King, and he sets out also to discredit the unfavourable impression which the recently-published memoirs have given of the Princess Dowager and her circle. In the *Quarterly Review* (Vol. XXV) Croker pointed out the danger of putting trust in the writers of memoirs, and said (p. 394) that "it is only their *admissions against themselves* which can be safely relied on". He particularly deplored the fact that the partiality in the case of the Waldegrave narrative was "so artful and so gentlemanlike", and, therefore, liable to be so disarming. Waldegrave, he said, was convinced that his removal from his post as the Prince's Governor had been due to the desire of Leicester House that he should make way for the Earl of Bute. Therefore (p. 397) "we must receive, with great caution and with much abatement, the character which he gives" of Lord Bute himself, of the Princess Dowager and of the Prince of Wales. Croker set out to show that the facts which formed the basis for Waldegrave's description of the Prince would bear a more favourable construction than the one that had been placed on them. In spite of the criticisms he had to make, he paid an unusual compliment to the Memoirs which he had under review.

> Though the facts were pretty well known, they are related with greater detail—with more extensive knowledge of all parts of the transaction, and with a juster appreciation of the characters of the several persons and parties than any other writer has had either the opportunity to collect or the ability to convey . . . and if his lordship had taken the trifling trouble of dating the proceedings as he went along, we should have been inclined to say that his Memoirs were the best we had ever read, and to have proposed them . . . as a model of the species of writing. [p. 413]

Both of the new sets of memoirs of 1821 and 1822 touched on the subject of the political education of George III. Once again the

Edinburgh Review, in its commentary on these works (Vol. XXXVII), took the line that the question at issue—this time, the alleged Jacobitism of George's teachers—had not by any means been disposed of. Horace Walpole, in his long account of the controversy on the subject in 1753, showed the absurdity of the charges made against those who had care of the Prince's education. The accusation had reference to a youthful prank on the part of one of them—the alleged drinking of the Pretender's health—and even this was stated to have taken place twenty years before. But Walpole managed to convey the impression that if the accused were acquitted this was because there had been some tampering with the essential witness—a man who had claimed to be present at the time of the alleged offence. The *Edinburgh Review*, therefore, was able to take the line that enquiry had been "stifled in the House of Lords in a manner that leaves an unfavourable impression against the accused". Again the reader was left with the feeling that the sub-preceptor, Stone, had not really been exonerated. The same article (p. 6) resurrects the story about the Prince's reading which, as we have seen, the Princess Dowager, in a conversation with Dodington, had explained away:

> Certain it is, that a book in vindication of the arbitrary and illegal acts of the Stuarts found its way into the hands of the young Prince, without the knowledge of his preceptor.

The discussions in the years 1821–3 on the rise of Bute and the education of Prince George had little effect on the controversy we are particularly considering—the question of the aims of the court and the relations between the Crown and its opponents in the period immediately after the accession of George III. The journals which were engaged in the discussions did, however, throw out on occasion a suggestion which concerns our main theme or touches its margins; and one or two of these suggestions may be worth noting at the point which our narrative has now reached. During a considerable part of the nineteenth century, such periodicals as the *Edinburgh Review* and the *Quarterly Review* did in fact serve some of the purposes of our modern learned journals, especially as the study of history was generally much less technical than it has become today.

First of all, the *Edinburgh Review* at this time differed a little perhaps, from Adolphus, in that it did not accept the idea of the Whigs as constituting a firmly consolidated "phalanx" in the middle of the eighteenth century. It accepted rather the view of Lord Waldegrave and said that, instead of being "united in one body, under one general, like a regulated and well disciplined army", the Whigs were to be compared with "an alliance of different clans, fighting in the same cause, professing the same principles, but influenced and guided by their different chieftains".

Secondly, the *Edinburgh Review* was ready to accept the case which Adolphus and other writers had made against the Whigs who had had the predominance in the reign of George II, and was prepared to admit in particular the charge of corruption which was so often levelled against them. It attempted to pursue the enquiry into the actual source of these evils a little further, however; and the very zeal of the partisan would seem to have driven it one stage deeper in its historical analysis, one stage nearer to the recognition of a process in history. At the same time, the responsibility for the evils in question was now thrown back on the Tories themselves, who are made to stand out as the culprits at an earlier point in the argument. In the eighteenth century, said the *Edinburgh Review* (Vol. XXXVII, p. 24):

> The Tories, forced to remain in perpetual opposition to the Government, learned to ape the language, and ended by adopting many of the opinions, of their adversaries. The Whigs, believing the preservation of their liberties depended on the maintenance of the Parliamentary settlement . . . and finding themselves a minority in the country, were constrained to employ measures and sanction

proceedings, from which their ancestors would have recoiled. To counteract the local influence of the gentry, they practised and encouraged corruption both within Parliament and without; and thus turned against their enemies the weapon they [i.e. their enemies] had invented under the Stuarts. To suppress tumults of the rabble, instigated by the vehicles of Tory sentiments annually exported from Oxford, and dispersed over the kingdom, they armed the magistrates with additional, and, till then, unknown powers; and to defeat the enterprises of foreign princes, acting in conjunction with the disaffected at home, they maintained a standing army.

On the other hand, the main story, as Adolphus had laid it out, received a further development in an article on Lord Waldegrave's *Memoirs* in the first number of the *New Edinburgh Review*. In reality, says the author of this article, George II was no more content than George III to see any diminution of the royal authority. If George III proved more able to assert his prerogative, this was not because he was peculiar in his purposes and intentions, but because he happened to be assisted by changing conditions and the processes of time. Now, more clearly than before, we are invited to pay attention to types of historical development which have a hand in the game that is being played, changing the terms of the conflict or bringing new forces and factors to help one side or the other. According to the *New Edinburgh Review* (p. 14):

In the contest maintained by the first Mr. Pitt with George II, the aristocracy and the people were leagued against the king, who, besides, was unskilled in the machinery of the constitution, and was not aware of the valuable weapons contained in the royal armoury for the defence of the prerogative. This was better understood in the succeeding reign, when the influence of the crown was successfully exerted to break the union of the great families; and it is of this that Burke, in his well-known work, "Observations on the Present Discontents" [*sic*], chiefly complains, when he contrasts that period with the constitutional reign of George II. But it is clear, from Lord

Waldegrave's Narrative, that George II was most reluctantly forced into constitutional measures, and that nothing could equal the aversion and the arbitrary temper which he displayed, before submitting to those compliances which were extorted from him. It was to be expected that these struggles between the crown and the aristocracy would gradually develope the full extent of the royal powers; that the crown, by constant practice, would naturally grow more expert in the tactics and discipline of party warfare; that all its resources would be strictly looked after, and called into activity; and that, as all violent use of the prerogative was now to be forborne, the patronage and power would naturally be used gently, to mould to compliance with its views those whom it could no longer compel.

When we are following the history of the historiography of a given subject, it is always interesting to note where a writer begins to pierce behind the obvious narrative of the doings and sufferings of individual people—begins in fact to carry his analysis below the mere surface story. At such a point—as in the passage which has just been quoted—an influence comes to be attributed to organic developments which take place in politics and society; and a certain role in the story—a role beyond that of a mere sleeping-partner —can be seen to belong to the processes of history itself. In the nineteenth century the resort to this kind of historical thinking or explanation could not by any means be regarded as a novelty. Before ever George III had come to the throne Bolingbroke had provided an example very similar to the one that we have just been observing. Rightly or wrongly, he had set out to show that in the decades after the revolution of 1688, the progress in society, and particularly the multiplication of offices at home and overseas, had increased the opportunities for corruption and greatly enlarged the harm that might be done by an unscrupulous king. It is by such reference to the processes which are taking place in time, or by such a reduction of parts of the narrative to general processes, that the chronicle is carried to a higher level and the material of the narrative is churned into history. At this stage in historical thinking one is most reminded of the way in which the natural scientist tries to bring his results to a higher level of generalisation. Before his analytical work is completed, the historian, who began by noting movements in the landscape—commotions only on the surface of the countryside—may find that he is embarked on a geological examination of the scene. Where in the first place he had recorded only superficial motions taking place above ground, he may end by referring a great part of these to a subsidence occurring far below.

CHAPTER THREE

THE PERIOD OF TRANSITION

1. *Variations on the Theme of Adolphus*

DURING THE 1830's and 1840's it was the publication of memoirs and documents rather than the appearance of new narratives and interpretations which constituted the significant feature in the history of the historiography of George III's reign. So far as secondary writers were concerned, the framework that was given to the story still corresponded to the general formula which Adolphus had presented—the Whig ascendancy providing a dark background, and George III appearing as the enemy of oligarchical abuses. This king was fortunate once again—fortunate at a new stage of the story—in the historians who chose to write about his reign. A revised edition of the work of Adolphus appeared in 1840, though its alterations do not concern us. The book which gained general acceptance from this period was Lord Mahon's *History of England in the Eighteenth Century*—essentially a Tory work. The most powerful critical mind which was brought to bear on the whole historical theme was that of the famous Tory, John Wilson Croker. George III was perhaps unfortunate in another respect, however. There was a growing tendency to emphasise the fact that he was determined to exercise his rightful prerogative, particularly in "the free and unaffected choice of his ministers". As the nineteenth century proceeds it would seem that the world gradually forgets the degree to which this devotion to the prerogative might have appeared natural to the men of 1760, natural even to early historians like Adolphus. While the description or definition of George III's purposes may remain the same as before, one begins to see that the changing outlook of the Victorian era gradually induces a different reaction to the resulting picture.

A typical example of those who follow the basic pattern of Adolphus is the Rev. T. S. Hughes, who in 1836 published Volume I of his *History of England from the Accession of George III*. He provides a description of that system of influence and corruption "which gave so much power to the duke of Newcastle, that he was enabled to dictate any terms he pleased to his royal master, and to keep him in a state of bondage, as far as regarded ministerial arrangements". In his portrait of George III he depicts a king "fully prepared, both by precept and by natural disposition, not only to demand the free, unfettered choice of his public servants, but to exercise personally a stronger power than was always thought consistent with ministerial responsibility". We are told that once he had "broken that chain with which the great whig confederacy had fettered his predecessor" it was George's object "to throw open the administration to men of all parties, especially those whose principles led them to support the royal prerogative". Hughes tells us that "the character of George III was not formed to cherish favoritism, or to endure domination of any kind". He says (p. 111) that:

> Few . . . at present are found, who believe in that interior cabinet behind the throne, over which a mysterious power was supposed to preside, counteracting the plans of nominal ministers, and paralysing the efforts of struggling patriotism.

The "mystery" of the influence which Bute was supposed to have exercised after his resignation is to be explained, according to Hughes, by the "natural affection" of George III and by the "ties of filial obedience" which that king was unwilling to dissolve.

A political intercourse was constantly kept up between him and his mother, their intermediate agent being Mr. Jenkinson, the private secretary of Lord Bute. [p. 112]

In one sense Hughes carried the argument a stage further; for he had a certain notion of the processes which take place in history and had the capacity to survey the whole landscape at a given moment and to look for signs of a general change in the basic conditions of political life. He attempted, for example (p. 232), to describe the advantages which followed the breaking of "the bonds of that oligarchical combination which had so long fettered the prerogative".

It soon became necessary for those who sought office under their new sovereign, especially if they fought under the banners of opposition, to found their claims on the confidence of the people rather than family connexions: hence the whigs began to embrace larger notions of liberty, and to conciliate adherents by a zealous advocacy of popular rights. From this period they declined rapidly from that character which they had established at the revolution, contracting the habits of an opposition, and giving a different tone to parliamentary warfare: this, instead of being a struggle, as before, between whigs and tories, soon became a contest between the friends of the crown and the advocates of the people; so that although the king had liberated himself from the domination of the great families, his prerogative soon became more subject to the encroachment of popular pretensions.

Besides this attempt to put his finger on something like an example of organic change, Hughes tries to examine the House of Commons itself in a more analytical way; and, working from very imperfect materials, gives (pp. 232–3) the following note of the new situation that was arising:

About this period also the very form and constitution of parliament admitted a change; many of the smaller boroughs rejected the influence of high families, or even of the crown itself; transferring their representation to persons who were recommended solely by their wealth: indeed about the commencement of this reign we first hear of the sale of seats in parliament; whence an opening was made in the legislature for the representatives of the monied and commercial interests, which were now making such rapid advances: in short, the house of commons appeared to consist of four different bodies of men: the crown had its immediate friends, who affected to belong to no party, to maintain no parliamentary connexions, and to hold no fixed opinions; the aristocratical families still retained a considerable portion of that influence which is inseparable from rank and property united; the popular interest found advocates through the change of sentiments; and the monied interests through the change of representation above mentioned.

It had been Hallam who, at the very close of his *Constitutional History*—a work which purported to reach only the end of George II's reign—had declared in 1827 that he could trace the actual sale of boroughs no farther back than the beginning of the reign of George III. Hallam's remark influenced Lord Mahon (later, fifth Earl of Stanhope) in his *History of England*, and would seem, perhaps through misunderstanding, to have played a part in the development of the idea that corruption in parliamentary elections became more intense from the time of the election of 1761. A letter from Horace Walpole to Sir Horace Mann of 3rd March, 1761, describes the election expenses as "incredible". It says "West Indians, conquerors, nabobs, and admirals, attack every borough", but adds: "Corruption now stands upon its own legs—no money is issued from the Treasury . . . and yet venality is grosser than ever!" Professor Namier in his *England in the Age of the American Revolution* (p. 175 n.) throws further light on the source-material which led to the emergence of "astonishing conclusions" about this particular election.

*   *   *

In 1839 Lord Brougham published in his *Historical Sketches* a portrait of George III which is in many respects refreshingly different from the usual accounts of that king. He tells us that, as he writes, he has before his eyes "the correspondence which he [George] carried on with his confidential servants during the ten most critical years of his reign". The years in question coincided with the administration of Lord North, and at the end of another of his essays—the one on Lord North himself—Brougham prints a number of very brief extracts from these letters. The most remarkable feature of the study of George III, however, is the defence of that monarch's determination to exercise a genuine authority in the conduct of public affairs and to make his prerogative real. This piece of argument does perhaps illustrate the changing attitude of the world—a world that now needed to be reminded of the function which monarchs had existed to perform.

But, though Brougham is ready to defend George III in the most contested of his regal pretensions, his portrait of that king is by no means a favourable one. He clearly regards George as a man of "narrow understanding" and "obstinate disposition", and says that "in all that related to his kingly office he was the slave of deep-rooted selfishness". He was a king who "unhappily . . . took the wrong direction" and who, having chosen an unfortunate course, "persevered in it with the tenacity that marks little minds". He was "thoroughly master of all the ordinary details of business" and admirably diligent in the work of a king, but constricted in his vision.

> No proofs remain, nor has even any assertion been made, that he had any familiarity with the nobler branches of information connected with state affairs; the constitution and privileges of parliament; the jurisdiction of courts; the principles, nay, even the details of banking, or of trade generally.

George's ambition, however, says Brougham, was by no means "confined within the range of his abilities". The essential theme of the essay with which we are concerned is George's attempt to make the role of the monarch a real and effective one.

He was impressed with the lofty feeling of his prerogative, and a firm determination to maintain, perhaps extend it. At all events, he was resolved not to be a mere name, or a cipher in public affairs; and whether from a sense of the obligations imposed upon him by his station, or from a desire to enjoy all its powers and privileges, he certainly, while his reason remained entire, but especially during the early period of his reign, interfered in the affairs of government more than any prince who ever sat upon the throne of this country since our monarchy was distinctly admitted to be a limited one, and its executive functions were distributed among responsible ministers.

Brougham admits that "such a sovereign was, for the servants he confided in, the best possible master. . . . He gave them his entire and hearty support". He will not agree that George III's conduct was unconstitutional; and on the question of whether the King should be the mere puppet of his ministers he seems to stand somewhat in the position of Adolphus. He writes:

> Some maintain, nay, it is a prevailing opinion among certain authorities of no mean rank, that the sovereign, having chosen his ministers, assigns over to them the whole executive power. . . . They regard the only power really vested in the crown to be the choice of ministers, and even the exercise of this to be controlled by the parliament.
>
> Now, with all the disposition in the world to desire that Royal prerogative should be restricted, and the will of the nation govern the national affairs, we cannot comprehend this theory of the monarchy. It assigns to the crown either far too much revenue, or far too little power. . . . To affect living under a kingly government, and yet suffer no kind of kingly power, seems extravagantly absurd. Surely the meaning of having a sovereign is that his voice should be heard . . . in the administration of public affairs. . . .
>
> It is not denied that George III sought to rule too much; it is not maintained that he had a right to be perpetually sacrificing all other considerations to the preservation or extension of his prerogative. But that he only discharged the duty of his state by thinking for himself, acting according to his conscientious opinions, and using

his influence for giving these opinions effect, cannot be denied unless by those who [are] averse to monarchy. . . . The example is worthy of imitation in all times, which he set, in refusing to be made a state puppet in his ministers' hands, and to let his name be used either by men whom he despised or for purposes which he disapproved. Nor could any one ever charge him with ruling by favourites. . . . He had intimate friends with whom much of his time was passed, but they were under his influence in all things and influenced him in none.

In the essay on Lord North, Brougham in a most positive manner—and on the strength of information which proceeded "directly both from George III and from Lord Bute"—denied that Bute had continued his political influence or held communication with the King after his resignation from office.

*   *   *

Even Macaulay accepts the general framework which Adolphus had given to the narrative of this period, and repeats the "Tory" case against the Whigs who had governed the country in the reign of George II. His famous essay on Chatham in 1844 sets the stage in the way that is already familiar to us.

> The Whigs, according to what was then considered as their pre-scriptive right, held by far the largest share of power. The main support of the administration was what may be called the great Whig connection, a connection which, during near half a century, had generally had the chief sway in the country and which derived an immense authority from rank, wealth, borough interest, and firm union. . . . The old King was content; and it mattered very little whether he were content or not. It would have been impossible for him to emancipate himself from a ministry so powerful, even if he had been inclined to do so. But he had no such inclination.

Macaulay does not hesitate to point out the abuses of the system. In particular, he asserts that "the Whig ministers of George the First and George the Second were compelled to reduce corruption to a system, and to practise it on a gigantic scale".

89

He does not for a moment pretend that in 1760 there existed a happy constitutional order which George III wickedly set out to overthrow.

In his case again, however, there is a development of the historical argument—another variation on the theme of Adolphus. Here, as so often in his work—and even in his great *History* to a degree that has hardly been recognised—Macaulay has a passion for historical explanation, and takes pleasure in producing a significant expository passage. He does not deny the charges that are made against "the Whig oligarchy" of 1760, but he tries to show that they are capable of historical explanation. On the other hand, while recognising that George III set out to remedy the evils that were associated with the existing system, he criticises the methods to which the King resorted for the achievement of the object. In his essay on Horace Walpole in 1833 he had asked the question whether the remedy might not have been "worse than the disease".

Already in this earlier essay he had explained his attitude to the main political issues of the middle period of the eighteenth century. Sir Robert Walpole, he wrote, "governed by corruption because, in his time, it was impossible to govern otherwise".

> Corruption was unnecessary to the Tudors; for their Parliaments were feeble. The publicity which has of late years been given to parliamentary proceedings has raised the standard of morality among public men. . . . But, during the century which followed the Restoration, the House of Commons was in that situation in which assemblies must be managed by corruption, or cannot be managed at all. It was not held in awe, as in the sixteenth century, by the throne. It was not held in awe, as in the nineteenth century, by the opinion of the people. Its constitution was oligarchical. Its deliberations were secret. Its power in the State was immense. . . . In the reign of Charles the Second, accordingly, the practice of buying votes in the House of Commons was commenced. . . . A large proportion of the members had absolutely no motive to support any administration except their own interest, in the lowest sense of the word.

Under these circumstances, the country could be governed only by corruption.

In the later essay on Chatham, which deals with the reign of George III, Macaulay gave further development to this point. "The real cause of the prevalence of corruption and faction", he said, "was that a House of Commons, not accountable to the people, was more powerful than the King."

The House of Commons was supreme in the state; and all the vices which had till then been latent in the representative system were rapidly developed by prosperity and power. . . . Thus, while the ministry was accountable to the Parliament, the majority of the Parliament was accountable to nobody. In such circumstances, nothing could be more natural than that the members should insist on being paid for their votes, should form themselves into combinations for the purpose of raising the price of their votes, and should at critical conjunctures extort large wages by threatening a strike.

Macaulay, furthermore, is near to Adolphus in his description of the measures by which George III proposed to remove the evils. He differs from the Tory historian rather in his evaluation of those measures. In his view, the situation could only have been rectified by bringing the House of Commons into closer conformity with the wishes of the nation. Nothing could have met the case except the publication of the proceedings of parliament and the passing of a Reform Bill.

He had seen Walpole's *Memoirs of the Reign of George III* while that work still existed only in manuscript. But he was not dominated by it, in the way that later writers came to be; and he does not suggest that George III inherited a liberal constitution which it was his object to undermine. It was probably in Walpole that he discovered the alleged connexion between the ideals of George III and those of the *Patriot King*. Even on the subject of Bolingbroke, however, he does not fall into the conventional heresies of a later generation. He saw that the ideals of the

"Patriots" attracted many intelligent people in the eighteenth century, "particularly among men of letters".

Their political creed was a peculiar modification of Toryism. It was the creed neither of the Tories of the seventeenth nor of the Tories of the nineteenth century . . . but of the sect of which Bolingbroke may be considered as the chief doctor. This sect deserves commendation for having pointed out . . . some great abuses. . . . But . . . the reforms which Bolingbroke proposed would either have been utterly inefficient, or would have produced much more mischief than they would have removed. . . . [His] doctrine was that a vigorous use of the prerogative by a patriot King would at once break all factious combinations, and supersede the pretended necessity of bribing members of Parliament. The King had only to resolve . . . that he would not be held in thraldom by any set of men, that he would take for ministers any persons in whom he had confidence, without distinction of party, and that he would restrain his servants from influencing by immoral means either the constituent bodies or the representative body. . . .

Fundamentally, therefore, Macaulay is in the tradition of Adolphus when he sets out the ideals of the court in 1760. He differs from Adolphus because he disapproves of those ideals in spite of their plausibility; but he accepts the older way of formulating them and describing their nature.

The watchwords of the new government were prerogative and purity. The sovereign was no longer to be a puppet in the hands of any subject, or of any combination of subjects. George the Third would not be forced to take ministers whom he disliked, as his grandfather had been forced to take Pitt. George III would not be forced to part with any whom he delighted to honour, as his grandfather had been forced to part with Carteret. At the same time, the system of bribery which had grown up during the late reigns was to cease. It was ostentatiously proclaimed that, since the accession of the young King, neither constituents nor representatives had been bought with secret service money.

*   *   *

In 1844 Lord Mahon, later Earl Stanhope, produced Volume IV of his *History of England*, the volume which embarked upon the reign of George III. For a time this book occupied something like the position which had previously been held by Adolphus. It was a standard work, Tory in sympathy but moderate and central in its views, and regarded by Croker as remarkable for its impartiality and its eagerness to reach the truth. It was as an enemy of the Reform Bill that Mahon had made his début in the House of Commons in 1831. He was to gain the gratitude of historians and writers for the stimulus that he gave to the passing of the Copyright Act, the founding of the National Portrait Gallery, the creation of the Historical Manuscripts Commission, and the establishment of an Order of Merit for men of letters. He put forward the case that in the period after 1714 the role of Whigs and Tories became inverted; but the growing tendency to read our eighteenth-century history in terms of nineteenth-century party politics made the idea seem too paradoxical for people less expert than Croker. In 1898, the *Dictionary of National Biography* regarded this passage as the most unconvincing part of his narrative. Yet the idea would not have appeared strange in the early decades of the century.

Mahon was free, then, from some of the prejudices which lay behind the Whig interpretation, and it is clear that he came to this part of his history without having any unfriendly feeling towards George III, concerning whom he wrote in general (Vol. IV, p. 310):

> To the exalted duties of his station he devoted himself with conscientious and constant attention. The more the private papers of his reign come to light the more it will appear how closely, during fifty years, he superintended all the movements of the great political machine. At all times, and under all vicissitudes,—whether in victory or in disaster,—whether counselled by Ministers of his own choice, or in the hands of a party he abhorred,—he was most truly and

emphatically an honest man. "Though none of my Ministers stand by me, I will not truckle",—was his saying on one occasion, and his sentiment on all. I shall not deny that his prepossessions for or against any statesman were mostly too strong and difficult to conquer, nor that his firmness sometimes hardened into obstinacy. The earlier years of his reign were not free from errors of conduct or intervals of consequent unpopularity; but the longer he lived, and the better he was understood, the more his subjects felt how closely his general views and principles, his tastes and habits, were in accordance with their own. And thus in the latter half at least of his reign, after he had shaken off the sway of the northern Favourite,—the report of that sway which so long survived its reality,—the taint of the factions which Junius adorned and envenomed,—and the odium of the North American contest,—no monarch, not Henri Quatre, not Marie Theresa, not even our own Elizabeth, were ever more deeply rooted in the hearts of the people that they ruled.

According to Mahon, George III's early predilection for Bute, though it sprang from certain admirable qualities in him, was a serious mistake. "It is undoubtedly the part of a wise Sovereign on his accession to dismiss any partiality not founded on the public service."

> From the first moment of the new reign the ascendancy of Bute had been foreseen and foretold . . . and Bute appears henceforward to have been consulted on all the principal affairs. The quick-eyed tribe of Courtiers at once perceived that this was the channel through which the Royal favours would most probably flow, and to which their own applications would most wisely be addressed. [p. 312]

Yet Mahon, who had been allowed to see the Hardwicke Papers before their publication by Harris, had no sympathy with Newcastle or with the figure that he cut in his own letters in that collection. On the accession of George III, he wrote, Newcastle "made at first a show of resignation, with a view, no doubt, of enhancing his importance, but as he took care to consult only such followers and expectants as had an interest in his stay he did not fail to receive earnest entreaties in support of his real inclinations, and magnanimously consented to resume the Treasury". And Mahon—referring to Dodington's *Diary* and to the Mitchell MSS. in the *Chatham Correspondence*—adds a further example of this man's inconsistency:

> Nay, so keen was he at this very time in his race for Court favour against his colleagues, that he sent most abject messages to Bute, hoping to see him in some high employment, and declaring his own readiness to serve not only with but under him! [pp. 312–13]

Mahon gives (pp. 319–20) the following account of the policy which was adopted at the beginning of the new reign:

> It had been the peculiar happiness of Pitt's administration to dissolve the ancient ties of Jacobitism, and to blend the hostile ranks of Whig and Tory. Yet still many great families had continued from habit what had begun in aversion,—their estrangement from St. James's,—and had never appeared at the Court of George the Second. The accession of a new sovereign, born and bred in England, and wholly untainted with Hanoverian partialities, gave them a favourable opportunity to renounce, even in outward form, their obsolete political faith. Thus, then, the members of the old Jacobite connexion came flocking to the Levee-Room, and found a gracious reception confirm their new-born attachment. . . . In the new Household several noblemen of this old Jacobite connexion were appointed Lords—and several gentlemen Grooms—of the Bedchamber; an excellent policy, promoting the reconciliation of a party without any approximation to its principles in government.

To Mahon, therefore, the accession of George III entails a new system chiefly in the sense that it crowns the work already begun by Pitt—the work of reconciling Whigs and Tories, creating harmony, and bringing the former outcasts into official positions around the King. In this respect Mahon follows the thesis which had been put forward in the work of Bisset in 1803; but the harmony of parties, he says, existed for a moment only in appearance;

for the group which had long maintained a policy of proscription were determined not to surrender their share of power. According to Mahon, therefore, it is the Whig faction under the Duke of Newcastle which is determined to spoil the music almost as soon as the new reign has begun. The essential issue, the real reason for conflict in the early years of George III's reign, is the one which had already been pointed out by Adolphus—namely the assumption on the part of the Whig oligarchy that they had the right to both power and patronage.

But, however fair and specious seemed the unanimity which greeted the new reign, it was no more than apparent. Beneath that smooth surface jealousy, rancour, and ambition were already beginning to stir and heave. A small knot of grasping families among the Peers,—which wished to be thought exclusively the friends of the Hanover succession, and which had hitherto looked upon Court offices, honours, and emoluments as almost an heirloom belonging to themselves,—viewed with envious eyes the admission of new claimants, not as involving any principle of politics, but only as contracting their own chances of appointment. Such malcontents found a congenial mouth-piece in the Duke of Newcastle. [p. 321]

Mahon's conception of the history of party in this period was affected by his interpretation of the resulting conflict.

These new accessions to the Court [he writes],—who for the most part took shelter under the wing of Bute,—were called Tories, and . . . the name speedily extended to all those willing to support Bute's person or policy, while his opponents combined under the appellation of Whigs. Such was the first revival of those party nick-names which had been so gloriously extinguished or intermingled in Pitt's administration, and which, after some further phases during the reign of George the Third, came at length, in the reign of his son, to that remarkable counterchange from their early principles which I have elsewhere endeavoured to portray. [pp. 320–1]

2. The New Evidence, 1838–53

THE SERIOUS historical attack on George III had still to appear; but the ground was already being prepared for it by the mass of new material which was being presented to the public. *The Chatham Correspondence* came out in the years 1838–40, and the *Bedford Correspondence* between 1842 and 1846. Some of Horace Walpole's letters had been published at an earlier date, but in 1833 a first series of the ones to Sir Horace Mann had been produced and a second series in four volumes was issued in 1843–4. In the meantime a six-volume collection of Walpole's letters had appeared, the edition of 1840. In 1844 came the *Correspondence of Edmund Burke*; in 1845 Walpole's *Memoirs of the Reign of George III* and the *Memoirs and Correspondence of George, Lord Lyttelton*. In 1847 Harris's *Life of Hardwicke* brought to light some of the significant letters written by the Duke of Newcastle after the accession of George III. The *Rockingham Memoirs* appeared in 1852, the *Grenville Papers* in 1852–3, and the *Memorials of Charles James Fox* in 1853–7.

The *Quarterly Review* for March 1852 summed up the situation (p. 507) in the following manner:

> There is something resembling common consent in the publication, within the last few years, of the papers of those who played the most conspicuous part in that drama which began with the fall of Walpole and ended with the rise of North. The collection is nearly complete, and perhaps will be quite so when the papers of Lord Bute are added to the number.

The *Edinburgh Review* said in the following July (p. 114):

> Neither Aikin, Belsham nor Adolphus solved, or indeed had it in their power to solve satisfactorily, the Whig or Tory problems which they had respectively proposed. It was unsafe to put trust in [Horace] Walpole. . . . The North papers have been suspiciously destroyed;

but with the Bedford, Chatham and Rockingham correspondence before us, and the Grenville in course of publication—and we should rejoice if the archives at Luton [those of Bute] were similarly exposed to view—we are in the position to estimate fairly the claims of the King and of his ostensible or secret counsellors to the praise or blame hitherto accorded. . . . We are become, with the advantage of distance, spectators of the passions and intrigues which, whether in the Royal Closet, or in the conciliabula of Hayes, Stowe and Richmond, broke up the "Whig connexion" [and] reanimated the Tory party.

In reality—and not for the only time in the nineteenth century —the release of great quantities of additional source-material carried historians further away from the truth. The striking results were postponed a little; the materials were not immediately digested; and, for a time, the historian may go on patching the new materials into the old story. Now, however, George III had to suffer once again because the great men of the land—the Chathams, the Newcastles, the Rockinghams, the Burkes—had been his bitter enemies. Through their papers and memoirs they acquired a new kind of dominion, for they were to influence the historiography of the reign at an important point in its development. When politicians like Lord John Russell edited and selected the published materials (or wrote the biographical introduction), the defects in the nature of the evidence were greatly multiplied and enlarged. Unless a man had some particular reason—unless he were stimulated by a counter-balancing political prejudice, for example, and set out therefore in a determined way to vindicate George III—it was extremely difficult for him to resist the general impression which the mass of new publications produced.

The *Chatham Papers* were supported by a considerable amount of material which was given in the footnotes—letters of Lord Barrington and others from the Mitchell Manuscripts, and letters from Horace Walpole to George Montagu. Though not quite consistent in regard to the matter, this work tended to confirm the charge (that Bute continued to exercise an influence behind the scenes after his formal resignation.) It supported also a suggestion, which appears in the memoirs of Horace Walpole, to the effect that Bute in any case left heirs to carry on his work—men like Charles Jenkinson and Gilbert Elliot, who were destined for important offices. And it revealed Bute as securing extraordinary rewards at the close of his ministry both for his own followers and for those of his recent collaborator, Henry Fox. At this stage in the story it appears that the *Edinburgh Review* has changed its attitude, and that it is more anxious to speak on behalf of Scotland than to defend the cause of Whiggism. In dealing with the work (Vol. LXX, p. 94), it seeks to counteract those features of the *Chatham Papers* which seem to confirm "the common error of supposing that Lord Bute had some influence over and communication with the King after . . . 1763".

> This impression is visible throughout most of the letters in this collection in which any reference to Lord Bute is made. The truth is, nothing can be more utterly groundless than the supposition of his ever having interfered in public affairs after he resigned. We have the most positive assertions to that effect, on the authority of both George III, and the family of Stuart in Lord Brougham's Historical Sketches. . . . Mr. Wilberforce once in the House of Commons made the same statement distinctly and authentically; and these volumes [the *Chatham Correspondence*] contain a remarkable confirmation of it in the conversation between Lord Chatham and the King himself in August 1763.

The chief object of the writer of this article, however, was to reprove "the vulgar outcry" which had been "raised against Lord Bute on account of his birthplace":

> His defects as a statesman may have been considerable, although we verily believe they were much exaggerated; for he was a man of perfectly sound judgment, possessed of more plain good sense than fell to the lot of some more brilliant persons; and far better informed

than most politicians of his day. . . . He was sincerely attached to the constitution of the country; and no man ever had a more true or a more judicious friend than George III and his family possessed in him. That he wanted the decision which was required in whoever would guide the state at a crisis of complicated difficulty . . . is not to be denied. That he possessed none of the bold original views . . . which marked out Lord Chatham for universal admiration, which happily were attended with dazzling success, but which might have nearly ruined the country—is readily admitted; and the want of them was, indeed, one of the qualifications for filling the place of a sage councillor which Lord Bute relied on. . . . He professed to be "fit for a calm" and not one that would "steer too near to the shore to show his wit". . . . His was a compromising spirit, much more resembling the character of Lord Chatham's prudent and practical son, than the genius and the fire of the father. . . . He had, indeed, but small force of speech; spoke as much below his abilities as many others have done above theirs. . . . Some favouritism towards connexions and north-countrymen, he might perhaps be accused of; but assuredly not one whit more than might be found in the proceedings of all ministers in those days. Nor could anything be more clean-handed than his whole conduct as regarded himself. . . . He was a Scotchman, and that was all. [pp. 95-6]

There follow some reflections on the attacks which Wilkes, Barré and Shelburne had made upon the Scottish people; also some happier allusions to the improvement which had taken place in Anglo-Scottish relations during the subsequent hundred years.

The *Bedford Correspondence*, the *Life of Hardwicke* and the *Rockingham Memoirs* were of considerable importance because of the Newcastle letters they contained, and particularly their revelation of Newcastle's attitude to the régime of Bute. The students of those days, unfamiliar with the repeated whinings and constant querulousness of this magnate, would be all the more prone to accept his judgments, and his account of the way in which he was treated after the accession of George III. That a great change was contemplated by the new court, though its execution was postponed for a time, was suggested by a communication which Newcastle received from Bute only a little more than a week after the death of George II. Bute had said:

> The King would have everything go on for the present as it was in his Grandfather's time, and 'til the several officers are appointed, after the expiration of the six months; but when the new appointments are made, the King will then declare whom he will call to his cabinet council. [G. Harris, *Hardwicke*, Vol. III, p. 230.]

The evidence, though it may have helped the enemies of the King, was by no means always fortunate for the reputation of Newcastle himself, however; and Lord Mahon, as we have seen, found in the *Bedford Correspondence* and the Hardwicke papers, the basis for a hostile treatment of this Duke. The moderate attitude which the old Earl of Hardwicke had maintained in the early years of the reign, and his frankness about Newcastle's errors, helped, if anything, to put the case for George in a better light. Certainly Hardwicke was more prepared for what happened after the opening of the reign than Newcastle himself, and he advised the latter to resign, while making it clear that he, personally, had no love for Bute. After Newcastle had resigned, however, Hardwicke showed that it was not his intention to insist on the resignation of three of his younger sons. He made the following significant comment on the attitude of the Duke:

> And you will forgive me, my dear lord, if I express some surprize at your general observation—*that you see interest and corruption prevail so far, that you despair of doing any good.* This cannot possibly be new to your Grace, who has been conversant in courts and parties above these forty years. Have you not all along seen such motives to be the great hinges on which the generality of people's conduct has turned? [*Ibid.*, p. 326.]

Hardwicke, who may have been anxious that his family should not be exiled from political favour, was ready to believe that the power of Bute would have to be opposed, but wished to wait until opposition should have been justified by real offences on the part of the ministry. His note on corruption ought not to be overlooked by those people who are tempted to argue that corruption did not matter at all.

In reality, George Harris, the author of the *Life* of Hardwicke, adopted a fairly favourable view of George III, though attributing considerable influence to the Princess Dowager, and repeating the story that she told her son to "be a king". Harris's disapproval is directed rather against George II, whom he regards as having had "strong predilections for a foreign nation". He says of this king (p. 222):

> To a large extent . . . he was not only the chooser of his own ministers, but the director also of all the most important measures propounded by them; and into every political step taken he seems to have entered fully, even to the very details.

In George III, on the other hand, Harris saw (p. 228) "a king who was divested of the strong personal, political and national prejudices which had animated his grandfather".

> No hereditary sovereign ever did so much by his own individual measures to advance the real power and welfare of the country as he did, or was more jealous of his own and his people's honour.

Even those publications of the mid-nineteenth century which related more particularly to the associates of Bute—the Duke of Bedford and George Grenville, for example—influenced historiography chiefly through the adverse evidence which they had to contribute. The *Grenville Papers* do comprise (Vol. I, pp. 392–3) a letter of 2nd October, 1761, from Bute to Grenville, in which occurs the significant sentence: "Mr. P[itt] has taken leave of us, and the K[ing] left in a most perilous situation to form a new Ministry." In other words, Bute was by no means happy to see the departure of Pitt at this time. Even in this work, however, the critics of George III were to find further material for their attack on the system of Bute. On 13th October, 1761, for example, Grenville produced a number of rough notes of the ideas and intentions which Bute had just been communicating to him. The meaning of these is not always clear, but the document (*ibid.*, pp. 395–6) was to prove useful to later critics of the régime of George III.

> General conduct of the Duke of Newcastle, and reasons to show the impossibility of him or his friends acting the [formidable] part which I [Grenville] suspected; immediate punishment, crazy old man. Young King, young nobility . . . D[uke] of N[ewcastle] does not look upon him as formidable: detail of N[ewcastle]'s conduct during the last reign: odious in his, B[ute]'s opinion; pusillanimity in the Closet, . . . foreign ideas, sole access, power of calling people rascals and Jacobites: since the accession B[ute] has no reason to find fault with his [Newcastle's] behaviour: great change in his situation in regard to the King: knew his own power diminished: would insist on nothing: would press for his friends and acquiesce where it would not do . . . had certain information that after the Peace N. would resign when called upon: thought it therefore better to let this old man tide over a year or two more of his political life: saw many among his people who were worthy and fit to be brought forward in the King's service.

The publication of the new materials in this period gave Lord John Russell the opportunity to formulate an extremely partisan Whig version of the reign of George III. This is already set out in his Introduction to the *Bedford Correspondence*, which shows that the editing of the new materials was itself a factor in the development of historiography. Some of the evidence quoted by Russell would in reality have served to support rather the interpretation given by Adolphus. There is a passage, for example, from a letter written by Gilbert Elliot to his father—a letter quoted from the Minto manuscripts. It suggested that a large-scale attack on the Whig oligarchy was in contemplation; for

Elliot wrote: "Nor is it to be expected that in such critical times, ancient systems of power will fall to the ground without a struggle." This remark of 24th June, 1762, though it followed Newcastle's resignation, preceded his open hostility to the government. It is curiously reminiscent of the words of Dodington in the very first weeks of the reign about the difficulty and danger of the attempt "to recover monarchy from the inveterate usurpation of oligarchy".

Russell seems to have been disposed to put a more sinister interpretation on language of this kind. He regarded the materials he had collected as evidence of a design against the constitution at the opening of the reign of George III:

> The letters of the King, the letters of Sir Gilbert Elliot, the friend of Lord Bute, the statement of Mr. Adolphus [that the Whig families were no longer necessary to guard the parliamentary title of the House of Hanover] . . . all corroborate the general view taken by Mr. Burke in his "Thoughts on the Causes of the Present Discontents". Not that the plan of Lord Bute and his royal pupil was of so systematic a character, nor the government to be subverted of so beneficent a nature, as the great Whig statesman portrayed to the world; but that the project of restoring to the Crown that absolute direction and control which Charles the First and James the Second had been forced to relinquish, and from which George the First, and George the Second had quietly abstained, was entertained and attempted by George the Third, can hardly be doubted. [Vol. I, p. xxix.]

From Burke's *Thoughts* Russell took the view that George III, from the time of his accession, set out to dissolve party connexions, to free the Crown from ministerial tyranny and to assert the supremacy of the King over parliament. He described Adolphus as a writer "who in many points is singularly accurate", but used him in support of the view that George III and Bute had had a "plan for breaking the power of the Whig aristocracy". He brought evidence from a period somewhat later than the one we have been considering to justify his version of George's original policy; for he quoted (pp. xxvi–xxvii) from the *Chatham Correspondence* the letter in which the King in 1766–7 asked for help "towards *destroying all party distinctions* and restoring that subordination to Government, which alone can preserve . . . liberty". He introduced further letters in which the King talked of the effort "to rout out the present method of parties banding together" and condemned "that evil called connection". These things are no longer described as a necessary remedy for the abuses that we associated with the Whig oligarchy. They are now recounted rather as evidence of George III's determination to advance the royal power. Some of the documents in the *Bedford Correspondence*, including Rigby's defence of the dismissal of Newcastle's followers after the debate on the preliminaries of peace, might have suggested that there was another side to the story. Historians seemed content rather to follow general impressions, and paid too little attention to discrepant pieces of evidence.

In the case of the *Rockingham Memoirs* the views of the editor, Lord Albemarle, which were amply dispersed amongst the documents, governed the character of the whole work. Albemarle reproduced (Vol. I, p. 6) the statement made by Hardwicke in 1770:

> In the beginning of the new reign no apparent alteration happened to our situation—we were cajoled and courted for the first weeks of it . . . but, in reality, Lord Bute had the sole power and influence; and he was determined to work out the old servants of the crown.

For half a century the evidence of Bubb Dodington had been the central factor for the historian—the basis for an exposition of George III as the enemy of a corrupt oligarchy. Now, however, Albemarle's work showed how new forms of evidence were coming to be strategic—coming to hold the first place in the mind

—and were producing a picture of George III as rather the enemy of Whig constitutional ideals. The hostile views of Newcastle, Hardwicke, and the elder Pitt were bound to provide the student at the very start with a different picture of the situation. Apart from the new sources which have already been considered, the *Memoirs* of Horace Walpole, which must be examined shortly, were beginning to exert their influence. The effects of the ideas of Edmund Burke become more perceptible than before, and are attested by explicit allusions, although even now his judgments are not slavishly followed. All the main evidence against George III seemed to be appearing at once, and the different contemporary versions of the case for the prosecution were being compounded into one version. With the passage of time, moreover, some of the traditions which had hitherto helped to supply the historical explanation for George III and Bute had apparently dropped out of remembrance. It had become more difficult to avoid seeing the followers of Newcastle through the eyes of modern Whiggism, though for a time one might still go on believing that by 1760 that party had been spoiled by success. The programme of Bolingbroke came to be reconstructed by people who interpreted it in the light of traditional Toryism, and who either neglected the sources of his teaching or were unable to see it in its true context. Albemarle's description of the system of George III (Vol. I, pp. 3–4) shows how these various factors were producing a strongly Whig interpretation.

> The system, indeed, was not altogether new. It originated in the factious court of Frederick, Prince of Wales . . . denominated the Leicester House School of Politics. Its inventor was Bolingbroke, and its leading features are shadowed forth in the . . . "Patriot King." . . . The primary object of the Leicester House system was to break up the powerful Whig confederacy. . . .
>
> But since the Whigs, collectively, were too powerful and too popular a body to be summarily dismissed, the leading men were to be

removed, one by one, from the Cabinet and the Household. . . . They virtually wished to supersede both the old Whig and Tory parties, and to create a third party, which might form a barrier against the attempt of any future cabinet to act independently of the royal will . . . a cabinet or household of favourites was to be placed around the sovereign. . . . A confederacy of renegades from every political section of the state was accordingly formed. . . . The [King's Friends] . . . abjured all party distinction, and professed to regard the pleasure of the sovereign as the sole source and condition of power. Although holding many of the offices under the crown, they acted irrespectively of the King's constitutional advisers, and voted with or against ministers according to the expressed or supposed predilections of their royal master.

The powerful Whig confederacy which George III was alleged to have set out to destroy might be regarded as suffering from abuses and from the effects of a long tenure of power; but in the middle of the nineteenth century it was beginning to be seen as essentially a good thing—a barrier against the most dangerous of evils, monarchical authority. And the measures which George III had been regarded as taking in order to free himself from imprisonment by a powerful oligarchy were now interpreted as the means by which he meant to establish arbitrary government.

CHAPTER FOUR

THE CRITICAL CONTROVERSY

---

1. *Horace Walpole's Memoirs*

AT AN early stage in the development of the historiography of a subject it is often the case that memoirs play a particularly important part in the work of recovering and reassembling the past. They are capable of exercising at any time perhaps greater power over the historian than any other kind of source, unless the reader is aided by an unusual degree of critical awareness. Over and above the new facts which such a work may carry, or the fresh light which it may throw upon events that are already familiar, it is likely to provide a ready-made framework for the story of an entire period, its evidence coming to us inextricably entangled with a particular interpretation of it. Such a work may induce the historian to imagine that he is exempt from the trouble of making his own reconstruction—exempt from the task of reassembling the drama out of the raw materials for himself.

Amongst the most famous and interesting of all the memoirs in our literature—and amongst the most important in the history of our historiography—are the ones written by Horace Walpole about the reign of George III. After their publication in 1845 they were regularly quoted by historians and they were used by the editors of other papers relating to the same reign—the *Bedford Correspondence* and the *Memorials of Charles James Fox*, for example. At the crucial point in the story they were most influential of all, perhaps, not for their concrete evidence but through their "tendency"—through the author's superadded comments, and through the way in which he "mounted" the story and set the scene. Walpole's main charges against the court in the early years of the reign were rarely new, though he added to their vividness by the fervour of his presentation or by the pointedness of his anecdotes and illustrative details. But whether he was discussing personalities or policies or deeds or states of mind he knew how to flavour his account with a wealth of imagination. He brought the innuendo also into his larger narrative, so that it coloured his whole version of the general political history of the time. In his work, the supposed change of system at the accession of George III is alleged to have been an imposture—a mere plausible covering for what was really a revival of Toryism and high prerogative. The events from the very beginning of the reign are now reinterpreted in the light of a supposed conspiracy to establish absolutism in the country.

Horace Walpole certainly knew what he meant when he called himself "a Whig", and indeed he was a Whig of the traditional type. In 1756 he had described how on one side of his bed hung "*Magna Charta*" and on the other side the warrant for Charles I's execution "on which I have written *Major Charta*". To be a Whig, in his view, meant to oppose the personal power of a king, and to be a Tory meant to support that power, in other words, to favour the prerogative. He tells us in his *Memoirs* that, at the accession of George III, government was in the hands of a "firm" administration, the members of which were "in good harmony with one another". Unfortunately, he says, "a passionate, domineering woman, and a Favourite, without talents, soon drew a cloud over this shining prospect" (1894 ed., Vol. I, p. 4). Concerning George's mother, the Princess Dowager, "whose ambition yielded to none", he insists that she was "desirous to figure in the new era" (p. 10). She was "ardently fond of power, and all its appanages of observance, rank, and wealth" (p. 14).

And "mankind was not inclined to think that her morals could have imprinted much devotion on the mind of her son". At the same time,

> [George III] was accessible to none of his Court but at the stated hours of business and ceremony: nor was any man but the Favourite, and the creatures with whom he had garrisoned the palace, allowed to converse with the King. [p. 14]

Walpole gives an unfavourable description of the personality of the King—one which tallies in a curious way with the portrait which Lord Waldegrave had provided in the *Memoirs* quoted earlier in the present essay.

From 1760, according to Walpole (p. 42), the court "conducted themselves by the advice bequeathed by Lord Bolingbroke, who had, and with truth, assured the late Prince of Wales that the Tories would be the heartiest in the support of the prerogative". And Walpole will not allow us to believe that it was the object of the new régime merely to annihilate the difference between "Whig" and "Tory". This, he says, had certainly been the object of the elder Pitt in the period before 1760. "The extinction of parties had not waited for, but preceded, the dawn of his [George III's] reign" (p. 4). The new king had other objects than this; or, supposing that nothing more than this had been in his original intention, his plan had been diverted—diverted perhaps through the conduct of the Tories who benefited from the abandonment of the old policy of proscription.

> The countenance shown to the Tories, and to their citadel, the University of Oxford, was at first supposed by those who stood at a distance from the penetralia, [to be] the measure of Mr. Pitt, as consonant to his own desire of uniting—that was breaking—all parties. [p. 13]

Walpole quoted Pitt as saying in parliament, some months after his resignation, that he himself "had contributed to annihilate *party*, but it had not been to pave the way for *those who only intended to substitute one party to another*" (p. 130). In reality the principles of Toryism were being brought into favour at court and the doctrine of the prerogative was achieving the ascendancy again.

> The Tories, who were qualified for nothing above a secret, could not keep even that. They came to Court, it is true; but they came with all their old prejudices. They abjured their ancient master, but retained their principles. . . . *Prerogative* became a fashionable word; and the language of the times was altered before the Favourite dared to make a single variation in the Ministry.
> These steps did not pass unnoticed; nor was the nation without jealousy, even in the first dawn of the reign. [p. 13]

Walpole had always been what we might call an "old Whig", as we have seen; and when he produces the *Memoirs* in the form in which they were published he sees in the early years of George III's reign the conflict of traditional Whiggism with traditional Toryism.

> The Tories, triumphing in the partiality of the Court, and rather offended than alarmed at the jealousy with which they were beheld by the Whigs, who in power, property, and credit were beyond comparison the preponderating part of the nation, took every occasion of displaying their old prejudices and resentments. On every contested election they acted in a body against the old Whigs, or later converts, however attached to the Court. Thus they exerted all their interest against Lord Gower and Lord Orford on election causes, and against the Duke of Bridgwater and Lord Strange, on a bill for a new northern navigation—points, on every one of which the Tories were rancorous and unsuccessful. . . . Nor did his partisans do more than was practised by the Favourite himself. If they insulted the nation, he ruled the Court with a rod of iron. [p. 109]

If the *Memoirs* dispose in this way of the vaunted policy of annihilating the difference between "Whig" and "Tory", they are no less severe in their handling of the claim that the projects of the new reign involved the abolition of corruption. The court is described as crying out against the corruption and the jobbery with which the Whigs had so long been associated; but Walpole, like the opposition writers of the time, taunts the men around Bute for their priggishness, and charges them with insincerity. "It was given out that he [George III] would suffer no money to be spent on elections", he says (p. 16). He tells us that "the King's declaration against corruption in elections was much "vaunted"; but adds that such announcements were made only to undermine the influence of the Duke of Newcastle—the Duke was the one who would be the loser if such forms of parliamentary influence were abandoned (p. 42). When he deals with the election of 1761, Walpole says (p. 31):

> All attention was engrossed by the approaching general election of a new Parliament. It had been propagated that the King had forbidden any money to be issued from the Treasury. Nothing was less true, in fact, or proved less true in effect. Both the Court and particulars went [to a] greater length than in any preceding times.

Though he is so hostile to George III, to the court and to the Tories, Horace Walpole has little sympathy with the Duke of Newcastle. He describes him as "a ridiculous old dotard, who had ever been in everybody's way, and whose feeble hands were still struggling for power, when the most he ought to have expected, was, that his flattery and obsequiousness might have moved charity to leave him the appearance of credit". According to Walpole, it was the deliberate object of the court to make Newcastle more and more uncomfortable in his position at the head of the Treasury. "At first it was designed by disgusts to drive the Duke to resign. [Gilbert] Elliot and [James] Oswald were instructed to treat him rudely at his own board" (p. 122). After Newcastle had resigned and tried forces with George III, we are given (p. 134) a withering picture of the changed face of politics in Great Britain.

> That he might taste the full mortification of being deserted by those whom he had most obliged . . . the clergy gave the most conspicuous example of ingratitude. For thirty years Newcastle had had the almost sole disposal of ecclesiastic preferments, and consequently had raised numbers of men from penury and the meanest birth to the highest honours and amplest incomes in their profession. At this very period there were not three bishops on the bench who did not owe their mitres to him. His first levée after his fall was attended by but one bishop.

Walpole's influence on the historiography of this period was considerably increased by the liveliness of the account which he gave of the political contest between the court and the main body of the Whigs. The following is his description (p. 157) of the methods of Henry Fox, who acted as Bute's parliamentary manager during the crucial conflict over the peace treaty with France:

> Leaving the grandees to their ill-humour, he [Fox] directly attacked the separate members of the House of Commons; and with so little decorum on the part of either buyer or seller, that a shop was publicly opened at the Pay Office, whither the members flocked, and received the wages of their venality in bank-bills, even to so low a sum as two hundred pounds for their votes on the treaty. Twenty-five thousand pounds, as Martin, Secretary of the Treasury, afterwards owned, were issued in one morning; and in a single fortnight a vast majority was purchased to approve the peace!

The victory of Bute in this conflict is interpreted (p. 158) as a vindication of monarchical power against parliamentary government as such:

> The Court having secured the obedience of Parliament, it was determined to assume a high tone of authority; to awe, and even to punish, the refractory. "The King", it was given out, "*would* be

King—would *not* be dictated to by his ministers, as his grandfather had been. The prerogative was to shine out; great lords must be humbled. . . ."

Finally Walpole describes with great relish (pp. 184-5) the way in which the court followed up its victory against the Duke of Newcastle, pursuing the members of the defeated party with unprecedented cruelty:

> A more severe political persecution never raged. Whoever, holding a place, had voted against the preliminaries, was instantly dismissed. The friends and dependents of the Duke of Newcastle were particularly cashiered; and this cruelty was extended so far, that old servants, who had retired and been preferred to very small places, were rigorously hunted out and deprived of their livelihood. . . . Schutz, who had been seven years of the King's bedchamber, was turned out, for no reason but that he had not a seat in Parliament, and could be of no use there.

It was left for the editor of the *Memoirs* to point out that Mr. Schutz was a very rich man.

For the historians of George III's reign, who seem not always to have read the *Memoirs* with a very close regard to details, and indeed not always to have read them through, these opening passages of the work served to set the tone for the whole reign. To the author of these *Memoirs*, the alleged new system of George III and Bute was in reality no attempt to rectify the constitution, but merely the cover for a revival of Toryism and high prerogative principles. At one point, however, Walpole seems to admit that he is bringing his knowledge of later years to decide the way in which the opening period of George III's reign shall be interpreted. He writes (p. 14):

> The views of the Court were so fully manifested afterwards, that no doubt can be entertained but a plan had been early formed of carrying the prerogative to very unusual heights.

He confesses, furthermore, in one place, that his judgment of the reign of George III had not always been as severe as it was at the time of writing. He tells us (p. 167):

> The truth was, I had been civilly treated on the King's accession, and had so much disliked Newcastle and Hardwicke, that few men were better pleased than myself to see a new administration; and had not the standard of Prerogative been hoisted, and disgrace brought on this triumphant country, I should probably have remained a satisfied spectator.

These two pieces of self-revelation are worth noting, for they remind us that the *Memoirs* of Horace Walpole are written after the passage of years; the work is loaded with the author's afterthoughts; it has the advantages and the disadvantages of a retrospective survey. One of the many tests which a critical student would apply to a source of this kind would be a close comparison of its contents with the ideas and the information which its author can be shown to have possessed at the time when the events were actually happening.

If we compare Horace Walpole's *Memoirs* with the letters which he wrote to one person and another in the early 1760's, the surprises are very great indeed. No doubt it was because he was so hostile to men like Newcastle and Hardwicke, and so grateful for being "civilly treated on the King's accession", that he welcomed the new reign and looked forward to the establishment of a new régime. In fact we find that Walpole at the time was surprised to note how few were the changes which occurred after the accession of George III; and it is interesting to see that he praised the Earl of Bute for his moderation (e.g. in a letter to Sir Horace Mann of 17th March, 1761, but also in his *Memoirs*, Vol. I, p. 10). Whether for private reasons or for public reasons—and probably for a confused mixture of the two—he rejoiced as he came to observe the discomfiture of the people who up to the moment had seemed to dominate the country. When Newcastle fell and George III was seen to be in conflict with the magnates of the Whig party, Horace Walpole, like many of his contemporaries, welcomed the reassertion of the monarchical principle. He writes to Sir Horace Mann on 9th November, 1762:

> It is very amusing to me to see the House of Lords humbled. I have long beheld their increasing power with concern. . . . I am convinced that nothing but the crown can reduce the exorbitance of the peers.

In the *Memoirs*, however, he desires that the power of the Whig magnates shall be increased, in order to counterbalance the undue influence of the Crown.

It was from Walpole's *Memoirs*—though not from this source alone—that there came into the school-books the assertion that George III's mother was the sinister influence behind the throne. Yet, in the letters written while she was still alive, Walpole insists that "no petticoat ever governed less". And even when she dies, he is still on her side, and he still pities her because of the unjust things that have been said about her. In 1765 he was so far from regarding George III as a tyrant that he wrote to George Montagu on 26th May:

> Prerogative—alack! he is grown so tame, that . . . you may stroke him. George the Third is the true successor of George the Second, and inherits all his grandfather's humiliations.

During the crisis which developed in 1769–70 out of the controversies over Wilkes and the Middlesex Election, he was afraid that the mob would overthrow the constitution. He condemned the conduct of the parliamentary opposition, and we find him still writing: "The King is much to be pitied." He praised the prudence and the moderation of Lord North, and rejoiced as he came to realise that, under North, the administration was going to survive the storm. In the published *Memoirs*, however, the existing Lords and Commons are both condemned, as having "sold" themselves to the King. And now Walpole writes as though he had been in opposition during the crisis of 1769–70.

It would appear that the original draft of the *Memoirs of the Reign of George III* was more closely conformable to the views that Walpole had expressed in his letters—the views he had had at the time when the events were taking place. Those views changed later in the reign, and particularly from 1775, when Walpole greatly resented the conflict with the American colonies. Once the change had taken place Walpole made it retrospective— he revised very radically the attitude he had adopted towards George III in the early 1760's. He then set out to alter at strategic points the draft of the *Memoirs* which he had previously written. Sometimes he would seem to have patched the revised portions in a slovenly manner into the text of the old; for he now produced a passionate diatribe against Lord North, but seems to have forgotten to delete what must have been an earlier passage—quite a panegyric of the same minister—leaving us a conflict of mood, a sign of geological rift.

It is not to be assumed that Walpole's later views were less sincere than his earlier ones; and it cannot be mechanically taken for granted that the verdicts of the *Memoirs* are unreliable—that we must give credit only to Walpole's letters and to the judgments which he made when the events were happening. The *Memoirs*, as we have seen, are likely to possess both advantages and disadvantages. Information acquired later, moods and attitudes that belong to the after-period, second-hand knowledge transmitted by new political friends—all these new factors have their effect on both the narrative and the commentary. When memoirs are of the nature and the structure of Walpole's they are not merely contemporary evidence—if they embody the afterthoughts of the historian, he will not necessarily be the unprejudiced historian. Letters which are genuinely contemporary may have a utility of their own precisely because they are written without this after-knowledge. As sources they are in a more raw and un-prepared state, and for certain important purposes their reporting may be more useful for the historian than the more carefully prepared results of retrospective enquiry. Letters, too, however, may suffer from prejudice or frivolity, and the fact that they are contemporary does not mean that they will not be defective in their information or ill-considered and unfair in their views. Horace Walpole, therefore, has left for the historian two great bodies of material and two imposing sets of opinions and reactions, both of which require a careful critical apparatus.

2. John Wilson Croker and the Tory View

THE NEW tendencies in historical writing were not allowed to proceed unchallenged, and the new printed sources did not secure an unthinking acceptance. The critical articles which were produced by John Wilson Croker bring the history of the historiography of this subject to one of its exhilarating points. In spite of his obvious Tory partisanship, Croker is important to us because he had so much of the specialised outlook of the technical historian. In his own day he was charged with paying too much attention to *minutæ* and attaching too great importance to dates. (See *The Croker Papers*, I, 27.) He was the kind of historian who is primarily intent on the recovery of the concrete narrative, and on the precise laying-out of the facts of the case. At crucial points one discovers that a certain scientific passion which he possessed might even override his Tory prejudices.

Now that we have begun to examine more closely the way in which critical methods developed amongst historians, we find that some writers, like the Catholic Lingard, are emerging into unexpected significance. Croker is one of these; and if his importance came to be overlooked after his death, this was partly because he was so well known as a Tory, partly because his work appeared in anonymous articles in the *Quarterly*, and partly because he produced his history in the process of reviewing other people's books. Also, very soon after he had passed off the stage, the Whig interpretation came to hold the field.

Yet the world did not forget in the same way his services to French Revolutionary studies, where his work was even more important. In this field he collected the masses of pamphlets and periodicals which ultimately were to enrich the British Museum; and though, here again, he was provoked into writing by the appearance of other people's books, he built up more positive studies of his own, and came somewhat nearer to the production of narrative history. So far as the French Revolution was concerned, he stood as the disciple of Burke, and he follows Adolphus in a central stream of English historiography, which is moderate in its outlook, though it regards the Revolution as an evil that might have been avoided. His Toryism added fire and vigour to his pen, and in 1831 the debates on the Reform Bill inaugurated his long conflict with Macaulay, who believed that more concessions by the French nobility would have prevented the Revolution. Croker held that the French nobility betrayed their own cause by their timidity—their over-readiness to make sacrifices or to retreat in the face of threats. In his French Revolutionary studies he had many opportunities for stressing the unreliability of memoirs at a time when historical writers were depending greatly on this kind of source. His critical procedures in respect of such memoir-material would seem to place him well in advance of his English contemporaries, in spite of certain defects in his application of his principles.

We may feel ourselves one stage nearer the world of modern scholarship as Croker surveys the state of George III studies on occasion—discussing the range of sources now generally available, referring to others which he has privately seen or located, and noting others again—the papers of Bute and the letters of George III, for example—which have still to appear. Partly because of his involvement in this whole field of study, and partly because of his connexion with John Murray, the publisher, Croker himself played a significant part in the publication of the manuscript sources for the reign of George III. He might encourage or propose the printing of some papers; his advice might be taken in the selection of an editor; sometimes he assisted in the preparatory work, and even—as in the case of the *Grenville Papers*—where he was not initially involved, he might become a collaborator in the later volumes. He talked of his own times as "days when the possessors of original papers are generally ready to open them to the inspection of the literary world". Sometimes he expressed the view that the editors or the owners of papers showed too little reserve in their publication policy. He questioned the propriety of the printing in 1827 of letters between George III and Lord Chief Justice Kenyon on the coronation oath. When Twiss's biography of Eldon appeared, he regretted the inclusion of private letters of recent date, particularly "a number of most secret and confidential notes from George III to his Chancellor on most delicate subjects" (*Quarterly*, Vol. LXXV, p. 408). Even if permission had been granted for the publication of these, he felt that the permission had been applied for too soon. On the other hand, he disliked the "family biography" and regretted the publication of a man's papers either by his relatives or on their behalf; for, he said, "the interests of truth might be best served by telling what should be *un*satisfactory to [the] family" (LXXXVIII, p. 217). In his view, "the generous sentiment that '*wars not with the dead*' supposes even in its most indulgent latitude, that the dead shall not be evoked to make war on us". He insisted that critical methods should be applied to all the details of the newly-published works, but predicted that, while these works would survive to affect the future, the world would soon forget the reservations with which they had been received at the time of their original appearance—a time which, he was thankful to say, was sufficiently close to the reign of George III to allow the poison to be recognised and the antidote administered. In connexion with his exposure of Wraxall's *Memoirs*, he wrote (Vol. LVII, p. 448):

> The fables of Sir Nathan are now capable of detection but the detection will not accompany them down to posterity; and we even doubt whether the conviction of Sir Nathan for libel, if it should occur, will reach many readers . . . fifty years hence.

He had begun his devastating criticism of Wraxall's *Memoirs* in 1815; and in 1821, as we have already seen, he had reviewed the work of Lord Waldegrave. Here he had avowed the great eagerness with which he was looking forward to the appearance of Horace Walpole's *Memoirs of the Last Ten Years of the Reign of George II.* When he came to review this further work (*Quarterly*, Vol. XXVII), he made the significant declaration (p. 184) that "Horace Walpole is an old hero of ours". In fact, in 1820, the publisher, John Murray, knowing his interest in this subject, had asked him to edit Walpole's *Reminiscences*; but he had advised that Miss Berry should be invited to undertake the task, as the work was one which had been written for her. He never did lose his special interest in Walpole and in 1828 he was pressing for a collected edition of his letters. Murray, who had lost money on the *Memoirs* of George II's reign, declined, however, to risk this further venture. Some of the letters had appeared in an edition of the works of Walpole in 1798, and a number to George Montagu, as well as a volume of letters to the Rev. William Cole, had been printed in 1818. These documents—and especially the letters to Montagu—had been quoted in subsequent years in favour of George III's conduct at the beginning of his reign.

The actual *Memoirs* of George II's reign had come as a great blow to Croker, however, and, according to his account, had cured him even of the faith that he had had in Walpole as a letter-writer.

> A great familiarity with Walpole's correspondence had, we confess, discoloured in our eyes most of the public characters of his day; and, neither seeing nor guessing any secret cause of malevolence, we gave credit to assertions which we are *now*—by the perusal of the Memoirs—convinced to be either absolute falsehoods or gross exaggerations. [*Ibid.*, Vol. XXVII, p. 182.]

The only valuable parts of Walpole's new work, said Croker, were his "reports of the debates to which he was a party in the House of Commons, and particularly of some of the speeches of

Mr. Pitt". A critic in the *New Edinburgh Review* dissented from this opinion, and wrote: "Except for two miserable speeches by Walpole himself, which he has given us at full length, there is not in these volumes a tolerable report of any single speech spoken in either house of parliament." Croker considered, however, that Walpole's rapid strokes sometimes captured the genuine atmosphere of the occasion; and an example which he quotes makes it possible for us to see his point (p. 184).

In regard to the main facts of the story, he concedes that Walpole's *Memoirs* are accurate. At this level, however, he takes the line that in reality they furnish the historian with little that is new. At the same time, he says,

> we have to complain of the *suppression* of circumstances which ought in candour to have been given, and, above all, to deplore the injuries done to private character by attributing the lowest and basest motives to almost every person whom he happens to mention. [p. 179]

Even on internal evidence, the *Memoirs* can be discovered to be untruthful, he says. "Writing . . . from day to day, and under the impulse of the moment, Walpole was unable, at last, to reconcile his discordant statements."

Furthermore, he says, "of the thousand names which [Walpole] mentions, one, and only one . . . escapes vituperation"—and that is the man's first cousin, General Conway, to whom he was particularly devoted. Over and over again, it was "*after* his private differences" with the famous politicians of the day that Walpole appeared to have turned the malice of his pen against them. And it was not even fidelity to his father that provided him with the motive, as he sometimes liked to pretend. It was not even the semblance of a public cause—not even resentment against the men who had brought about the downfall of Sir Robert Walpole. The men in question had not intrigued against his father, in fact, and at one time or another he had shown that he knew this to be the case. But he had hated his own uncle, another Horace Walpole, and he would not forgive anybody who remained friendly with the man—anybody who even tried to make peace between them (pp. 189-93). And if any minister refused to accommodate him in respect of his sinecures (which were so much more valuable than he pretended)—then his bitterness would be uncontrollable. These factors were to be operative again when he wrote his *Memoirs of the Reign of George III*.

Furthermore, Croker sets out to show how, even in this earlier work, the narrative becomes particularly minute in its detail and particularly malicious in its tone, when it is dealing with affairs in which Walpole had himself intervened with a piece of intrigue, but had only shown his own ineffectuality. The trial of Admiral Byng, and the controversy which was provoked by his condemnation, afforded an example of this; and Croker, tearing the narrative to pieces, set out to expose the mean and unattractive spirit of the author at this point. Another example can be found in the dispute already mentioned concerning the alleged Jacobitism of the men around George III when he was Prince of Wales. Walpole admits in a footnote to the *Memoirs* that he himself was the author of a document which in the narrative he had described as though he were ignorant of its origin. At the same time his own work demonstrates the mischief which this document had caused. It had purported to come from some of the nobility and gentry; and it had complained that a certain faction was trying "to engross the education of [the] Prince of Wales to themselves"; that "books inculcating the worst maxims of government, and defending the most avowed tyrannies" had been placed in the Prince's hands; that "none but the friends and pupils of the late Lord Bolingbroke [were] entrusted with the education of [the Prince]; and that there had been no proper enquiry into the charge of Jacobitism which had been made" against one of the Prince's preceptors. Walpole himself showed how this document had helped to provoke the famous charge against Stone and others, who were accused of having drunk the health of the Pretender years before.

If Horace Walpole was to have undue influence upon future historians, this was not for lack of warnings against him, particularly at the time when his *Memoirs* began to appear. The *Edinburgh Review* received Walpole's *George II* more uncritically; but the *New Edinburgh Review* (Vol. IV, p. 1), after describing the political effectiveness of the author in actual life, presented him as contriving

> to solace his wounded feelings by composing these Memoirs, in which he was secretly preparing such pictures of his successful rivals —of those very men before whom he could maintain no honourable or open competition—as he expected would give him a late but a very sure revenge for that superiority which he could neither contest nor forgive.

To the critic in this *Review* Walpole was more offensive in that his work—"More detestable than any ordinary libel"—had been arranged to appear "after every chance of personal responsibility [on the author's part] and every fair opportunity of refutation should have gone by". Walpole, we are told (pp. 18–19),

> never had the vigour or the talent to push his opposition by any open means in parliament. All his blows . . . were aimed in private, after the most laborious preparation to make them effective.

Croker, who dared to attack Macaulay's *History of England* in 1849, when its popularity was unmistakable, was not daunted by the flood of publications which after 1838 brought the historiography of George III's reign to a new stage. He had not lost his attachment to Horace Walpole, and in 1840, while a general edition of this man's letters was appearing, he said that this correspondence,

> besides its unequalled gaiety and brilliancy, has the more important merit of being the liveliest picture of manners and the best epitome

of political history that not only this but any country possesses. [*Quarterly*, Vol. LXVI, p. 195.]

The *Memoirs of the Reign of George II*, however, had prepared his mind for the further series on the reign of George III, which was published in 1845. He greeted the latter (*ibid.*, Vol. LXXVII, p. 253) as "these more solemn chronicles of libel and malignity", and wrote (p. 261):

> We will not . . . permit the mean and dirty spite of a disappointed jobber to sully the fountains of history.

This new attempt by Walpole to deceive posterity required, in his opinion, a separate work of refutation.

> If any reader should be inclined to think that we assign too much importance to this detection and exposure, we beg leave to remind him that, from a variety of concurrent causes, Walpole is likely at first sight to obtain a confidence which he in no degree merits, and that his pertinacious efforts to poison history require that *at each successive attempt* the antidote should be administered. . . . Few readers can have the means, and still fewer will have the diligence, for a minute and critical examination of his details, while the public will greedily swallow the potion so suited to the general appetite for scandal, without attempting to distinguish the ingredients. [pp. 274–275]

It was his view that "Walpole's Memoirs are little else than an apocryphal chronicle of 'motives'". In both the old series and the new there were "very few facts—hardly one, that we recollect, of any real historical importance". If these works purported to contribute anything new, it could only be in regard to the "motives" which they assigned to the various actors "in scenes and circumstances already superficially known". At these very points, however, "no historian reverent of truth should quote one line from Walpole, without a minute investigation of the individual fact, and of the possible *temper* in which Walpole may have related it".

As to naked facts and the mere succession of events, the skeleton, as it were, of history, Walpole is in general accurate, and no doubt brings to light many small details . . . which, *valeant quantum* are obviously entitled to credit; but his natural inclination was to grope an obscure way through mazes and souterrains rather than walk the high road by daylight. He is never satisfied with the plain and obvious cause of any effect. . . . His Memoirs tend to lower mankind to one common size and level of mere selfishness. [p. 277]

By collating the *Memoirs* with a statement which Walpole himself had drawn up about the history of his sinecures, Croker was able to achieve what he called his "elucidations" of the man's literary character.

We are satisfied that Walpole's anxiety about his offices, combining with the constitutional peculiarities of his temper, became the *primum mobile* of all his misanthropical feelings and led him . . . to calumniate by every indirect means, under every false pretence, but with inveterate and indefatigable malignity, everybody whom he knew or fancied to have interfered with his incessant endeavours to place his income on a more permanent footing. This was clearly the first and chief motive of both sets of Memoirs. . . . [pp. 255-6]

Croker collated the *Memoirs* also with the letters which Walpole had written at the actual date of the events in question; and showed that at the opening of George III's reign he "attempted some cajoleries of His Majesty and Bute on their love and patronage of the arts", though he only sneered at the "would-be Augustus" in the *Memoirs*. He quotes also Walpole's confession that, after a disappointment over a sinecure, "he took occasion of fomenting the ill-humour against the Favourite". Though the *Memoirs* did so much to spread the conviction that Bute retained his influence behind the scenes after his retirement, Croker discovers their internal inconsistency, and finds Walpole confessing that he had often changed his mind on the subject—finds also that in one place Walpole designates Charles Jenkinson as the man who replaced Bute in the confidence of the King after the latter's retirement. He also quotes a letter of 28th February, 1763, in which Walpole declared: "It is already obvious that Lord Bute's levée is not the present path to fortune." From this he inferred that Walpole had not believed at the time in that extraordinary influence of Bute which would secure him a continued ascendancy even after his ostensible fall.

Croker's method comes to quite a sensational climax when he deals with Horace Walpole and the Treaty of Paris. He quotes a letter in which Henry Fox reports the intention to provide an emolument for Walpole's nephew, Lord Orford, and crudely announces to Walpole himself: "This is offering you a bribe." Orford, he says, accepted the proposed gift and Walpole voted for Bute's peace-treaty. Yet, in the *Memoirs*, Walpole talks of this latter as "a scandalous peace"—a thing "ruinous and shameful to the country". He says that "thunder was wanting to blast such a treaty" and he speaks of "the infamy of the peace". He notes that the *numbers of* the parliamentary division on the subject of this treaty were printed, and he adds: "had they printed the *names* the world would have known the names of those who were *not* bribed". Croker is withering on the subject. Walpole himself voted with the majority, he says (pp. 265–6):

> and in that majority we doubt whether there was any man more open to the imputation of bribery than himself. Probably he was the only one of them all that had accepted a *Bribe*—offered directly *eo nomine*.

While he is so bitter against the innuendoes and the tendency of Walpole's narrative, Croker claims that in fact George III comes well out of the story.

> Every *act and fact* that he [Walpole] relates are highly to his Majesty's credit. . . . The time during which he was nearest the court, and best informed as to the conduct of the King, is that in which he expresses the most favourable opinion of him. [p. 282]

Croker's treatment of Walpole and the other memoir-writers of his time is a typical example of the development of a more critical and analytical treatment of sources. But there is a sense in which he never lost his attachment to Walpole, of whom he still wrote in June 1848:

> He was during a great part of his life a very dishonest politician; but he really loved liberty, and well understood that it was inseparable from good order. His own temper, too, was cynical and selfish almost to infirmity, but he had a sure and prompt taste for kindness and generosity in others. . . . Walpole readily hated and ridiculed individuals, but he loved mankind; and under the surface of his wayward passions and strong prejudices there is always an undercurrent of good feeling and, above all, of good sense. We have before applauded the sagacity and humanity with which from the very outset he reprobated the American war. [*Quarterly*, p. 16.]

Even so, Croker had his own passions and prejudices, and trusted too much to his own sense of what was plausible or credible in an historical source. He has the virtue of agility in his criticism of memoirs, but we must not be surprised if he carried destructive criticism too far. In connexion with the *Memoirs of the Last Ten Years of George II*, he confessed the fault with a fairness that was typical of him. His work on an edition of Lord Hervey's *Memoirs* opened his eyes to the fact that Horace Walpole's narrations were supported by other evidence which he felt bound to regard as independent. He wrote therefore in his Introduction:

> I for one must confess, that most of my former doubts of Walpole's accuracy have been entirely removed by Lord Hervey's Memoirs; and that, on the other hand, there are some things in [Hervey's] Memoirs which I should have deemed incredible, if we had not been in some measure prepared for them by the previous revelations of Walpole.

Walpole's letters, as we have seen, are often curiously at friction with his *Memoirs*; yet it seems clear that this man, who could be so "laborious" in his attempts to deceive, must have intended his letters as well as the *Memoirs* to be published. He himself confesses to inconsistencies in the *Memoirs*, and says that these reflect the changes that took place in his ideas with the passage of time. Croker charges him with having recognised in his last volume that, after all, Bute's influence did not survive his resignation. But the inconsistency may be interpreted as implying that where Horace Walpole misleads us, he is capable of providing the corrective himself. Croker sometimes seems to transform the memoir-writer into a sinister and malevolent figure; but Miss Berry set out to show that such a view was itself an exaggeration. And Croker, for his own part, was capable of definite mistakes—he takes as the crowning proof of Walpole's infamy the accusation that Edmund Burke "jobbed in India stock". Sir Lewis Namier has commended the care and accuracy of Walpole's narrative in the few years after 1765, and has quoted no less an authority than the Duke of Grafton as witness to Walpole's knowledge of what was going on behind the scenes at that time. Croker was not blind to this particular point.

> Up to the year 1765, [he says] Walpole was in Parliament . . . imperfectly acquainted with the real views or principles of the Government . . . well acquainted with the intrigues of the several opposing factions.

For a few years, from 1765, however, owing to his connexion with the minister, Conway, he was "better informed than he *ought to have been* on many cabinet questions—not indeed, it would seem, on any great national concerns, but very much as to the difficulties and embarrassments in the conduct of the King's Government". And at this point in the story, where Walpole's inclination is on the side of the ministry, Croker asks us to note:

> how sensible he [Walpole] had become of the indecency and mischief of a factious and interested opposition, and how much less

disposed to doubt the good sense of the King, his sincerity towards his ministers and his love of the people.

On the other hand, from about 1769, "Walpole's escape from the actual whirlwind of party had somewhat sobered and rationalised his mind".

This is on the whole the portion of the volumes that instead of "falling short" as he supposed of the others, may, we think, be read with the most satisfaction and the greatest approach to confidence. But it contains little that is new—particularly to the readers (and who have not been readers?) of Walpole's Letters . . . especially the two first volumes of the last series to Sir H. Mann, which contains in truth the substance of these Memoirs in another form. [Vol. LXXVII, 275–7]

Croker showed something of the modernity of his outlook— or perhaps, rather, one should say, his historical-mindedness—in the interest which he took in the analysis of party in the eighteenth century. Speaking of the decades before 1760 he wrote:

It was the happiness of England at that period to have no question on which a Party could be raised; and in a representative Government, where there is not a Party there must be faction. [Vol. LXXVIII, p. 256]

He says of Godolphin and Marlborough, Harley and Boling-broke, that "there was no real *principle* of Whiggism or Toryism in question between these ambitious intriguers, they were all contending for place, power, and personal aggrandisement" (Vol. LIV, pp. 370–1). He quotes from Horace Walpole the remark that it was a "peculiarity" of the Hanoverian dynasty to have the heir-apparent always in opposition to the reigning monarch. He himself sees the characteristic as not at all strange, but "more or less universal"; though, he adds, "our political system developed it with peculiar force and more remarkable effects in the royal family" (Vol. LXVI, p. 193). He recognises that the party or faction in power would be on the side of the King, while those who were in opposition would tend to fix their hopes on the prospective successor. For this reason, a genuine significance attached to the quarrelling which took place within the royal family.

> This was the mainspring of the most serious part of the political troubles of the last century and will, we doubt not, be revived—if our present constitution should last so long—whenever a similar occasion for rivalry shall arise in the royal family. [Vol. LXVI, p. 193]

In this situation of things, everything depended on whether one's political group was in power and held the favour of the King. "The *Ins*, however they might originally have belonged to the Whig connexion, adopted the Tory policy"; and for this reason Croker accepted the view of Lord Mahon that, though "we talk *now*, as they did *then*, of *Whig and Tory*, the tenets of the two parties . . . have been so completely *counter-changed* (as the heralds express it) that a Whig of that day very much resembled a Tory of ours, and *vice versâ*". He ridiculed the new error of "fancying that the *Toryism* of Bolingbroke had the slightest affinity to that system of political opinion which is at present denominated Toryism". In one respect only did he admit that the traditional party distinctions survived—the supporters of the Church inclined to feel themselves Tories still; and the Dissenters naturally leaned to the side of the Whigs.

Since factiousness had tended to take the place of the old party-conflicts based on principles, Croker allowed great importance to Burke's *Thoughts on the Cause of the Present Discontents*. He did not accept it as evidence for the aims of George III, and he rejected its attempt to reconstitute that monarch's system—rejected the supposition, "which we now know to have been imaginary of a secret party behind the throne to thwart and control ostensible ministers". But, he wrote in the *Quarterly* (Vol. LXXVIII, p. 258):

> Mr. Burke opened those enlarged and just views of *Party Allegiance*, as a high political duty, which at once raised it from the obloquy to which the selfish corruption of its *locum tenens*, *Faction*, had for

half a century exposed it. This—which we may venture to call a great moral and political discovery—startling as it was to the public opinion of the day, and though made while in pursuit of another and we admit visionary object (as useful chemistry sprang from the dreams of alchemy) has effected a great revolution in practical politics.

In spite of the Toryism of both his politics and his historical outlook, Croker, in fact, saw much merit in the Rockinghamites whom he described as "the best tempered and most moderate" of the parties.

In the years when the documents were being published which were to bring so much ammunition to the Whig historian, Croker resolutely set himself against the tendencies of the time and defended the reputation of George III. He wrote in 1842:

Every additional light which time throws on his public or his private character raises him in our esteem and reverence; but it was long before he was justly appreciated. He had a hurried utterance—particularly in his youth, and when addressing strangers—which made an unfavourable impression; and the eh? eh? and what? what? which were in truth only symptoms of nervous excitability, were quoted by ignorance or malevolence as proofs of a trivial mind. No man in his dominions had a mind less trivial; . . . and if he was not what the world called a *great* king, it is only because he lived in times and under a constitution in which the personal action of the sovereign on public councils is concealed under the responsibility of his ministers; and, like the spring of a watch, is to the common eye only visible by the ostensible movement of the hands on a dial: but we speak advisedly when we assert, that if ever, and to whatever extent, his daily correspondence with his successive ministers upon the varied business of the state shall be published, the world will then, and not fully till then, be able to appreciate his virtues and his talents; his unwearied affection for his people, too often ungrateful . . . and his steady support of the constitutional liberties of England, of which he always considered himself as the first representative and official guardian. [*Quarterly*, Vol. LXX, pp. 281-2]

Faced with the task of reconciling the alleged indecision with the supposed obstinacy of George III, Croker declared:

> The truth is, the King was firm and decided in *his own* opinions and conduct, but felt as a constitutional sovereign in our mixed government that he was bound to submit his public acts to the advice of his responsible ministers.

He noted (Vol. LXXVII, pp. 283–4) the King's "*active, accurate and intelligent despatch of business*".

> He never postponed anything—never left a letter unanswered . . . he understood foreign affairs better than any minister he ever had, and took a lively interest in that department. . . . We do not believe that any human being ever acquired a more accurate knowledge, or executed with more intelligent regularity the details of what is in truth a most complicated and difficult office—which the law allows, or rather obliges, the sovereign to exercise, in a great measure, by his responsible advisers, but on which an honest, a brave and an intelligent monarch like George III felt it to be his duty to satisfy also his own conscience, and to exercise his constitutional influence and control.

The editor of Horace Walpole's *Memoirs* of the reign was able to make use of a portion of the correspondence between George III and Lord North; and Croker tells us that this had been obtained for him by the intervention of Lord Brougham from North's daughter, Lady Charlotte Lindsay. The bulk of George III's papers, however, were lost for a very long time and only rediscovered in 1912. Croker, writing on Walpole's *Memoirs*, wishes that more of this correspondence had been inserted by the editor; but the extracts which are given, he says (*ibid.*, p. 284),

> fully confirm our opinion, that whenever and to whatever extent George III's correspondence with his successive ministers shall be disclosed, his character as an able judicious and conscientious sovereign and statesman, and an honest and amiable gentleman in the highest sense of the word, will be additionally confirmed.

Croker's conclusion was that:

> Every new circumstance of evidence that arises or transpires—
> even those that, like Walpole's Memoirs, were designed for the very
> contrary object—have the effect of vindicating the character of the
> King, and raising him above the gross misrepresentations and
> malignity of faction in all the lustre and purity of his blameless
> character as one of the best of kings and the honestest of men. [*Ibid.*,
> p. 297]

3. "The Quarterly" versus the "Edinburgh Review"

IN THE *Quarterly Review* for March 1852 there appeared an important article under the title "The First Decade of George III" —a reply to the new tendencies in the historiography of this period, and an attempt to reconstruct a Tory version of the story. The author writes:

Nearly a century has elapsed since the accession of George III, yet misrepresentation is as busy [as ever] with his name. . . . This cannot be from ignorance—for the most secret events of the early years of his reign are disclosed. . . . The personal qualities and motives of the young King have been illustrated . . . authentically by recent publications. . . . That Lord John Russell, indeed—in editing the Bedford Correspondence, should write of the "foolish prejudices", the "narrow intellect", the "brooding sullenness" and the "uncharitable temper" of George III might not excite much of our surprise, considering that he had to support the credit of family tradition and to maintain in full force that antipathy to the king, which, strange as it may seem, forms a very important part of the . . . Whig stock-in-trade. But that Lord Albemarle—with all the Rockingham papers which he has printed before him—and especially with the letters of the king himself, which on any fair construction, establish beyond the possibility of doubt or cavil his firm good sense and undeviating honesty—that a man of obvious ability, and not, to our knowledge, much mixed up hitherto with the movements of faction—that he should endorse all the wretched inventions of old malignity, does really move our wonder. . . . We object very decidedly to such "cooking" of historical papers as he [Lord Albemarle] has resorted to. [pp. 503–6]

According to this article, in the years before 1760, "our government was degenerating into an oligarchy of the worst kind".

That mischievous principle, from which France in our own day has reaped such infinite misfortune—*le roi règne, et ne gouverne pas*—

had been uniformly acted on by English ministers from the death of Anne; and as the result of the absolute authority intrusted to the Whig ministry formed by George I on his arrival, the Government remained for nearly half a century in the hands of men who scrupled not at the most shameless corruption to maintain themselves in power. During the whole, or nearly the whole, of that period, the principle of popular representation may be said to have remained in abeyance, so completely was it overlaid by that system of management which enabled the government to gain a majority and to keep it together by open and direct bribery of the members. [pp. 510–11]

George II "had sense to perceive the tyranny of his ministers, but not force to resist it". After George III's accession in 1760, however, the first acts of the King were decisive of his intention "not only to reign but to govern". The writer argues that "fortunately for the success of the King's project, the Whig party at his succession was broken up". And in the first ten years of the new reign, we are told, "a revolution was proceeding not assuredly less worthy of study" than the convulsions of a later period—the convulsions, that is to say, of 1789 and after:

It is not often in great affairs that any man can fix his mind on a definite object, to be attained only after years of struggle and the conquest of innumerable obstacles. Still less frequently is it permitted him to march straight forward towards his design, and accomplish it by the very means he had projected. But this is what George III did. On his accession to the throne it was scarcely a secret that he contemplated the overthrow of that Whig domination which had enthralled his two predecessors, and made the legitimate head of the nation the slave of a party. The courtiers most eager for royal favour soon learnt the leading idea in the King's mind, and adopted it with more zeal than discretion. They put it forward in an offensive shape, and thus aggravated their master's struggle. "To recover monarchy from the inveterate usurpation of oligarchy" wrote Dodington to Bute . . . "is a point too arduous and important to be achieved without much difficulty and some degree of danger". True; and had not the King possessed far more sense and nerve than any of those

who ostentatiously ranked themselves among his friends, the enterprise must have been abandoned almost as soon as commenced. . . .
As he had not to make concessions to his ministers for the sake of
gratifying personal predilections in foreign policy, he felt the less
disposed to give up to them that share of discretionary authority
which the constitution has lodged in the hands of the monarch.
[pp. 509–10]

Here, where the Tory interpretation of George III's reign seems
to come to a climax, we find an extreme statement of the view
that this monarch ascended the throne with a deliberate plan for a
change of system, an overthrow of the "Whig domination". Once
again we learn that the project was endangered by the inadequacy
of the King's collaborators; but now the success of George III's
new order is triumphantly announced. By about 1772, we are
told (p. 542), "the Walpolean system of management was at an
end".

> To the firmness and virtue of the King are due that purification of
> our political system, and that higher standard of public and private
> morality, which so remarkably renovated the whole structure of
> English society soon after his accession to the throne. [p. 543]

Confronted by the power of the Duke of Newcastle and his
associates, George III was induced to make use of Henry Fox at
the time of the controversy over the peace-treaty with France.
But, says this article, besides disliking Henry Fox personally,
George III in reality "had the strongest objection to the system
on which he acted". The trouble was that the existing system of
parliamentary management "was too deeply rooted to be overthrown in a day". The King is quoted in fact as saying that "he
must employ bad men to govern bad men"; but also he repeatedly
asserted that this "was but for a time—the expedient of the
moment only". It is one of the arguments of this author that
George III "decidedly set his face against bribery as an engine of
government".

In fact, though the King might be forced, from the necessity of his situation, to the old Whig mode of securing majorities, he soon succeeded in establishing a purer system. Lord Mahon notices the decline of venality at general elections as the reign advanced (VI, 27) while the vile plan of purchasing majorities on particular occasions fell altogether into disuetude. [pp. 519–20]

Even in regard to the details of the story this article has considerable interest for us at the present day. It is marred by its extravagances, but now (though not at the time of its publication) its arguments in favour of George III seem more incisive than the counter-arguments of the Whig historians. This author is naturally severe in his discussion of the Duke of Newcastle and quotes the latter as writing:

> Never was man who had it in his power to make, to choose, so great a part of the members of both Houses, so abandoned as I am at present.

He is severe on the Earl of Hardwicke, whom he describes as refusing to rally to the ministry of Bute on the ground that "the great Whig lords with whom and their families he had acted for forty years were now displaced". The article adds the comment:

> as if the forty years' prescription had given to these great Whig lords and their families an indefeasible right to the government of the country for ever. [p. 518]

On the question of the influence which Bute was alleged to have exercised behind the scenes after his resignation, the author of this article has some trenchant things to say. He asserts even that "all well-informed writers on the Whig side have long since repudiated the idea of a secret intelligence between the King and Lord Bute". He notes, however, that Lord Albemarle still clings to the dogma "as an indispensable article of the orthodox creed".

> It is not possible for evidence to be clearer on any historical point, than that Bute had no intelligence with the King after Lord

Rockingham took office. We have Lord Bute's own "solemn word of honour", given in 1778, that from the date when the Duke of Cumberland was called in he never saw his Majesty but openly at court, and never presumed to speak to him one syllable on any political matter. We have the King's word to the same effect, and a mass of corroborative testimony sufficient to bring conviction to any mind not hermetically sealed by inveterate prejudice. [pp. 532–3]

At the same time the Whig version of the story was hardening, and, three months after the important article in the Quarterly, the Edinburgh Review in July 1852 described George III and Bute as treading the path of Charles I and the Duke of Buckingham, "with more adroitness but with less excuse". Here Albemarle is described as a "zealous" disciple of the Rockingham school, "writing under the conviction that [Rockingham himself] had hitherto been treated unfairly by even Whig historians, and had recently been strangely undervalued by no less an authority than Lord Mahon". And now the judgment of the Quarterly is reversed:

> Of the contemporary documents which now enable us to explore the maze of royal and party intrigues at the commencement and during the first twenty years of George III's reign, none are upon the whole more instructive than the Memoirs of the Marquis of Rockingham. . . . We believe that there is an opinion current in many quarters that the reputation of George III will "improve with keeping". The Rockingham Memoirs do not favour that expectation. [pp. 111, 114]

Furthermore, says this article, "The 'Grenville Correspondence' and especially the 'Diary' afford us glimpses into the royal closet . . . which fully confirm Lord Albemarle's account".

According to the Edinburgh Review, "the Princess Dowager had instilled into her then docile son the maxims of Bolingbroke rather than those of Somers or Walpole. The doctrines sketched in the 'Craftsman' and the 'Patriot King' had passed from

Leicester House to St. James's palace". George III, "from his youth upwards", had been "trained in distrust of the Whigs as a body. . . . He had mounted the throne with the fixed intention to burst the bonds and cast away the cords of the Whig connexion". It was admitted that "the Whig Cabinet had rested upon three main pillars—family connexion, borough influence, and Pitt's eloquence".

> Nor was the great Whig party itself at the time by any means blameless. In the pages of the "Rockingham memoirs" we trace its gradual return to the pure doctrines of Somers and Halifax, but we behold it at first in a divided and degenerate condition. [pp. 116, 119–20]

According to this article, Bute "began by cajoling [the Duke of] Newcastle with assurances that he was more acceptable to the King than his eloquent and popular colleague [Pitt]". It was apparent that "the responsible advisers were not the real counsellors of the Crown", however; and Newcastle's "almost hysterical joy at Pitt's resignation was speedily followed by equally hysterical distress". Newcastle's patronage "could not now procure a tide-waiter's place", and "a series of slights and affronts at length drove him to resign". The new régime

> broke up the "Whig connexion", reanimated the Tory party, committed the Crown and Legislature to direct collision on grave political questions with an able and profligate adventurer [Wilkes], paralysed the genius of Chatham, barbed the arrow of Junius, and severed from Great Britain the fairest portion of her colonial empire. [p. 115]

*   *   *

It is relevant perhaps to note that Croker had very strong feelings about the personality of the elder Pitt. It was his view that the publication of the *Chatham Correspondence* had raised the reputation of George III while making the defects of Pitt more

141

flagrant than before. "We can neither esteem nor respect [Chatham]", he says. "His was, we believe, the most disastrous glory that ever intoxicated—and when the intoxication was over—enervated our country, and planted the first germs of revolutionary disease in the constitution." Croker was puzzled by Chatham's illness during his administration of 1766–8, for he held that gout could not be the explanation and he felt that the "suspicion of insanity has been supported by some plausible arguments". He was unwilling to allow the validity of this latter "excuse" for Chatham, since "as soon as he was out of office, there was a sudden improvement of his health". He thought that Chatham "surprised at the sudden loss of popularity . . . felt some reluctance to come forward in his new character" (*Quarterly*, Vol. LXVI, p. 254). He admitted that "the private letters of [Chatham's] family represent his malady as more real and more severe than his contemporaries were inclined to believe". Finally, he confessed that, until he saw the *Chatham Correspondence*, he had had "no idea . . . how entirely and how pertinaciously Lord Chatham had withdrawn from all share in his own administration" (*ibid.* p. 252).

Though he greatly disapproves of Chatham he says that, in regard to the conflict with America, "on the whole his motives were honest—his councils wise, and the abilities with which he developed them transcendently admirable. It is in this part of his history that this great man seems to us to be greatest". In a similar way Croker gave great credit to Horace Walpole for his hostility to the conflict with the American colonies. He was clearly not an obscurantist on this issue, and he tells us in one place that "the truth was, the Colonies had outgrown their tutelary institutions". (p. 263).

The author of the article in the *Quarterly Review* in 1852 actually speaks of "the perfidy which alloyed the higher genius of Chatham". In regard to the colonial question he writes:

It has been a favourite assertion with Whig writers that America was lost through the obstinacy of George III. We might reply to this that the King seldom attempted to control the general policy or measures of his government. He was jealous of his executive power as that fell legitimately within his kingly province; but he left to his Ministers the part which constitutionally belonged to them, of originating and carrying forward all legislative business. . . . We do *not* find . . . that he attempted to control the discretion of his Ministers, by dictating to them any line of policy. He left to them the responsibility of their acts and the management of the Legislature, confining himself to the exercise of his duties as chief magistrate of the State. We do not know any single statute of his reign, with the exception of those which immediately concerned his person and family, which can justly be ascribed to his suggestion or influence. [p. 536]

4. Compromise and Synthesis in Massey

EVEN AFTER the appearance of the printed sources which have been mentioned, it is remarkable to what a degree the shape of the traditional story still persists in the narrative produced by William Nathaniel Massey. This man was a liberal in politics and Volume I of his *History of England*, which appeared in 1855, dealt on a considerable scale with the early years of George III's reign. He seems to be affected by the evidence and the controversies which had been produced in the 1820's on the subject of George's education. He mentions Jacobitical teachers and books, and the influence of the Princess Dowager; and he sees the youth "in the hands of persons who insinuated unconstitutional principles into his mind". He follows Macaulay in the view that something unsatisfactory in the development of parliament itself provides the historical explanation for the evils of the Whig ascendancy. And if he resembles Adolphus in his picture of George III as the enemy of oligarchical abuses, he comes near to Horace Walpole in the view that this King used the plan for the annihilation of party-distinctions in order merely to break the Whigs and advance the royal prerogative. He combines the views of his predecessors, attempts an all-embracing policy and collects into his narrative the elements of inconsistent systems and alternative types of interpretation. He seems to be trying to accept both the opinions of previous historians and the objections that had been made to those opinions. He manages in a way both to follow Burke's *Thoughts on the Cause of the Present Discontents* and the criticisms of that work. One imagines that Massey must provide the average and the common mean of all views on George III, though it is true to say that he ends by being hostile to that King—hostile, indeed, for reasons of his own. And yet—perhaps because he is hostile—he seems to try to englobe in his text everything that had ever been said on the man's behalf.

Massey was prepared to see the accession of George III as the beginning of a change in the system of government; and he was ready to define the change in a more radical way than his predecessors had done. He saw the King as attempting to recapture an authority which in the period before his accession had actually been taken over not merely by the Whigs but by parliament itself. He was prepared, however, to see that there was something to be said in favour of the new policy, and he guarded his mind from certain forms of judgment that would have been anachronistic. It was his view that "the King had, from his earliest years, been taught that his first duty as a sovereign was to cast off the thraldom in which his grandfather had been held by political combinations". Bute, he thought, had taken care to give him this notion of what his office demanded. And it was in the light of this that Massey interpreted the opening years of the reign:

The commencement of this reign was remarkable for an attempt on the part of the Crown to recover that power and influence which since 1688 had been appropriated by the Parliament. Nor was the adventure so hopeless or so devoid of plausibility as it would appear to a generation fully reconciled to that system of parliamentary government in which the constitution has long since practically determined. The mode in which parliamentary government first developed itself in this country was not such as to entitle it to the respect and confidence of the nation. The ancient prerogative, which, though often oppressive, was still regarded with reverence and affection by the people as a rightful rule, and as a simple and intelligible principle of government, was now superseded by a new form of policy, which enabled factions, and even individuals, to exercise supreme power by means of a packed and venal House of Commons. The result of this mode of administration has been imbecility in the national councils, and the abuse of the public service throughout every department. But of the four sovereigns who had filled the throne since the Revolution, three were foreigners and strangers, and every one of them had reigned by a title *de facto* rather than *de jure*. It was in vain for princes so situated to appeal to the loyalty of the people against the dictation of a cabal. But the case was now altered. The new King was avowedly an Englishman both by birth and education, and in his person the lawful demise of the Crown was at length practically admitted. The present, therefore, seemed to be a favourable opportunity to raise the Crown from the powerless and dependent condition into which it had fallen. The Whigs had hitherto assumed to take the House of Hanover under their exclusive protection; and almost every public man who had held high office since the accession of that family was a member of the great Whig connection.

But it was neither expedient nor becoming that the King of England should always depend upon one party, however great their services might have been. The necessity for doing so had undoubtedly ceased. There was no longer any reason why the Tories should not be admitted to power and employment. . . . That George the Third, fortified by the support of this great party, thus happily reconciled to the Crown, should assert the regal authority in a tone which his immediate predecessors were not in a condition to assume, seems to be perfectly intelligible, without resorting to any farfetched theory for an explanation. The Tories might also be justly called "King's Friends", because their ruling tenet had been that of loyalty and implicit obedience. [pp. 63–5]

Massey, then, managed to enter into the older ways of thinking when he envisaged the relations between the King and those politicians who were connected with the Duke of Newcastle. It is not clear, however, that he was not anachronistic in his picture of the Whig and Tory parties, and in his view of the role which the emancipated monarch could be expected to play. He becomes clearly critical of George III when he moves on to the ground covered by a famous passage in Burke's *Thoughts on the Cause of the Present Discontents*. It will be seen, however, that he makes both reservations about Burke's thesis and allowances for the King himself.

But the term "King's Friends" has been ascribed to a class of courtiers, the members and agents of a secret interior cabinet, which was the real council of the Sovereign; where the real policy of the Government was dictated, and from whence all rewards and honours were dispensed. According to this scheme, the ostensible administration consisting of the great officers of state, was a mere pageant; its policy thwarted, its credit undermined, and its existence terminated, at any time, in the face of Parliament and the country, by an unseen, mysterious power. There was some foundation, in fact, for this ingenious theory. The King certainly showed no favour to ministers neither chosen by himself nor recommended to him by the confidence of Parliament, but brought into office by the force of party connection. He made no secret of his repugnance to such ministers. Occasionally, perhaps, to suit a temporary purpose, he might wear a face of dissimulation towards them; but his fixed and avowed purpose, from the commencement of his reign, was to break up party connection, and to emancipate his government from the domination of great lords. With this view, he hurried on the peace, and openly defied the whole Whig connection. . . .

There is no doubt he intrigued against the ministers he abhorred, and that he employed irresponsible agents to communicate with his loyal friends in Parliament, as well as others who were disposed to his service from less honourable motives. But the deep-laid, complicated scheme of a double cabinet, as described by Burke, would have been unintelligible to the limited and practical understanding of George the Third. If he resorted to mystery and secret influence, it was not for the purpose of setting up a cabinet within a cabinet: but simply to disperse the haughty cabals which had enthralled his predecessors, and to recover what he thought fairly belonged to a king —the right, namely, of choosing his own servants, and being their master, instead of a puppet in their hands. [pp. 66–7]

In many respects Massey prefers Bute to Newcastle, and if he passes judgment even against the former he seeks to be fair in his exposition of the man's purposes. In his view, Newcastle's "only notion of government was the coarsest management of the House of Commons", the dispensing of "the whole of the ordinary patronage", the "art of 'gratifying' Members of Parliament". Bute, on the other hand, reprobated "those odious means which former administrations had employed for the purpose of securing parliamentary support". He himself "did not resort to those means until he found he could not go on without them". It is Bute who has misgivings in respect of the "bold step" of "dismissing the popular minister [Pitt]"; and it is Newcastle who exults at the latter's fall. Bute is to be commended for his policy of "restoring peace, and severing England from a connection with German politics"; and his peace-treaty, though open to criticism, secured to this country "everything worth having, or that she was likely to maintain". While Newcastle was still in office, "boroughs were disposed of, places were given away without his knowledge, or in opposition to his wishes".

> His complaints were unheeded; and his recommendations were met with significant hints that power had passed into other hands. Convinced at length that such was the fact, Newcastle prepared for the dreaded hour of resignation.

In Massey's view "it was almost a matter of course that the chief political instructor of George III should be the minister on whose counsel and aid he first relied in bringing the new system of government into operation". But, he says:

> the court favour which Sir Robert Walpole enjoyed was founded entirely upon his merit as a public servant; that of Bute had no other origin than royal caprice. There had been no royal favourite thrust into state affairs since the ill-omened precedent of George Villiers; and Bute had none of the brilliant qualities which dazzled the people in the person of Buckingham.

Bute's system of government, however, was "plausible" enough, according to Massey, and the revival of royal authority was connected with the plan of restoring the country to political health. "Prerogative was to be rescued from the hands of faction, and restored to independence; while the system of government by bribery and corruption was wholly to cease." He lacked the political realism which would have enabled him to see the fallacy in the theory that an independent King and an independent parliament would be mystically at one.

We are ill-informed as to the extent to which Bute proposed to carry his scheme of prerogative. To suppose that he meant to follow the example of Strafford in superseding parliamentary government and setting up the will of the crown in its stead, is to deny him credit for ordinary knowledge of history, and of the temper and character of the times in which he lived. But a politician so shallow as Bute, might have thought that the exercise of a wide discretion by the Sovereign in the choice of his public servants was compatible with the character and pretensions of a popular legislature. In fact, he did believe, at first, that the strength of the public men of England really lay in the corruption of the House of Commons; and, consequently, that by restoring purity and freedom to the electoral system, he should obtain a representative assembly submissive to the pleasure of the crown. On discovering his mistake, he went into the opposite extreme. (p. 137)

When he proved incompetent for the task, George III "cast him aside and sought for abler services. It is now well ascertained that, instead of being the ruling genius of a court cabal for years subsequent to his retirement from office, Bute had scarcely any communication with the court after that period, and complained, not without reason, of the King's neglect and ingratitude."

Massey quotes George III as saying "Never more shall those Whig grandees be admitted to power". And if his final criticism is an adverse one, it is substantially different from that of the ordinary Whig historians:

Though Parliament had been tampered with, the great nobility insulted, and small men ruined, prerogative, so far from having had its ascendancy secured, was in fact not advanced a step. These measures had, indeed, an effect just the contrary to that for which they were intended; instead of erasing party distinctions, and teaching public men to look for preferment to the crown alone, they revived that old party spirit which had languished for nearly half a century. The entire predominance of the Whig interest at the accession of the House of Hanover left room for jealousies to spring up in the bosom of the party itself; and the schism which took place in the year following that event, under the guidance of the Earl of Sunderland, had never yet been healed. The opposite party, divided again into Tories and Jacobites, were unable to profit by these dissensions, and whatever changes took place in administration, whether Walpole or Newcastle were driven from power, their places were generally supplied from the great Whig connection.

George the Third, coming to the throne with advantages which neither of his predecessors possessed, might, indeed, have abolished those old party distinctions which there was no longer any plausible pretence for maintaining. But instead of inviting to his service able and eminent men, without reference to the obsolete banners under which they had been ranged, the course which his Majesty pursued made it sufficiently plain, that his idea of suppressing party distinctions meant no more than the suppression of that great constitutional party whose leading principle it was to restrain monarchical power. Even this design was not hopeless, had it been attempted with caution and tact. The nation was disgusted with party, which, for the last twenty years, had meant an unprincipled struggle for place and power. The Whigs had no hold on public favour; they were considered, not without justice, as a proud and selfish aristocracy; and George the Third might have calculated on popular sympathy in shaking off the irksome domination of a few great families which had oppressed his predecessors, if he had not outraged popular prejudices by the means which he employed. A combination of two characters most odious to the English taste—a reputed minion and a Scot—was set up as the minister whom the King delighted to honour. [p. 130]

Massey's criticism is worthy of note, then. He complains that prerogative was "not advanced a step", that party-spirit revived—in fact, that George III failed to achieve what Adolphus had regarded him as trying to achieve. This work does at least show us that in 1855 the Whig interpretation had not yet come to hold the field.

CHAPTER FIVE

THE VICTORY OF THE WHIG INTERPRETATION

1. *Erskine May and his Contemporaries*

THE ESTABLISHMENT of a new interpretation of George III's reign —a counter-system to that of Adolphus—comes in the 1860's, particularly in the early pages of Erskine May's *Constitutional History*. The old Whig charges against the King—the party attacks, recently reviewed by Lord John Russell—were now transmuted into a form of academic orthodoxy. By this time the point had been reached at which the eighteenth century was so remote that the structural differences between the world of 1760 and that of 1860 could be entirely overlooked. Up to this date, men like Croker had had their roots sufficiently far back in the *ancien régime* to save them from serious misconceptions about the situation at the time of George III's accession. There now occurred that effective lapse of memory or break in tradition which made it easy even for the historian to slip into anachronisms. It became possible to imagine that, prior to 1760, there had flourished a regularly-established system of ministerial and parliamentary government, and that George III had wickedly set out to secure its overthrow.

The case against this King was developed in a remarkable manner in the opening pages of Erskine May's *Constitutional History of England*, which appeared in 1861. It was perhaps of some significance that this work started only at the accession of

George III, so that the author, before he interpreted the new reign, had not been compelled to examine carefully the antecedent situation. Also he does not seem to have taken any account of the evidence or the explanations of Adolphus. His book was greatly influenced by Horace Walpole's *Memoirs*, but he had made use of the other printed sources which had recently become available, and particularly the letters from Newcastle to Hardwicke which had been printed in the *Rockingham Memoirs*. The effect of these Whig influences was heightened by the fact that they gave him greater confidence than his predecessors had had in the evidence of Edmund Burke and the interpretation embodied in Burke's *Thoughts on the Cause of the Present Discontents*. This means that, in respect of three kinds of sources—contemporary letters, pamphlet literature and memoirs—the author made an uncritical use of what (for his particular subject) were extremely doubtful authorities.

Furthermore, Erskine May must be a good example of the way in which an historian may fall into error through an excess of brilliance. His capacity for synthesis, and his ability to dovetail the various parts of the evidence in order to form them into a system, would seem to have carried him into a more profound and complicated elaboration of error than some of his more pedestrian predecessors would have been able to achieve. Because he was a constitutional theorist he inserted a doctrinal element into his history which, granted his original aberrations, was calculated to project the lines of error, carrying his work still further from centrality or truth.

Erskine May agrees with the previous historians of George III's reign in one thing. He sees that down to 1760 the authority of the king had been eclipsed by the power of the combined Whigs. He cannot conceive, however, that in the eighteenth century it would be the Whig domination which appeared to be the anomaly, such an ascendancy being interpreted in those days as a

mere cornering of power. He merely imagines that modern constitutionalism was already in existence before 1760—a system of
government by "responsible ministers, upheld by party connexions and by parliamentary interest". He regards it as having
been established by 1760 that the prerogatives of the Crown
should be separated from the person of the ruling monarch and
exercised only at the discretion of ministers who were responsible
to parliament.

From Horace Walpole he takes over the view that George III,
having been educated by Jacobites, set out from the very first to
overthrow a constitution which was already established. From
Burke he takes over the theory that this king, instead of relying
on ministers who had the confidence of parliament, ruled by
means of an "interior" cabinet, a cabinet of people who were
dependent on himself. It was natural that he should condemn
George III in a much more radical way than Macaulay had done.
His verdict was: "To revert to a policy under which kings had
governed and ministers had executed their orders, was in itself a
dangerous retrogression in the principles of constitutional government." In fact he produced that interpretation of George III
which in a popularised form retained its currency until very
recently.

> A succession of sovereigns less capable than William [III], and of
> ministers gifted with extraordinary ability . . . rapidly reduced
> to practice the theory of ministerial responsibility. . . . Upon
> ministers, therefore, devolved the entire burthen of public affairs:
> they relieved the crown of its cares and perils, but, at the same time,
> they appropriated nearly all its authority. The king reigned, but his
> ministers governed.
>
> To an ambitious prince, this natural result of constitutional govern-
> ment could not fail to be distasteful. . . . The young King, George
> III, on succeeding to the throne, regarded with settled jealousy the
> power of his ministers, as an encroachment on his own; and resolved
> to break it down. His personal popularity was such as to facilitate

the execution of this design. . . . So far back as in 1752, complaints had been made that the prince was surrounded by Jacobite preceptors, who were training him in arbitrary principles of government. . . . [Lord Bute] had taught him that his own honour, and the interests of the country, required the extension of his personal influence, and a more active exercise of his prerogatives. The chief obstacle to this new policy of the court was found in the established authority of responsible ministers, upheld by party connexions and parliamentary interest. Accordingly, the first object of the king and his advisers was to loosen the ties of party, and break down the confederacy of the great Whig families. The king desired to undertake personally the chief administration of public affairs, to direct the policy of his ministers, and himself to distribute the patronage of the crown. . . .

Lord Bolingbroke had conceived the idea of a government under "a patriot king"—who should "govern as soon as he begins to reign" . . .

. . . It was the king's object not merely to supplant one party, and establish another in its place; but to create a new party, faithful to himself, regarding his personal wishes, carrying out his policy, and dependent on his will. . . . Instead of relying upon the advice of his responsible ministers, the king took counsel with this "double" or "interior cabinet" . . .

. . . His courtiers represented that he was enthralled by the dominant party, which had become superior to the throne itself; and that in order to recover his just prerogative, it was necessary to break up the combination. But what was this, in effect, but to assert that the king should now be his own minister? that ministers should be chosen, not because they had the confidence of Parliament and the country, but because they were agreeable to himself, and willing to carry out his policy?—And this was the true object of the king. . . .

It is possible that no other writer on the early years of the reign of George III has managed to put his finger on so many errors, heresies, anachronisms, points of misunderstanding and perversities of interpretation—all collected from various quarters but never hitherto combined—and by drawing a line from one to another succeeded in making a system calculated to be so plausible to unhistorical minds. This new interpretation did not merely qualify the version of Adolphus, or provide a variation, but superseded it; and, though it is rare to find the entire combination of errors repeated, its general argument gained considerable currency in the academic world. Because historians are not always closely mathematical in their reasonings or their dove-tailings, the reconstruction of Erskine May might still be combined with the older system, however, the one being somewhat inconsistently patched into the other. The deepest source of error was perhaps not party prejudice; perhaps it was not even the flood of opposition evidence which had been produced during the previous decades. It was rather the tendency to read the assumptions of 1860 into the now forgotten world of 1760. This occurs in the very decades in which European historiography had come perhaps to its period of most signal progress—the period when historical scholarship appeared in general to be becoming more scientific. It would seem that in this very period the Whig interpretation of history was definitely gaining ground in this country. John George Phillimore, in his three-volume work on George III in 1863 complained that "by far the greater number" of previous writers on the reign of this monarch had "erred on the side of adulation". And Miss Crosby, in the volume of essays presented to Professor Abbott, tells us that Alison stopped writing history in 1861 because he felt that it was vain to try to resist the tide of Whig interpretation any longer.

Even now, however, we must be careful not to exaggerate the victory of the new interpretation, particularly amongst those writers who were engaged in authentic researches in this field. In 1867 W. Bodham Donne produced an important two-volume work: *The Correspondence of King George the Third with Lord North from 1768 to 1783*; and in the introduction to this he repeats much of the older criticism of the mid-eighteenth century Whigs, as well as much of the older argument in favour of George III.

He describes the Whigs as being more devoted to civil and religious liberty, while the Tories regarded both Church and King with greater loyalty and reverence. The Whigs tended to be more abstract and philosophical, while Tory thinking was more in accordance with the "average disposition of mankind". The former regarded the King as the head of the aristocracy and thought that ministers ought to be chosen from a select circle. The latter regarded the King as "the Prince of the People" and thought that he had the right to choose his own ministers, the right to have a say in the government of the country in general. "In the political logic of the Whigs there was something chilling; in the sentimental bias of the Tories there was a chord that vibrated in the heart of a people."

Donne, however, repeats the old "Tory" opinion that "so late as the year 1819 we find power regarded by the Whigs in the light of an heirloom". He echoes an older view of the causes of the Whig domination:

> Their dependence for the conduct of home affairs upon the Whig leaders, so far from being felt as a grievance, was accepted by George I and his son as a relief from cares that diverted their attention from Hanover, while in all that related to the Electorate those sovereigns were not merely supported but even indulged by their Whig advisers. [Vol. I, p. xxxi]

He refers to the account in the *Parliamentary History* of a speech made by the Earl of Sandwich in the house of Lords in 1770—a speech directed at this point primarily against the Earl of Chatham. Sandwich says:

> Give me leave to take some notice of what a noble earl has been pleased to say, with respect to the propriety of an hereditary gratitude in the Crown to the great Whig families; his Lordship talks much of the merit which these families had in bringing in the House of Hanover, and it is a merit I am very ready to acknowledge; but will the noble Earl say, that . . . they are therefore to make a perpetual

monopoly of the royal favour. . . . Is the booby descendant of a Whig, to be employed in the first departments of the State, because his ancestor was a man of abilities; or is the deserving offspring of a Tory to be overlooked, because his father's principles were obnoxious? . . . The noble Lord wishes, he tells us, to abolish all party distinctions, yet he is greatly offended that the distinction of Whig and Tory is not inflexibly kept up; the King must govern by a faction to please his Lordship, he must not be the common father of his people, but only the monarch of the Whigs. [pp. xxix–xxx]

Donne refers to George III's "known aversion to Whig dicta-tion" and says that "partly for this reason, loyalty revived" at the beginning of the new reign. He quotes Lord Hardwicke as the authority for the view that "the purpose of superseding gradually and removing finally the Whigs from Office and Household" dates "from the accession of George III". "Whether it were the fact or merely rumour", says Donne, "it was evident that George III was not walking in the ways of his immediate pre-decessors". He describes this as equivalent to "the transition from a passive to an active sovereign" and says that now "the position of the ruling parties was reversed". He speaks of the "imperfect and vicious education" of George III, of his "limited understand-ing and obstinate disposition". He repeats this criticism of the King and is insistent in the view that "of the badness of his educa-tion there can be no doubt". George, he says (p. xiii), was

> a blunt, busy, positive, shrewd, but not very sagacious man; one well acquainted with public business—better versed in it indeed than many of his advisers; a restless inquisitive man . . . rising early, and, when work was to be done, sitting up late. . . . Punctual, even minute in his mode of transacting business . . . a good hater. . . . The Chatham Correspondence proves him to have been most indulgent to a really great [but wayward and provoking] Minister.

Furthermore, he says, this king had no Hanoverian propensities, but had "a strong if unenlightened sense of duty to his people"—indeed he was "sincerely attached to his people".

The idea of power to do what he thought good and to hinder what he thought evil presented irresistible attractions [to him]. . . . Nor can I subscribe to the doctrines of such historians as represent George III deliberately aspiring to put himself above the laws. Neither can I blame him, in the early days of his reign, for his desire to conciliate all classes of his subjects and to welcome home again dissidents from the Hanoverian succession. He had been taught, erroneously and perhaps factiously, to regard his predecessors as bondmen to their advisers . . . [but] as his experience was enlarged he failed to profit by its lessons. [p. lxii–iii]

Donne thought that it might never be possible to settle the question whether Bute had ceased to have political influence after his retirement from the Treasury. "So far as silence goes", he said, however, "the evidence of these letters [the correspondence between George III and North] is unfavourable to the theory of such *influence*".

It seems more in accordance with the Royal disposition to believe that *favouritism*—his friendship for Lord North must not be dishonoured by that term—was not likely to be among George III's failings. . . . He was inclined . . . to be his own counsellor-in-chief. [p. lix]

In many of his incidental opinions Donne does not stand at any great distance from Adolphus; and on the main issue he places the narrative in a framework so similar that he may be counted as merely another variant of the same tradition. He does not insist that George III's predecessors were in fact under bondage to the Whigs, and even suggests that they rather accepted ministerial government in home affairs in return for special indulgence in respect of their Hanoverian policies. But George III had been taught that the earlier Hanoverians had been the prisoners of an "oligarchy". And this misconception of his is part of the explanation of his policy.

2. Lecky and George Otto Trevelyan

ALTHOUGH IT has often been said that Lecky was responsible for the hostile views of George III which prevailed in the later decades of the nineteenth century, this historian was more moderate than Erskine May in his description of the early years of the reign and in his judgment upon the initial policy of the King. Volumes III and IV of his *History of England in the Eighteenth Century* came out in April 1882, and carried the narrative from 1760 to 1784. Lecky traversed a very great amount of material—two or three hundred volumes of manuscripts and about a hundred volumes of pamphlets in one summer, by his own account. There were eighty large volumes of papers in London on the subject of Ireland alone, and he reckoned that in Dublin there were two hundred and eighty volumes of pamphlets relating to English history in the period with which he was concerned. For his first two volumes his Irish work had comprised "the informations and presentments of all the grand juries, the correspondence of the English authorities with the Lords Justices, the correspondence of country gentlemen with the Government, newspapers of the first half of the last century, and the magnificent collection of pamphlets at the [Irish] Academy". He admits that on the Irish side of the story the bulk of the materials used and the "originality of research" were "of disproportionate magnitude"—he would seem to have been particularly anxious to answer Froude. His survey of the materials was rapid, however, and even in the Irish sections, it is clear that he picked out from the documents the things which fitted the framework of story already existing in his mind. He did not treat the evidence microscopically and tear the story to pieces, re-assembling the framework after detective-work on the primary materials. It has been said of him with some justice that he strove to find the mean between the two kinds of history which were represented respectively by Carlyle and Buckle. He had declared in 1872:

> I want greatly to write a kind of analytic history explaining as well as describing all English politics for the last century and a half. [Memoir of Lecky, p. 88]

A considerable part of Volumes III and IV was devoted to the American Revolution, and it is clear that Lecky felt himself to have been too impartial—too fair to the English cause—to please the citizens of the United States. Before the volumes actually appeared he wrote to the American historian, Lea, about his apprehensions on this subject. "But", he said (*ibid.*, p. 160), "you can hardly expect a somewhat conservative English or Irish man to write about the American Revolution in the spirit of Bancroft". In reality the volumes were well received in America. But it is clear that Lecky did not feel himself to have been producing merely a Whig diatribe against George III.

He was ready to do justice to the private virtues of this monarch and wrote of him:

> Simple, regular, and abstemious in all his tastes and habits, deeply religious without affectation or enthusiasm, a good son, a faithful husband, a kind master, and (except when he had met with gross ingratitude) an affectionate father, he exhibited through his whole reign, and in a rare perfection, that type of decorous and domestic virtue which the English middle classes most highly prize . . . his constant attendance and reverential manner at religious services; his solemn and pious resignation under great private misfortunes, contrasted admirably with the open immorality of his father, his grandfather, and his great-grandfather, and with the outrageous licentiousness of his own brothers and of his own sons. He never sought for popularity; but he had many of the kingly graces, and many of the national tastes that are most fitted to obtain it. He went through public ceremonies with much dignity, and although his manner in private was hurried and confused, it was kind and homely, and not

without a certain unaffected grace. Unlike his two predecessors, he was emphatically a gentleman. . . . He was also a very brave man. . . . His habit in dating his letters, of marking, not only the day, but the hour and the minute in which he wrote, illustrates not unhappily the microscopic attention which he paid to every detail of public business, and which was the more admirable because his natural tendency was towards sloth. . . . He was sincerely desirous of doing his duty, and deeply attached to his country, although stronger feelings often interfered both with his conscientiousness and with his patriotism. . . . In his hatred of innovation and in his vehement anti-American, anti-Catholic, and anti-Gallican feelings, he represented the sentiments of large sections—perhaps of the majority—of his people. [Vol. III (2nd ed., 1883), pp. 12–14]

Lecky, in point of fact, does put before the reader the arguments which the court party in the early years of the reign, and the Tory historians in the first half of the nineteenth century, had used to vindicate the initial policy of George III. The supporters of the new régime, he said, "had no wish to restrict or override the authority of Parliament, or to adopt any means which were not legal and parliamentary".

Their favourite cries were abolition of government by party or connection, abolition of corruption at elections, emancipation of the sovereign from ministerial tyranny. No class of politicians were . . . to be allowed to dictate their policy to the King. The aristocracy, it was said, had obtained an exaggerated place in the Constitution. A few great families, who had been the leading supporters of the Revolution, who were closely connected by family relationships, by friendship, by long and systematic political co-operation, had come to form a single coherent body possessing so large an amount of borough patronage and such vast and various ramifications of influence, that they were practically the rulers of the country. This phalanx was beyond all things to be broken up. [p. 20]

Lecky quoted from Adolphus the remarks of Bubb Dodington about the "set of undertakers" who in the reigns of George I and

George II had "farmed the power of the Crown at a price certain". In support of the argument of Adolphus, he drew attention to a further pamphlet which had appeared in 1761—the *Seasonable Hints from an Honest Man on the new Reign and the New Parliament*. The author of this pamphlet asked the King "whether he is to content himself with the shadow of royalty while a set of undertakers for his business intercept his immediate communication with his people, and make use of the legal prerogatives of their master to establish the illegal claims of [factious] oligarchy". This writer, says Lecky,

> complains that "a cabal of ministers had been allowed to erect themselves into a fourth estate, to check, to control, to influence, nay, to enslave the others"; that it had become usual "to urge the necessity of the King submitting to give up the management of his affairs and the exclusive disposal of all his employments to some ministers, or set of ministers, who, by uniting together, and backed by their numerous dependents, may be able to carry on the measures of Government"; that "ministerial combinations to engross power and invade the closet", were nothing less than a "scheme of putting the sovereign in leading-strings"; and that their result had been the monstrous corruption of Parliament and the strange spectacle of "a King of England unable to confer the smallest employment unless on the recommendation and with the consent of his ministers". He trusts that the new King will put an end to this system by showing "his resolution to break all factious connections and confederacies" . . . and by steadily pursuing this course, the true ideal of the Constitution will be attained, "in which the ministers will depend on the Crown, not the Crown on the ministers." . . . With the destruction of oligarchical power the reign of corruption would terminate, and undue influence in Parliament was never likely to be revived. [pp. 22–3]

According to Lecky (p. 16), George III was determined "to restore the royal power to a position wholly different from that which it occupied in the reign of his predecessor". Lecky himself recognises, furthermore, that "this design was in many respects more plausible than is now generally admitted".

> The power of the English sovereign had for many years been steadily declining, and the limitations to which he was practically subject went far beyond the mere letter of the law. . . . What the position of the English sovereign was in the eyes of the English Church was sufficiently shown by the long series of theologians who proclaimed in the most emphatic terms that he possessed a Divine right. . . . The language of English law was less unqualified, but still it painted his authority in very different colours from those which an historian of George I or of George II would have used. The "Commentaries" of Blackstone were not published till George III had been for some time on the throne; but Bute had obtained a considerable portion of them in manuscript from the author, for the purpose of instructing the Prince in the principles of the Constitution. "The King of England" in the words of Blackstone "is not only the chief, but properly the sole magistrate of the nation. . . . He governs the kingdom: statesmen, who administer affairs, are only his ministers".
>
> It is not surprising that the contrast between such language and the actual position of George II during the greater part of his reign should have vividly impressed a young sovereign surrounded by Tory followers, and naturally extremely tenacious of power. . . . The propriety of breaking down the system of exclusion seemed manifest. The Tory sentiment of the country had long found no adequate expression in the Government. . . . There was something manifestly unhealthy in the continuance during many years, of a Government like that of Walpole, which was supported chiefly by a majority of members of nomination boroughs in opposition to the large majority of the county votes. [pp. 16–19]

Lecky is cautious in his attitude to Burke's *Thoughts on the Cause of the Present Discontents*. He thinks it probable that the author of this treatise "considerably exaggerated the systematic and elaborate character of the plan that was adopted" by the court of George III at the beginning of the reign. He points out that Burke himself appears to have been in favour of the plan for the abolition of parties in the year 1762. He quotes the *Annual Register* for that year and draws attention particularly to the passage which said that "From the beginning of the reign it had been professed, with the general applause of all good men, to abolish those party distinctions [of Whig and Tory]". Lecky recognises that, in his attacks on corruption and on political connexion, George III was following the methods adopted by the elder Pitt in the period before 1760.

From all this it is clear that Lecky reproduced on a considerable scale the arguments of the traditional Tory historiography in favour of George III. It is possible to see, furthermore, that to a certain degree, Lecky recognises the reasonableness of that Tory case. He does justice to the situation of things in 1760, and does not pretend that there already existed at that time a regular system of ministerial and parliamentary government. He points out that the constitution of 1760 was not the Victorian one, and he does not suggest—he specifically rejects the idea—that George III was seeking to override parliament. In any case he tells the whole story at sufficient length and in sufficient detail—with sufficient qualifications in fact—to enable the critical reader to undermine many of his conclusions on the internal evidence of his own book.

On the other side, however, he maintains (p. 14) that George III "inflicted more profound and enduring injuries upon his country than any other modern English king".

> Ignorant, narrow-minded, and arbitrary, with an unbounded confidence in his own judgment and an extravagant estimate of his prerogative, resolved at all hazards to compel his ministers to adopt his own views, or to undermine them if they refused, he spent a long life in obstinately resisting measures which are now almost universally admitted to have been good, and in supporting measures which are as universally admitted to have been bad. . . . In a word, there

is scarcely a field of politics in which the hand of the King may not be traced—sometimes in postponing inevitable measures of justice and reform, sometimes in sowing seeds of enduring evil. [pp. 14–16]

If he summarises the virtues of this king on the one hand, he reproduces on the other hand Lord Waldegrave's account of his defects, and deplores the influence that his mother had had on the development of his mind.

In fact Lecky qualifies in a serious manner (or in a way that carried serious consequences for him) the interpretation that Adolphus had presented. He takes over from Horace Walpole the idea that George III at the beginning of his reign did not in reality follow the aims of the elder Pitt, though this might have appeared to be the case. George may have used the same means, but he did not intend merely to check corruption and abolish distinctions of party in the way that Pitt had hoped to do. He intended that the Tories should supersede the Whigs, because the Tories were in favour of monarchical authority.

> "Prerogative", as Horace Walpole said, had once more "become a fashionable word", the Divine right of kings was once again continually preached from the pulpit, and the Court party never concealed their conviction that the monarchy in the preceding reign had fallen into an essentially false position, and that it should be the first object of the new sovereign to restore it to vigour. [pp. 19–20]

Lecky, then, slides between the interpretation put forward by Adolphus and the version that was set out in the *Memoirs* of Horace Walpole; but he never accepts either of these fully, and he never adopts the extremist system which had been worked out by Erskine May. He is hostile to George III—perhaps as hostile as if he had held him to have been an unconstitutional king. But the basis of his hostility is to a considerable degree a new one, and he provides us with the mathematical formula for a more subtle kind

of Whig interpretation. It is his argument that George III was
wrong not because he violated an existing constitution but because
he persistently opposed all those movements which in the fullness
of time were to turn the government of 1760 into the government of 1860. George III was opposing a Whig demand for the
development of the constitution in a certain direction. In other
words, he opposed the cause which was to be retrospectively vin-
dicated in the nineteenth century. Over and over again, in fact,
George III took a strong line over matters on which subsequent
history has proved him to have been in the wrong.

The more extreme form of the Whig interpretation is represented by Sir George Otto Trevelyan, whose *Early History of
Charles James Fox* was published in 1880, before the third of
Lecky's volumes had appeared. He claimed that "the popular
impression of George III" had been derived from the latter half
of the reign, and especially from the time "when he had Pitt for a
master and Nelson for a servant"—when "happily for his own
fame", he had "yielded himself to the dominion of a stronger
will than even his own". According to Trevelyan (p. 121),
George III possessed

> all the accomplishments which are required for doing business, as
> business is done by kings. . . . Punctual, patient, self-willed, and self-
> possessed; intruding into every department; enquiring greedily into
> every detail; making everybody's duty his own, and then doing it
> conscientiously, indefatigably, and as badly as it could possibly be
> done.

He "never scrupled to exert his authority" or "to foster disunion
among politicians". Indeed we are now informed that he
knocked "Chancellors of the Exchequer and First Lords of the
Treasury down like ninepins". Trevelyan speaks of "the round-
ness and vehemence with which he invariably declared himself
upon the wrong side in a controversy". He complains of him as
a king "so formidable, so pertinacious, so insatiable of power and

so very far from particular as to the means which he employed in the pursuit of it". His mother, "a narrow-minded intriguing woman, with the Continental notion of the relations between royalty and the rest of mankind", had had an enduring influence upon him; for she had been "ambitious to see him govern as arbitrarily as an Elector of Saxony", and she had "willingly allowed his strong mind to remain uncultivated by study, and overgrown with prejudices".

As far as any knowledge of the duties and the position which were before him were concerned, she kept him in the nursery till within two years of the time that he mounted the throne. All that bedchamber women and pages of the backstairs could tell him about royal prerogative and popular rights she took care that he should learn; but at this point his political education ended. . . . One of the very few books, which [he] was ever authentically known to have read, was a Jesuit history of [the] great and glorious Revolution. [p. 119]

The issues of 1760 assume a new form in the hands of this Whig historian; and George III is now seen as bringing his country to the verge of ruin by his abandonment of the policy of his grandfather—his attempt to establish a "system of personal government".

[George II's] solid and unambitious intellect had taught him that the true secret of kingcraft was to get the best ministers he could find, and then leave them responsible for their own business. . . . A different policy from his, pursued during the next two-and-twenty years, mutilated the Empire, loaded the nation with debt, reduced the military reputation of Britain lower than it had ever stood before or since, made formidable inroads upon freedom, and rendered the Crown itself so irksome a burden that its wearer thought very seriously of resigning it.

And now it is argued that George III, far from cherishing a vague dream of the abolition of "corruption", set out to take advantage of the prevailing system in order to build upon it a more powerful monarchical authority.

> The venality and servility of Parliament presented an irresistible temptation to a monarch who aimed at extending the influence of the Crown. [p. 117]

The King is not charged with initiating corruption, but "*he protected and prolonged a bad system* which, but for him, would have died an earlier death by at least sixteen years". At this point in the argument the interpretation put forward by Adolphus and his successors would seem to suffer an almost complete inversion. Trevelyan adds however (p. 132):

> The nucleus of the Liberal party, as it has existed ever since, was formed during the turbid and discreditable period that intervened between the fall of Pitt in 1761 and the fall of Grenville in 1765.

"Loathing the corruption which was rising around them like a noisome tide,—and foreseeing the perils of that deliberate warfare against the freedom of the press, which began with the arrest of Wilkes", the men who were attached to Rockingham, and who followed the teaching of Burke, opened a new era by the stand that they made against the new menace of monarchy.

CHAPTER SIX

THE RETREAT FROM THE WHIG INTERPRETATION

---

1. *German and British Scholarship Compared*

BY THE very fact that he was soaked in a modern kind of constitutionalism, essentially British in character, Erskine May was in a sense perhaps incapacitated for the task of interpreting the reign of George III. It should not be surprising to us that, on a number of occasions, a continental historian, standing outside our system, and unfettered by the notions of the modern political Englishman, has been able to throw a refreshing light upon our history, and, in particular, to curb our natural propensity for the fallacies of the Whig interpretation. The foreigner is sometimes less ready than we are to take for granted the uniqueness of our political and parliamentary tradition—less ready in any case to appropriate modern constitutionalism and then to read it back into the earlier centuries of our history. Unhampered by those ideas and assumptions which we have unconsciously allowed to become the framework of our thinking—ideas and assumptions which in complete absence of mind we often carry with us when we enter even the remoter fields of history—he sometimes finds it more easy than we do to regard an ancient system of government as a thing which has the right to stand—the right to be judged—on its own footing. He is less anxious to envisage it as merely an imperfect form of the governmental system which exists at the present day, and which is presumed to have existed always in aspiration—

presumed sometimes to have existed in an ideal form at the very beginning of history. The eye of the outsider easily catches the anomalies and the discrepant facts—the things in English history which remind him of something in the history of his own country. Some of them will be anomalies which we who are Englishmen may find it comfortable to ignore precisely because they cut so inconveniently across our conventions or our expectations. In fact, we tend to assume that our own system has always been essentially the same, and from that very cause has always been unique. For many reasons, therefore, the continental historian (though, to be sure, he may add some new errors and misunderstandings of his own) may escape some of our aberrations, particularly those which are associated with the Whig interpretation of history.)

The decade of the 1890's has a special importance in the history of historical scholarship in Great Britain. It sees the flowering of a generation that reacted to a considerable degree against Seebohm, Freeman and Stubbs, and established fresh foundations for much of our medieval history. Foreign scholars played an important part in this movement—Vinogradov, Liebermann, Petit-Dutaillis, for example. The historical revisions which stirred many of us when we were young—on the meaning of *Magna Carta*, for example, or the origins of the House of Commons—have their roots in the scholarship of this decade. An advance towards a view of the past which should be less "unhistorical" was achieved when scholars began to try to see feudalism from the inside in a way that Stubbs had failed to do. In general it was not merely the work of Stubbs that was being revised, however; for an older historical structure—a traditionally English way of formulating the whole history of this country—was being taken to pieces and reassembled in a different manner. Above all, it was the deep-seated Whig interpretation that was being overthrown—the ancient tendency to read the past state of the British constitution too much in the light of the present. It was in the revision of our medieval history that foreign scholars played a particularly important part; and some amendment in this field was necessary, no doubt, before a proper basis could be found for the revision of our modern history. Before McKechnie published his famous book on *Magna Carta*, which so greatly qualified the Whig interpretation of that document, Petit-Dutaillis in the 1890's had begun to react not only against the accepted idea of the Charter but also against Stubbs's whole approach to the problem of English constitutional development.

In 1886 the fourth Earl of Chichester presented the five hundred volumes of the Newcastle Papers to the British Museum; and within a very short time this massive body of evidence was beginning to alter the very basis of George III studies. By 1892 the German historian, Albert von Ruville was working on this material, as well as on diplomatic papers in the Public Record Office, for a dissertation entitled *Die Auflösung des preussisch-englischen Bündnisses im Jahre 1762*. In this work, von Ruville set out to show that the treatment of Prussia by George III and Bute in the closing stages of the Seven Years' War, though not impeccable, was by no means so discreditable as had been imagined, when considered in relation to the code of conduct then followed by other governments, not excluding that of Prussia herself. In 1895, in a study of *William Pitt (Chatham) und Graf Bute*, von Ruville claimed to show that Pitt and Bute shared the desire to destroy faction and exalt the power of a ministry dependent on the King, though the former might have in mind primarily the welfare of the nation, while the latter worked rather for the benefit of the monarch. Bute's concern to put an end to the Seven Years' War was bound to mean his alienation from Pitt. His great ambition, once the difficulty over the peace-treaty had passed, however, was to see Pitt at the head of a ministry.

In 1905 there appeared in Germany von Ruville's famous three-volume life of the elder Pitt. It was characterised by a conscious and avowed effort to counteract the peculiar tendencies which the author had observed in the historical scholarship of this country. Von Ruville criticised the Englishman's habit of regarding the whole history of his own country as unique—utterly separate from that of continental countries—and he opposed our way of imprisoning the story of our constitutional development within a private system of interpretation, as though that story were a purely insular one, and our government had been peculiar from the very first. He wrote [Engl. transl. Vol. I, pp. 1–2]:

> The opinion is widely and generally entertained, that the English state is the purest form of constitutional government, and that it was impressed with this form at a very early date. While other states were labouring under great uncertainty or entire confusion of constitutional form, or were burdened by the weight of despotism, England is supposed to have secured a careful delineation of spheres of influence and a balance of power between co-existing forces.

In England itself he saw uncertainties and confusions—saw at given dates the possibility of constitutional developments quite different from the ones which were actually brought about. Even within the terms of the constitution as it had been established in 1688, he held that wide realms had been left undefined, and areas existed in which action was neither prohibited nor prescribed. On the question of the rights and wrongs of a given case, therefore, he held that authentic differences of opinion might exist. He insisted that one should make allowance for a sphere of legitimate competition—a sphere in which kings and ministers fairly fought for position, and royalty and aristocracy still had to struggle in order to settle the extent of their rights.

> Utterly false is the opinion that there was at any time in England an equilibrium of different forces with constitutional right above them as a final court of appeal. . . . To regard a constitution as something above and beyond the human administration of it, is to adopt a fictitious point of view: a constitution can, at most, be considered as the established basis of action which is used by successive

generations until some advisable reason for change appears. . . .
[pp. 1–3]

This writer was certainly jealous of England's claim to uniqueness—anxious to show that, prior to the victories of Bismarck,
Germany herself had had a parallel right to be considered as the
home of constitutionalism. But his whole view of English constitutional history enabled him to be much more flexible than
Erskine May in his handling of the problem of the English constitution in the middle of the eighteenth century. Since he was a
continental historian, he was able to envisage the England of the
elder Pitt as an example of the *ancien régime*—able to see not only
the king but also the House of Commons as capable of aggression.
And he did not construe the eighteenth century as merely the age
of the "unreformed" Parliament, did not hamper himself with the
assumption that it ought to have been like the nineteenth century,
or that it was a corrupted form of the Victorian order of things.

The result was that von Ruville reverted to something like that
interpretation of George III's plan of government which had been
current in England itself in the earlier part of the nineteenth
century. George III, he said,

> was anxious to free himself from dependency upon the whigs, who
> had hitherto used the royal prerogative for their own purpose; he
> thought he might stand aside from party politics and make the
> monarchy to some degree independent. He was particularly anxious
> to gain the power of choosing his servants with reference solely to the
> welfare of the state. . . . He could not see that such a course of
> action implied any infringement of the constitution. . . . The
> King . . . was disinclined from the outset to step into the secondary
> position which his grandfather had held, from whom a large number
> of measures had practically been extorted by his ministers. [Vol. II,
> pp. 314–16]

In serious moral purpose and devotion to the general welfare, he
surpassed his egoistic predecessors and most of his contemporaries,
and consequently might well seem to be the suitable person to abolish

the numerous existing abuses and the evils arising from the system of party government. This party system was, as a matter of fact, most repugnant to him; he regarded it as a cancerous growth upon the English constitution. George had a highly developed sense of justice, and hence was imbued with that respect for the law and the constitution which the English people demanded of a ruler whom they were to trust and love. [Vol. III, pp. 2–3]

In other respects von Ruville was more startlingly original, however; and, amongst other things, his remorseless realism carried him to remarkable exposures of what he regarded as egotistical behaviour in Pitt himself. The controversies to which this side of his work gave rise would seem to have taken attention away from some of his novel suggestions in respect of constitutional history. He saw that the men of different parties who broke with their old connexions were admirably suited to develop into what he called "government servants"; though he did not use the more questionable term "civil servants", which has since been attached to them, and he did not base historical arguments upon the term itself or set out to over-stress a mere analogy. Partly because he had reason to remember the conflicts which had taken place between the young Frederick the Great and his father, he saw particular significance in the repeated quarrels between the successive Hanoverian kings of England and their heirs-apparent. He saw the relevance of these to the party-history of eighteenth-century England, and noted the importance of the fact that for a considerable period George III was not confronted by an heir who was in a position to behave as a political rival. Once again, however, he did not go so far as the modern school which has even claimed that this is the only difference between the situation of George II and that of George III. On this subject von Ruville wrote (Vol. II, pp. 313–4):

But the chief advantage that the new king enjoyed over his immediate predecessors was the fact that he alone represented the

174

strength and power of his kingdom, and that he need not fear the rivalry of a successor. This was an obstacle that had constantly hampered the efforts of his predecessors, and made them dependent upon groups of nobles or upon individuals; the presence of an heir-apparent who had attained his majority attracted general attention, while the strongest politicians shrank from opposing his views.

Von Ruville, furthermore, is distinguished from his English predecessors by his less hostile, less anachronistic, view of the essential purport of Bolingbroke's *Patriot King*. He insists that the "Patriot King" is required only to free Parliament "from all extraneous influence", that is to say, to abandon the practice of corruption. He rightly relies on a passage in which Bolingbroke stresses the fact that this single measure will be sufficient ro rectify all the disorders of the constitution. George III is regarded as being a follower of Bolingbroke in his attempt to break down the party-divisions in the country. But von Ruville criticises him for not being a follower of Bolingbroke in one important respect. He came short of the ideal of the "Patriot King", because he wanted "to take the reins of government into his hands and *rule*, which the last kings had not done". This is not imputed to George III as a crime. We are told that George's inclination was "to make himself, without violating the constitution, the predominant power in the state". But Bolingbroke had intended something different. He had regarded it as essential that parliament should "retain the powers it possessed". He had been in earnest when he argued that the "Patriot King" had one duty and one only: the abandonment of corruption.

Finally, says von Ruville, George III could not "dispense with the means which the Whigs had created for the maintenance of their power, namely corruption". In this again, he departed from the ideal of the "Patriot King"; though he did not depend on corruption entirely, but owed much to "the royalist feeling of the nation", much also to "the recognition with which a conscientious, wise rule could not fail to meet", and much again to "the tendency of people in general to side with those in power". According to von Ruville there existed in this period a natural tendency to monarchy, a predisposition in favour of the royal authority. This was counteracted, however, by the growing prosperity of the country, the march of political progress, and the extension of the power of the press. All these factors had their effect on the proceedings of parliament itself.

*   *   *

In the meantime, the Rev. William Hunt, who had made himself known by his work on the local history of the Somerset region, as well as his writings on ecclesiastical history, had been gaining an authoritative position in the field with which we are concerned. In the *Dictionary of National Biography* he had produced in 1890 a portrait of George III and an account of what he regarded as the "successful" but "costly" struggle waged by that monarch against the Whigs. Before 1760, he said,

> The affairs of the nation were . . . controlled by a party which had almost wholly ceased to represent principles, was held together by connection, and was strengthened by bribery and other corrupt practices, while the crown was fast becoming a mere ornament, adding lustre to a powerful oligarchy.

George III, he continued, "began his reign with a determination to break the yoke of the whig oligarchy, and to recover for the crown the power which it had lost since 1688".

> He had been taught that the royal authority could be best asserted by disregarding the ties of connection, and breaking up parties, and that a king should choose his ministers without yielding to the dic-

176

tates of a faction. He had seen in the success of Pitt the triumph of a statesman who disregarded party connection. He therefore resolved to overthrow the system of exclusion, to open office to the tories, and not to allow any party to dictate to him.

By using politicians who were attached to him personally, by taking patronage out of the hands of the ministers, and by maintaining "a crown influence in parliament which was apart from, and often opposed to, ministerial influence", he "renounced the proper sphere of a constitutional monarch in favour of that of a party leader".

In 1905, the very year in which von Ruville's *Pitt* was published, there appeared Volume X of *The Political History of England*, a volume by Hunt, which opened with the accession of George III. Now, as before, he described George as having been brought up "completely" under the influence of his mother, who "had the prejudices of a little German court". He repeats his former view that Bute encouraged the Prince to "exercise direct control over public affairs", and borrowed for him a volume of Blackstone's *Commentaries*, a work "in which the royal authority is magnified". He says that George's political system was "largely based" on Bolingbroke's *Patriot King*, and particularly on those parts of it which assert that the King should "begin to govern as soon as he begins to reign", choosing ministers who would conform to his principles. He adds, however, that the alleged teaching of Bolingbroke "seemed specially appropriate to the state of affairs at George's accession".

> During the last two reigns the power of the crown had dwindled. . . . [The] principles [of 1688] limited the exercise of the prerogative, but they did not involve depriving the crown of all participation in the government. The whig party exaggerated them, and . . . completely usurped the government of the country. . . . For nearly fifty years a small number of whig lords shared the government of the country among themselves.

Hunt does not follow Horace Walpole's view that George III attacked the distinctions of party with the secret object of bringing the Tories instead of the Whigs into power.

> He did not contemplate taking political power from one party in order to vest it in another. He designed to rule independently of party; no political section was necessarily to be excluded from office, but no body of men . . . was henceforth to dictate to the crown. To be willing and able to carry on the government in accordance with his will was to be the sole qualification for a share in the administration. Ministers might or might not be agreed on matters of the first importance; all the agreement between them which was necessary was that each in his own sphere should act as an agent of the king's policy.

Yet, as in the article of 1890, Hunt says that George III's plan of government "was in itself unconstitutional, for it would have made the ministers who were responsible to parliament mere agents of the king who was not personally responsible for his public acts".

> It necessarily made the king the head of a party. He needed votes in parliament, and he obtained them, as the whig leaders had done, by discreditable means. If his ministers did not please him he sought support from . . . his party, "the king's friends", as they were called, and so there arose an influence behind the throne distinct from and often opposed to that of his responsible advisers.

Hunt was not acute in analysis, and it was possible for him to accept at the first stage of the argument the complete framework which Adolphus had given to the story, but then to assert that George III was seeking to impose upon the country a plan of government that was "unconstitutional". At bottom Hunt follows the method of Horace Walpole's *Memoirs* and regards George III as using the occasion in order to establish his personal power and assert the principle of prerogative. It is not inconceivable, of course, that George III should have justifiably set out to overthrow the oligarchical Whigs and at the same time unjustifiably sought to impose upon the country a personal authority that was unconstitutional. But the work of William Hunt illustrates the point that no amount of learning can redeem historical work if the student is defective in imagination. Hunt declares that George III's relations with his ministers and with "the King's friends" are unconstitutional in the 1760's because the fact is self-evident to him—such relations would obviously have been unconstitutional in the closing decades of Victoria's reign. The relations themselves seem more sinister to Hunt because he does not understand them; and, though his article of 1890 contains reservations about Burke's *Thoughts on the Cause of the Present Discontents*, he sees "the King's friends" as an illegitimate kind of party, and regards them as working somewhat in the way that Burke had described.

He makes the mistake of imputing to the early 1760's (and interpreting as part of George III's initial intentions) the things which the King did, or the purposes he expressed, or the system that happened to develop, during the conflicts of later years. Horace Walpole, as we have seen, had even confessed to having used the evidence of later years to explain the King's policy at the beginning of the reign. Burke's *Thoughts on the Cause of the Present Discontents* had interpreted the whole scheme of George III through the things that had been taking place in the latter half of the 1760's. The evidence of the *Rockingham Memoirs*—and in general the experiences which the Rockinghamites had claimed to have had when they were in power in 1765–6—had increased the tendency to interpret George III's original purposes by events that happened later. Hunt regards George III as desiring to establish a "departmental" system of government, the King forming "the only element of coherence in a ministry" because "each of its members was to be guided by his will". He admits that "the idea of the cabinet as a homogeneous body, collectively responsible to parliament, was not yet established". He recognises that

> the factious spirit of the whigs, the extent to which they monopolised power, and the humiliating position to which they had reduced the crown, afford a measure of defence for his [George III's] scheme of government.

Yet because this made the ministers "mere agents of the king" while the King himself was "not personally responsible for his public acts", Hunt, as we have seen, regards the whole system as "unconstitutional". He over-simplified the issue; though it must always be remembered that such a system (or indeed any system that George III could be regarded as having adopted) might well have been "constitutional" at the time, but still not without danger for the future if left unopposed.

It is doubtful whether the extreme Whig interpretation of George III ever had a very considerable or very prolonged acceptance in high places. It would seem to have been more common for writers to behave like Hunt—accepting the Adolphus framework, sympathising with the idea of a royal attack on the Whig oligarchy, but still feeling that George III made dangerous assertions of his personal authority. And when they accused him of behaving "unconstitutionally" it is not absolutely clear that they squarely faced the issue whether his conduct or his intentions had been "unconstitutional" at the actual time. They thought they saw something which would be dangerous for the future, something which, if it had been left unopposed, would have prevented the constitution from developing in the way in which it actually did develop. If this was what Hunt had in mind he expressed himself with less clarity than Lecky and failed to make his readers really aware of the important distinction that required to be made. The point is not unimportant, as Hunt's work had considerable academic influence in the early decades of the twentieth century.

2. The Return to Adolphus

LORD ACTON was responsible for two of the most faulty statements ever produced by Whig historiography on the subject of British politics in the eighteenth century. In the first place, he asserted that "government by party was established in 1714, by party acting by Cabinet"; and here, through a mistake very similar to that of Erskine May, he antedated the establishment of a constitutional system of the modern kind. Secondly, he declared that by "about the year 1770 things had been brought back, by indirect means, nearly to the condition which the Revolution [of 1688] had been designed to remedy". In this case he assumed that after George III had brought about the discomfiture of the main body of the Whigs, corruption was so efficacious as to make the King the master of parliament itself. In other words, it became possible to circumvent the constitutional devices which had been adopted for the purpose of safeguarding the country against a despotic monarch.

The Whig interpretation could still appear in extravagant forms, even reversing the long tradition which had described George III as at least the enemy of corruption and political jobbery. We meet even in the twentieth century the repetition of Sir George Otto Trevelyan's opinion—the view that George III, observing the corruption that was prevalent, actually welcomed the existence of the abuses, because he saw how they would serve his purposes. In 1903 Edward Porritt published in two volumes his famous work on *The Unreformed House of Commons*, and he carried a stage further the argument of William Hunt, who had condemned George III for being the head of his own party, and himself a parliamentary manager. George, he said, "was intent on having ministers of his own choosing, and it was long his

181

steadfast purpose to maintain a party in the House of Commons which would support his ministers without question". He was a king who concerned himself with electioneering; and "to the House of Commons—to its management and the details of its business he gave closer and more continuous personal attention than any sovereign who had preceded him".

In the first thirty years of . . . George III, the electoral system was at its worst. The smaller boroughs were more under the control of patrons than at any previous time. Seats in the House were openly sold. Bribery was rampant in the larger boroughs. It was by turning these conditions to account that George III secured and maintained his control over the House of Commons. . . . He was determined that if Parliament was to be corrupted, and he had no objection to its corruption, it should be corrupted to serve his purpose; and . . . every minister [was to be] a mere instrument. [p. 409]

*   *   *

Even in English historiography, however, the Whig interpretation of the reign of George III was soon to be undermined, though in gradual stages. Hunt himself had held that Bute would have liked to work with the elder Pitt, if the latter had been more amenable; and in 1906 he published in the *English Historical Review* some of the papers that had been employed by von Ruville, making it clear that neither the Duke of Newcastle and his friends nor Bute himself "intended that he [Pitt] should resign office before peace was made". Harold Temperley published in the same Review, and during the course of the same year, some Hardwicke papers, apparently unknown to von Ruville, "showing the dissensions already rising in the council, and the isolation of Pitt and Temple, before the *pacte de famille* between France and Spain was guessed at by Pitt"—that is to say, before the emergence of the issue that brought about the actual resignation. By this time much more detailed work was being done in England on the very earliest years of the reign; and in 1902 D. A. Winstanley had published in the *English Historical Review* an article on "George III and his First Cabinet" which gave a close account of the triangular relationships between Newcastle, Pitt and Bute at that early period.

One of the first and most interesting attacks on the assumptions that had long prevailed in this whole historical field was an account of the politics of the early Hanoverian period, the epoch before 1760. It is contained in Volume VI—the volume entitled "The Eighteenth Century"—in the *Cambridge Modern History*, and is a curious example of the way in which, on rare occasions, that work could provide not a mere record of the existing state of scholarship, but a lively essay of a pioneering kind, remarkable for its originality. The volume in question appeared in 1909 and the article which concerns us is the one on "The Age of Walpole and the Pelhams", by Harold Temperley—a breezy piece of work which went out of its way to discredit many of the ideas that had long been fashionable. Much of the accepted teaching about the Whig ascendancy was drastically revised in this article, in such a way that criticism was focused upon the underlying ideas of Adolphus himself—upon the basic components of that whole enduring tradition of interpretation which had sprung from the work of Adolphus. Temperley insisted that there had been a great deal of exaggeration in the thesis from which almost all the interpretation of George III's initial intentions had derived—the thesis that, in the time of the first two Georges, monarchical authority had been under an eclipse. On this subject some of his remarks are perhaps reminiscent of the things which William Smyth had been saying in his Cambridge lectures a hundred years before; but Smyth, it must be remembered, had been expressing the prejudices of a Whig—one who indeed particularly suspected the principle of monarchy. Temperley wrote (p. 42):

Great as were the restrictions imposed upon the sovereign's power, his influence was still real, and might have been dangerous, if unscrupulously used. Eighteenth century statesmen were so deeply conscious of this fact that they continually suspect or accuse one another of intriguing in the closet, or of trying to catch the ear of the King; Walpole spent hours daily in the boudoir of Queen Caroline, telling her what policy he desired George II to pursue. . . . The authority of the two first Georges was exercised with less frequency and effect by reason of their ignorance of English parliamentary methods. Nevertheless, in his relations with his sovereign Walpole was anything but the autocrat that fancy has often supposed. In 1725, he reluctantly yielded to the royal will and permitted the recall of Bolingbroke to England; in 1728, he only secured his power over the new King, George II, by obtaining for him the substantial gratuity of an additional £100,000 yearly for the Civil List. Subsequently, the favour of the able and enlightened Queen Caroline assured Walpole's supremacy over the mind of George II; but her death in 1737 brought about a visible decline of his influence, which contributed, in some degree, to his subsequent fall.

Such arguments as these were bound to have the effect of weakening the case put forward by Adolphus and the Tory historians, who had regarded George III as justifiably attempting to rescue the monarchical authority from a state of bondage. The case for George III would at least require a certain degree of transposition, though it might still be said that this king at least imagined his predecessors to have suffered unduly at the hands of a Whig oligarchy, and that he resented this, as George II himself appears to have done on occasion. It would have been interesting if the article on the reign of George III in the same volume of the *Cambridge Modern History* had continued the argument and prolonged the analysis contained in this earlier chapter.

In general, Temperley seems to have set out to apply a powerful acid to various forms of anachronism which had been current amongst students of this period. In particular he seemed determined to avoid being deluded by appearances into thinking that modern constitutional principles had been established before men had in fact recognised them to be in operation. He deprecated the attempt to interpret the politics of the time on the principles of the modern party-system. He said that the old opposition of Whig and Tory had been superseded by the competition of political groups—that Walpole ruled "not over a large compact party" but over a number of allied leaders who were like the chieftains of separate clans. He anticipated the results of very recent scholarship when he reckoned that what is now called "the Court and Treasury Party" numbered just over a hundred, though he noted that the reliability of these might depend on the existence of a good understanding between the King and the First Lord of the Treasury. He said that "direct bribery has been proved against [Walpole] in a few cases", but that the evidence suggested this not to have been a common thing. He realised the existence and the importance of a considerable number of independent members of the House of Commons. Most of Walpole's "corruption", he said, consisted of the use of indirect means of securing party allegiance which every party leader employs.

In the same volume of the *Cambridge Modern History* there is an article by J. M. Rigg on the reign of George III. It speaks of the Whig oligarchy in a hostile manner; but regards parliamentary reform as the only cure for the evils of the eighteenth-century system. It criticises the Whigs under Newcastle and Rockingham —criticises particularly their notions of party cohesion—but chiefly in order to make a hero of the elder Pitt. George III is described as coming to the throne "with a mind made up to shake off the yoke of the Whig oligarchy, and form for himself a party which should secure him against the danger of ever again falling beneath their yoke". Rigg is very critical of Edmund Burke's *Thoughts on the Cause of the Present Discontents*. He says that the "truest admirers" of this author "must recognise that in this pamphlet the political sagacity of which his name has become a symbol is none too apparent". When he sees Burke imputing "all the disorders of the body politic" to "the secret and insidious influence of the court" he breaks out into exclamations and writes:

> as if the Whigs had been incapable of intrigue and quite unversed in the arts of corruption, and had not, by their jealousy of Chatham . . . and their own interminable dissensions, given the Court its opportunity.

This author particularly regrets that "Government by the collective Cabinet was still the pure theory of Whig constitutionalism, to which whatever savoured of a Prime Minister was abhorrent". He objects to the doctrine because it was one which set the followers of Newcastle against the elder Pitt and so helped the King and the court. Rigg admires Pitt, and values him most of all because of his recognition of the fact that the defective condition of the representative system was "the true cause of the confusions, and its reform the paramount need, of the State". Therefore, if Rigg is different from other writers, it is perhaps in being more Whig than the Whigs. And his interest in tangential questions prevented him from making any real contribution to the theme with which we are concerned.

Though there was much crudeness, much capriciousness and much thoughtless compiling, it would appear that the defects of British scholarship were slowly being remedied in detail. In 1914, Sir William Anson, in the *English Historical Review*, gave a comprehensive reply to the kind of heresy that Acton had put forward by pointing out the "unreality" of what had appeared to be "party government" in the eighteenth century. In the same journal in the same year, J. Holland Rose set out to correct the legend that George III and Bute had intrigued for the conclusion of peace in order to facilitate the overthrow of Pitt. More important than these detailed contributions was the work of the Cambridge historian, D. A. Winstanley, and the development which took place in his ideas in the years before the First World

War. In 1910 he produced his book on *Personal and Party Government in the Reign of George III*, in the introduction to which he declared that "it was no mere selfish lust for power that impelled George III to make war upon the men who had enslaved his grandfather". In the course of the same book he argued (p. 23) that George

> had been taught to dislike the party system, to distrust the whigs, and to despise his predecessor for the humiliation he had endured at the hand of his ministers ... He intended to inaugurate a new epoch in the relations between the crown and the cabinet, to wrest from his ministers the power which they had stolen from the monarchy, and, without transcending the limits of his prerogative, to exercise a decisive influence over the national destinies.

When, in 1912, he produced the sequel to this work, *Lord Chatham and the Whig Opposition*, Winstanley, however, chose to return at the very beginning of the book to the theme he had discussed in the earlier volumes. In a piece of recapitulation which was clearer and fuller than he had given in his previous account, he now produced what was really a re-exposition of the argument that Adolphus had developed over a century before. George III, he said, was "determined to regain for the monarchy the influence which it had lost during the reigns of the first two Hanoverian monarchs".

> It was never his intention to bring about a revolution in the government or to trample under foot the privileges acquired by the nation in its contest with the Stuarts; but he firmly believed, and with some justice, that the politicians, who had driven James II from the throne and excluded his son from the succession, had never intended to reduce the kingship to a condition of subservience. The constitution had developed on other lines than those laid down by the statesmen responsible for the Revolution settlement; and the royal authority had been usurped by a narrow oligarchy which had taken advantage of a disputed succession and a foreign dynasty to acquire supremacy in the state. [p.1]

Winstanley's language on this subject is in fact as radical as anything in the whole tradition started by Adolphus. In 1760, he says, "the royal power appeared to have reached the very nadir of its fortunes". George II had declared that "ministers were kings in this country" and "the cry was wrung from him by bitter experience". George II had claimed the right to choose his own ministers, but had once told Lord Waldegrave that "so far from having an option, he was not even allowed a negative". At the close of his reign he had been mortified to find that "he had sold himself into slavery to a few whig nobles who ruled the country in his name".

The supremacy of the Whig party "had been too oppressive to pass unchallenged". That there should be a reaction against it "is not surprising", and by 1760 "men had been taught to expect salvation from the court". According to the constitutional doctrines in which George III was reared

> an English king, though obliged to rule in accordance with the national will, had never been intended to become the puppet of the party predominant in parliament. It was the duty of the sovereign to lead rather than to follow, and the functions of the house of commons were those of a guardian, not those of a dictator. It was for the king to choose his own advisers; and it was incumbent upon parliament to support the ministers of the crown, unless they were guilty of a breach of the law or proved themselves so incompetent as to render their removal a matter of urgent necessity.

The King was to govern as well as to reign, and his advisers were to be "servants of the crown in something more than name".

> When all men thought that the power of the crown had passed away, never to revive, the court once more became the spring and centre of political life.

Winstanley attempted to rescue Bolingbroke from obloquy and misunderstanding, saying that "in the arguments which he advanced, in the most famous of his works, there is more truth and cogency than has often been allowed".

It is impossible to deny the justice of his denunciations of the political morality of the age; and when he called upon the monarchy to rescue the country from the slough of corruption into which it had fallen, it was not with the intention of restoring the absolutism of the Stuarts, but of bringing about an alliance between the crown and the nation, in order to effect the downfall of an immoral system of government.

Even Bute is granted a word of kindness; and we are told that his "political ability has been unduly depreciated".

In reality, Winstanley carries the thesis of Adolphus to the point of exaggeration; and, as a result of this error, he brings this interpretation of George III to a curious inversion in the final stages of the argument. If he had paid due attention to the article by Temperley in the *Cambridge Modern History*, he would not have been quite so extravagant in his account of the eclipse of monarchical authority under the first two Georges. If he had understood and developed some of Temperley's hints concerning Walpole's management of parliament, he would not have gone to so great an extreme as he did in assessing the success of George III, and the completeness of the hold that he acquired over the House of Commons. After the King had secured the discomfiture of the Whigs, said Winstanley (pp. 15–16),

parliament, which remained as corrupt as before, was now tied by gold chains about the throne. . . . There had been something little short of a constitutional revolution, the significance of which could not be measured by the ease with which it had been effected. No longer could parliament be considered an effective check upon the despotic tendencies of the crown, since the astute policy of George III had rendered the Bill of Rights and the Act of Settlement . . . almost constitutionally valueless. Parliament, which had previously been the puppet of the whig nobility, now became the slave of the court.

It had been the object of von Ruville to show how closely the ideas of George III and Bute coincided with those of the elder Pitt—the common source of their systems being the earlier programme of the "Patriot" party. It still remained difficult for the English historians to feel that Pitt was anything but the enemy of the system of George III, in spite of the correlations that had been established. And some of these English writers, like Rigg, favoured Pitt, while others were more inclined to sympathise with the Rockinghamites. Winstanley was impressed by the importance of creating a strong and coherent party system for the purpose of resisting the victorious George III. He who had written so contemptuously of "the Whig ascendancy" became therefore a strong supporter of the Rockinghamites, as against the elder Pitt.

In this connexion he was able to write (p. 18) a revealing sentence which suggests that by 1912 the mood of the world must have been changing:

> It is too often overlooked that if George III was fighting for a principle, so were his opponents.

BOOK THREE

GEORGE III

AND THE NAMIER SCHOOL

1. Introduction

UNTIL VERY recently the main contribution of the Namier school has been concerned with that early period of George III's reign, the historiography of which we have been primarily discussing. The question of the intentions of George III immediately after his accession has constituted one of the main challenges which that school presents to the student of the ordinary narrative history of the reign. In regard to this internal problem, Sir Lewis Namier, though his views are not always clear, seems to take his start from a point not very distant from the one we have reached—a point not far removed from that of Winstanley. His thinking begins here, but we must not imagine that he stays in this position, even in his early works. What we are concerned with now is rather the system of ideas which he is intending to overturn.

He does not quite take the system of Adolphus and Winstanley as his point of departure; and it is possible that this fact has affected the direction in which he has moved. Initially he describes the situation in a manner that might be called "Whiggish"; and the point may have helped to condition the mode in which he has reacted at the next stage in his thinking. From Adolphus to Winstanley, the main tradition of historical writing had described the Whig ascendancy under the early Hanoverians as a somewhat unpleasant affair—a case of the cornering of power. It was the Whig historians—Erskine May, for example—who envisaged the Whig ascendancy as an established form of constitutional government. Sir Lewis Namier, however, does not describe the situation before 1760 as anything irregular, or as a case of the mere engrossing of power; and he seems more ready than Adolphus or Winstanley to state the position in terms of modern constitutionalism. He tells us that, under the first two kings of the

Hanoverian dynasty, "certain forms and even principles of Cabinet government seem to have been established". He talks of government being "based on a party majority in the House of Commons" and says that the king had "to act and even think" through "the leaders or makers of that majority". It is almost he who is anachronistic; and though he is setting up what he means to undermine he is perhaps not choosing the correct point at which to start his argument; indeed he does speak of this in parenthesis as being only "in appearance" an "advanced constitutional period". At the same time, in his opinion this "early constitutional development" had been a "lop-sided" one.

In this section (pp. 51–2) of his *England and the American Revolution* (1930) Sir Lewis Namier points out that George III was to score against the Whigs under Newcastle "a (temporary) success" at the very point where his grandfather had failed. For the time being, he tells us, however, that the events of the early years of George III's reign have been ascribed too much to the "personal character" of that King and to "the principles he is said to have imbibed at Leicester House". Namier himself prefers to think that "the development"—that is to say, the conflict against the Whig ascendancy—was "in reality the logical outcome of the situation". It is not clear, however, that in this he differs greatly from that tradition of interpretation which runs from Adolphus at the beginning of the nineteenth century to Winstanley at the beginning of the twentieth. These writers were prepared to see that the reaction of George III against the régime which he inherited in 1760 was the logical outcome of the situation, the natural thing to expect when a king should emerge who was free from the special limitations under which the first two Hanoverians had laboured. Winstanley, in fact, had been ready to say that by 1760 men "had come to expect salvation from the court".

2. *The Rise of Structural Analysis*

ONE of the factors which have greatly altered our historical interpretation has been the development of a kind of history which is really analysis. The very form of our narratives has suffered change through the fact that events are now examined in relation to the type of society in which they occurred. Society is not merely a picture of still life, or a kind of background to the story which is being told—a passive piece of scenery to be described in an introductory chapter or mentioned on occasion in parenthesis. It is an active collaborator in the work of history-making; and for that very reason it turns out to be at all times an important source of historical explanation. And history is no longer merely a line or a stream of story, but has to be conceived at the same time in terms of an underlying structure. The result is more like a glacier, moving along a path but also possessing depth.

Before the end of the seventeenth century, we catch a glimpse of a profounder kind of history which again makes its appearance in this country at the close of the Victorian era. For a moment during the reign of Charles II the Whig interpretation is menaced; it is challenged by the assertion that *Magna Carta* has been treated unhistorically in the past and must be construed with reference to a feudal form of society. At the end of the nineteenth century and (in the famous work of McKechnie) at the beginning of the twentieth, an anachronistic view of the Charter was superseded by one which at least paid due attention to the kind of world taken for granted in its successive clauses. Since 1890, in point of fact, much of our European history also has had to be reshaped, because it came to be realised that a knowledge of social structure alters the bearings of a piece of narrative. If an extravagantly Whig-Protestant version of the French Wars of Religion or the

Revolt of the Netherlands has been superseded, this is because we have learned to take account of structure, and therefore—so to speak—to see the narrative "in depth".

It is not clear, however, that this more analytical treatment of historical problems necessarily operates only to the disadvantage of the Whig interpretation. And certainly it was the Whigs and the radicals who introduced the device of interpreting the parliamentary history of George III's reign by reference to the "structure of politics". Here was one of the favourite weapons of those reformers who wanted to expose the perversity of eighteenth-century voting and the irrationality of the whole electoral system. While George III was still alive they made it part of their propaganda to go through the constituencies one by one in order to show the workings of patronage and influence. The *History, Personal and Political, of the Boroughs of Great Britain* (1792) was compiled by T. H. B. Oldfield, who, amongst other things, set out to demonstrate that the ancient Britons "enjoyed liberty in its most unlimited sense". He confessed that he had produced the work in order to expose "the abuse of representation" and to bring together grievances hitherto seen only piecemeal—hitherto discoverable only in scattered publications. Until he had brought all the data together, he said, the evil had been "too divided for the mind to form a complete idea of its aggregate enormity". At the present day it is still not impossible that this kind of analysis, this detailed study of eighteenth-century constituencies, should provide the basis for a Whig interpretation of history—one that might well be more formidable than any of its predecessors. It is wrong to assume (as some people seem to do) that the historian who recovers the form of the ancient structure must necessarily feel that he has to defend not merely his interpretation of it, but the thing in itself, and the whole order of society for which it stands. The modern student is not under any necessity to condemn those people of the eighteenth century who were dissatisfied with the representative system, and desired to see the world become more rational.

The development of local history, the publication of family papers—especially the long series of volumes produced by the Historical Manuscripts Commission—and the research upon official sources, brought a considerable advance in the study not only of constituencies but also of elections and of controverted election cases. The parliamentary representation of particular regions—of Cornwall and the northern counties, for example—was subjected to special examination. The Newcastle Papers in the British Museum seem to have given the stimulus to work of greater precision. In 1897 Basil Williams used these manuscripts for a paper in the *English Historical Review* on "The Duke of Newcastle and the Election of 1734". In 1903 Edward Porritt produced his famous two-volume work on The *Unreformed House of Commons*—a history of parliamentary representation, of the bonds between electors and elected, and of the relations between the Crown and the representative system—a history also of the development of the House of Commons itself. He summarised his authorities as follows:

> the Journals of Parliament, Statute books, official returns and reports, Parliamentary histories, Hansards, calendars of State papers, State trials and Election Committee and Law reports, reports of the Historical Manuscripts Commission, municipal council books and municipal histories, and the publications of the numerous English and Scotch printing societies . . . memoirs, letters and diaries.

We are brought closer to the modern study of parliamentary history, however, in 1907, when William Hunt publishes a document of considerable significance under the title *The Irish Parliament, 1775*. The manuscript was one which had passed through the hands of a London bookseller a few years earlier, and, in point of fact, a similar but shorter document had appeared earlier still in Volume X of the privately-printed *Harcourt Papers*. It gave an account of the individual members of parliament, their careers, their political connexions, the claims of government upon them, their expected mode of conduct and their attitude to the existing administration. Nothing could be more intimate and authoritative; for here was the final detailed assessment of the state of both houses, and the political prospect in general, by the government's parliamentary manager. It was a type of document destined to have great importance in the future history of this branch of scholarship, and was calculated to give a new birth to the study of eighteenth-century parliaments.

Both for the politics of the time and for the historiography of this subject a special importance attaches to one of the parliamentary managers in Great Britain during the reign of George III —John Robinson, who was Secretary to the Treasury when Lord North was at the head of the ministry. A further development of scholarship in this field is registered by the appearance in 1922 of *Parliamentary Papers of John Robinson, 1774–84*. The volume was edited by an American historian, W. T. Laprade, who, by 1912, had been working on the Westminster elections of 1784 and 1788, and who, by 1916, was using transcripts of these papers for an article on "Public Opinion and the General Election of 1784", which appeared in the *English Historical Review* for April 1916. Before that date the Royal Historical Society had entrusted him with the task of printing the manuscripts themselves in what is called the Camden Series. The published papers provide important material relating to the management of three parliamentary elections during the reign of George III, as well as "Secret and Special Service Accounts". In connexion with the election of 1784, the work claimed to reproduce "perhaps the most detailed description extant of the actual forces represented in the parliaments of the latter part of the eighteenth century". Unlike William Hunt, however, Laprade ensured that even the Introduction to his book should mark a new stage in the study of our parliamentary history.

He made a number of remarks which point to the future, and which even today carry a remarkable flavour of modernity.

He writes, for example:

> The conclusion . . . from the information contained in Robin-son's papers is not that the people and parliaments of the last decades of the eighteenth century were corrupt beyond those of subsequent times. They were merely different instrumentalities for exercising political power, totally unsuited to later conditions.

In the eighteenth century, he said, "an election seldom gave evidence of the views of the ruling class one way or the other".

> Parliamentary seats were simply the perquisites of the members of the ruling group, whether they occupied them personally or others sat on their nomination.

Even in the few places where a constituency might have represented the voice of the people, "contested elections were dreaded as an evil and were seldom held if it was possible to avoid them". He tells us that "fewer than one in eleven of the members who sat for the counties of England and Wales" between 1760 and 1800 "met with even nominal opposition"; and "there was not in Yorkshire a single contested election". In fact, "measures or questions of public policy were rarely primary motives in the choice of members in an eighteenth-century House of Commons."

These judgments are of strategic importance, and when we begin to work out their implications we find that they carry us very far and produce displacements over a very wide area. They imply something like a change of intellectual system, for here, before the emergence of the Namier school, a whole set of relations has been radically transformed. Laprade's book, in any case, draws particular attention once again to a type of source which provides the student with remarkably intimate glimpses into the inner workings of eighteenth-century government.

During the first half of the present century the available sources were greatly multiplied, and the evidence of the supposed culprits of George III's reign was at last discovered—the long-lost correspondence of the King himself, for example, and the papers of Bute, which had once been thought to have been destroyed by fire. Methods of research were considerably refined, and in general the work of the historians came to be conducted with better microscopes and more delicate instruments. The relations between politics and society, between government and the structural order, came to be more profoundly appreciated in one field of study after another. So far as the reign of George III is concerned, the career and the work of Sir Lewis Namier bring the whole story to its interesting climax. This historian is not merely the product of the twentieth-century developments but a creative source within them, himself a pioneer and a stimulus, a tremendous fountain of energies. Using not only the correspondence of George III and Bute, and the papers of political managers like Newcastle and Robinson, but a whole universe of untapped sources, he has made it his object to reconstruct the world of eighteenth-century politics, and to work out in detail that system which Laprade had only begun to adumbrate. His *Structure of Politics* (1929) not only enriched this side of the study of George III's reign with new analyses and new techniques, but attained types of result which possess a remarkable precision, results that stand as a solid contribution to scholarship. It has rightly been said of Sir Lewis Namier that "he uses the microscope at one moment and the telescope at the next—both with equal effect"; and in him the kind of industry which is not merely patient but which generates high pressure is assisted by a brilliant imagination which does not refuse to take risks. It cannot be said that the judgment is always unclouded by passion, or free from the possibility of being deflected by "interferences"; but repeatedly one is made aware that the wires are carrying electricity at a high voltage.

Furthermore, the methods which Namier has employed in the study of the early years of George III's reign have been followed also by later historians working in the same field. They have been transposed for use in work on other periods of English parliamentary history. And those who are not Namier's disciples will not deny the value of the results which have been achieved by this kind of research.

Concerning eighteenth-century politics, Sir Lewis Namier made the important point that "between them and the politics of the present day there is more resemblance in outer forms and denominations than in underlying realities".

> A system of non-Euclidean geometry can be built up by taking a curve for basis instead of the straight line, but it is not easy for our minds to think consistently in unwonted terms; Parliamentary politics not based on parties are to us a non-Euclidean system, and similarly require a fundamental readjustment of ideas and, what is more, of mental habits.

This is an excellent formulation of what, surely, the historian must be having to do all the time—of the re-shaping which an original mind, authentically re-thinking things, and sincerely pursuing the consequences of its thought, will be liable to give to almost any kind of subject-matter. It is significant that the first chapter in the *Structure of Politics* proceeds in an analytical way with the fundamental question: "Why Men went into Parliament". And few things said about history can be more important than the statement in Sir Lewis Namier's Preface: "One has to steep oneself in the political life of a period before one can safely speak, or be sure of understanding, its language".

As a result of the developments which have taken place in the last fifty years or so—and most of all perhaps of the work and the methods of Sir Lewis Namier—historical research has taken a closer grip upon this whole aspect of our political history. We are ripe for the still greater project with which the same historian is so intimately associated—the new history of the parliament of this country. Besides the history of constituencies and of parliamentary elections we are to be provided once and for all with the biographies of the individual members of parliament. This will mean that the politics of any period may be studied with an intimacy and a sense for structure which have never been possible before.

Let it be clear from the first that the strength of the Namier school really rests on the massiveness of its detailed researches. Its contribution has been imposing in this respect, and such a contribution has a permanent value—an importance that is not going to be undermined by differences of opinion or fluctuations in intellectual fashion. The research is not always equally close or equally exhaustive when the reconstruction of the over-all narrative is in question; but the material in Sir Lewis Namier's *Structure of Politics*, the feat of Mr. Romney Sedgwick in dating hundreds of letters from George III to Bute, and the work devoted to the individual biographies of members of parliament (judging by the samples which have appeared) represent a type of achievement hardly paralleled in the historiography of our time. If differences of opinion arise, therefore, they are likely to come at a later stage in the work of historical construction—the point where there is an accretion of details into a definite shape, or where types of generalisation are produced—the point where one decides on the strategic thing to say in laying out the map of forces or the political situation. They come where an action or a piece of narrative has to be expounded, and the description of it is hardly separable from its interpretation. Even here, though there may be differences of opinion which produce a colossal displacement in one's picture of general history, it is not over the whole of the area that differences are likely to arise. But it is part of the thesis of the present work that the massiveness of detailed researches is not in itself sufficient to guarantee men from error in the work of historical reconstruction; and the case of Harold Temperley or of Laprade will even tend to show that a man of some insight may pierce into the essentials of a political situation without any vast apparatus, while there are other examples to demonstrate that, without the benefit of such insight, the most industrious research student is in danger of colossal errors. The researches of the Namier school have a great importance for us, however, whatever our view of history may be. And, though this does not guarantee the correctness of all their conclusions, it makes them a formidable squadron for any critic to have to face.

3. Narrative History and Structural Analysis

WE MUST not exaggerate the revolution produced by the new methods. Some of the good things which we are now told about the workings of eighteenth-century politics were available to discerning politicians who were living at the time. Such things had leaked into the literary evidence, and they had passed into historiography by another route. The plan of compiling the lives of all members of parliament is going to provide historians with a piece of apparatus that will be invaluable during an indefinite future. But whether scientific methods (statistical procedures and devices of correlation) can be applied to the resulting materials—whether these will produce more valuable conclusions about the politics of a period than were available to a contemporary statesman with a good nose—is not yet very clear.

It is necessary that we should not magnify too greatly even the importance of the study of "structure". It still has to be admitted (and the members of the Namier school seem anxious sometimes to remind us of the fact) that through a sense of responsibility or an attachment to principle, men in the eighteenth century might break with their party or act against what appeared to be their immediate personal interest on occasion. There were in any case many independent members of parliament who, though they might normally support the government, would be prepared to vote as their judgment dictated; so that the course of debate, the influence of popular passion, or the existence of a national crisis, would be calculated to affect their conduct. In such cases, which by their very nature are likely to be significant, the politics of George III's reign could not be regarded as responding to structure or as explicable solely in terms of structure. And where the votes of many people are affected—as in the case of Dunning's famous

motion on 6th April, 1780—it is necessary to resort to the
ordinary method of the narrative historian, who puts the microscope on the episode as such, and even studies very carefully (so
far as the evidence is available) the course of the parliamentary
debate itself. It would in fact be true to say that the whole policy
of stressing the significance of the independent members (or
bringing out the pivotal importance that these may have, as Dr.
Owen has recently done in *The Rise of the Pelhams*) automatically
increases the propriety of the older type of narrative method, and
even the analysis of parliamentary debates. This is being neglected
by the new school, and for this reason we hear too much about
structure and vested interests, and too little about those higher
political considerations which clearly enter the case at these important points in the story, and which help to turn the study of
history into a political education. In fact, it is just here that, over
and above the irrationalities of the world, the social pressures and
the sheer play of forces, there moves something of rational purpose, something of the conscious calculations of reasoning and
reasonable men. And surely the fault of the Whig historians was
that, though they would give long rambling *résumés* of parliamentary debates, they did not treat these on an analytical method.
On crucial occasions they assumed in too facile a manner that the
votes on one side of the question were given automatically—that is
to say were the mere effect of vested interests involved, the mere
counterpart of "the structure of politics". If it is important to study
parliamentary elections, individual members of parliament and the
various constituencies, we today can hardly neglect the activities
of the two houses and even the analysis of parliamentary debates.

We are in an analogous position when we are told that the
French Revolution cannot be explained merely by general causes
—merely by the operation of a standing system of historical necessity. And that is why it is so significant when Professor Labrousse
—the supreme student of the economic correlations that can be

made—insists so strongly that the Revolution emerges from the clash of personalities, the play of fear and passion, the interaction of purposes and cross-purposes, with the intervention sometimes of sheer mischance. At this stage in the argument the analysis of mere conditions, or of structure as such, loses that unique importance which some people like to give it; and much may hang on the things that human beings chose to do in regions of conduct where they could easily be imagined to have made a different choice. For the sake of historical explanation itself we must watch human beings deliberating and choosing their conduct; and we must examine the story of what happens between people, we must examine the considerations upon which men make their decisions. All this is a vindication of the older kind of political history, which did not overlook the part played also by conditions, though in all things it may have been less precise and microscopic than twentieth-century scholarship manages to be. That Professor Labrousse should have realised the position in respect of the French Revolution is remarkable, since his own peculiar studies might easily have led him to the opposite conclusion. But one of the theses of the Namier school is the authenticity of the independent member of the House of Commons and the pivotal importance he was capable of having. It means that, over and above the structure of politics, we must have a political history that is set out in narrative form—an account of adult human beings, taking a hand in their fates and fortunes, pulling at the story in the direction they want to carry it, and making decisions of their own. We must have the kind of story in which (no matter how much we know about the structure of politics and the conditions of the time) we can never quite guess, at any given moment, what is going to happen next.

All this should be considered in its bearings on the conception of an over-all history of the reign of George III. The older writers, who are now taunted and condemned, were above all things narrative historians. The relevant question to ask before they are summarily dismissed, and before the earlier historio-graphy of the subject is thrown into the waste-paper basket, is the question how the new kind of analysis affects the shape of the previously-accepted story. It is not permissible to imagine that the England of 1760 is unique in the sense that just here, and just at this particular date, the study of "structure" must replace other forms of history. To people who have studied the Glorious Re-volution, the Hanoverian Succession, the policy of Walpole and the role of William Pitt in the Seven Years' War, we cannot say that after the accession of George III mere story-telling must be over and done with—that just here the "narrative" method has been rendered obsolete. In any case the world cannot afford to sacrifice the kind of history which broadened a man's political outlook—the history which dealt with politics and statesmanship and the march of great events. It is curious that there has never been a more desperate cry from the teaching profession than the demand in recent years for light and help in respect of the interpretation of the reign of George III.

Perhaps the ideal kind of history is the kind in which a story is given and events are presented in motion, but the story is re-told so to speak "in depth", so that it acquires a new dimension; it is both structure and narrative combined. This has been achieved on occasion by scholars and writers; and here, where history is both a story and a study, one may gain a profounder insight into both the ways of men and the processes of time. For the rational purposes and the con-scious intentions of human beings on the one hand, and the histori-cal process, with its systems of necessity and ironies of circumstance on the other hand—these two together are the weft and warp of the fabric of human destiny. They are the ingredients of that history which in one aspect men make for themselves and which in another aspect they suffer, as they see it being manufactured over their heads.

In this present study we are primarily concerned with the things which affect the interpretation of what might be called the ordinary narrative history of the reign of George III.

4. The Occupational Disease of the Historians
of Structure

SIR LEWIS NAMIER tells us that *England in the Age of the American Revolution*, which his collaborators are fortunately to continue in a considerable series of volumes, sets out to provide "the chronological narrative of political events". But in his own original volume, as well as in the recent addition to the series by Mr. Brooke, it seems to be assumed that such narrative need be little more than the "structure of politics" extended in time and turned into a sequence. We are given a story which becomes silent or curiously neglectful as it touches the very things that governments and parliaments exist to do. There is little interest in the work of ministers within their departments; in the springs of policy and the origins of important decisions; in the actual content of the political controversies of the time; in the attitude of the public to measures and men; and in the thrust and counter-thrust of parliamentary debate. Nothing is added to the story of British policy in respect of the American colonies, and even of Townshend's disastrous intervention in this field, though the title of the whole series might have created a certain degree of expectancy here. These problems are dealt with only as they touch the fundamental theme of the whole work; and since the fundamental theme, even in this narrative side of the history, concerns rather the interplay of factions and the manipulative side of politics, even the topics that belong to statesmanship tend to be reduced to just such terms as these. We must not imagine that this is the only way in which a history of this particular period can be reconstructed. We must not imagine that what is being supplied is really "the history of the reign of George III".

Such tendencies are calculated to raise the question whether the new form of structural analysis is not capable of producing in the practitioners of the craft its own kind of occupational disease. Within the field with which the volumes are explicitly concerned, it would appear that the anatomising method may have its defects, unless it is complemented by the activity of a sympathetic—even a synthesising—mind. In the two volumes of narrative which have so far appeared, it is remarkable to see how often the things which are most clearly true are by no means new, and how often the points of interpretation which are novel and paradoxical are inadequately demonstrated. One may have misgivings about the selectivity in the use of sources, and about the processes of inference which are brought to bear upon the evidence. In any case there are certain points which must always be borne in mind by those who, in reading the writings of this school, mean not to suspend their critical awareness.

There may seem to be something unanswerable in the thesis that the Labour party opposed the Suez adventure because it was their business to defeat the Conservatives. And some people feel that it would be too much of a coincidence if we accepted the members of that party as also sincerely attached to the ideals of the United Nations. It is possible, therefore, to describe the activities of such an opposition on such an occasion in terms of interests; and when we are in a certain mood we may find it even satisfactory to discount, or quite explain away, all the evidence of higher purpose and rational discussion which may appear amongst the papers or the speeches of the men in question. In reality, however, the egotisms of human beings do in every age of history find subtle and complicated ways of combining with higher purposes, though the mode of combination may well be different in every generation. It seems to be true that the Whig historians will tend to assess the virtues of the Rockinghamites by their ideals, but that still they may be content to measure the followers of Lord North only by their interests—a procedure which is not improved if the opponents of the Whigs merely reverse the formula. Antagonistic political parties must be examined from both points of view, and even individual people may require very sympathetic treatment from the historian. John Wilson Croker could pretend to demonstrate how powerful a motor behind the actions and the writings of Horace Walpole was his selfish concern for his sinecures. Croker could also show in a moving passage, however, the genuineness of certain aspects of Horace Walpole's Whiggism, and the wisdom of his opposition to the conflict with the American colonies. How easy it is for the historian to rest his mind in the first of these demonstrations, and to close his eyes to the fact that the second may be at least of equal significance!

It is not clear that the Namier method possesses the kind of receiving-set that is capable of catching all the relevant wavelengths. At a certain level, recognition is given to the fact that, particularly on critical occasions, politicians think of their country and have regard to the public cause. Men do not support the government merely because they enjoy profits and places; and corruption itself is not sufficient to bind the House of Commons when a serious issue has been raised. Even in Ireland, where the corruption was more notorious than in Great Britain, it was explicitly realised in the reign of George III that "the occasional favours of government" could not be relied on to secure the vote of the House of Commons against the interest of the country or the passions of an awakened people. On this point the Lord Lieutenant, the Earl of Buckinghamshire, for example, once expressed himself in a most insistent manner. Precisely where the issues were more than the routine ones (in which "party discipline" might operate effectively) political conduct was not unlikely to have its reference to the things that men were thinking on public questions. Let it be remembered (though there are people who forget the point) that this was true of the regular opposition

as well as the customary supporters of government. As Winstanley put it, in a remarkable sentence already quoted above: "It is
too often overlooked that if George III was fighting for a principle,
so were his opponents". Human beings are the carriers of ideas
as well as the repositories of vested interests. And political history
requires the over-all narrative—the account of policies, legislative
projects, diplomacy, wars, etc.—for it is about such things as these
that the practitioners of politics are apt to have ideas. And for
these reasons it is never sufficient to study even eighteenth-
century politics with too exclusive a concentration on the manipulative side or the play of faction. Horace Walpole in the eighteenth
century and Croker in the nineteenth knew the quality of faction.
They did not even need historical imagination for its understanding, since they had been in a position to learn the "feel" of it
practically at first hand. Like the polemical literature of the early
1760's, however, they recognised also that there were important
political and constitutional issues to discuss.

Because the Whig historians took ideological pretensions too
much at their face value, the modern school tend to drain the
intellectual content out of the things that politicians do. The
dramatis personæ are portrayed without that outer framework of
ideas and purposes which affects political conduct, and which
statesmen and monarchs—even a George III—could scarcely
unload from their minds if they tried. This framework of ideas
and conscious purposes may appear only in partial glimpses—
though it certainly does appear—in the correspondence of political
personages who generally write to one another rather to discuss
detailed decisions and day-to-day moves. The parts of the correspondence which are here in question are the ones which the
new writers are apt to neglect or to slur over, as we shall see
(e.g. pp. 217–18 and 287–9 below). These are the things, however,
which give some coherence to political history and rescue it from
mere atomisation; and one may despise them over-much if one is

too intent on delving into structure and self-interests, or even into the darkness of man's unconscious mind. There is a danger that the study of the under-side of the piece of embroidery will be puffed and exalted, and turned into an end in itself. Even U.N.O. today would provide a sorry picture if we examined it from the point of view of the "structure of politics", leaving the other dimensions of the story out of account.

There is a way of studying history which atomises everything, especially if one slurs over the very kind of evidence which gives intellectual content to the things that politicians do. There is a form of fundamental analysis, excellent in itself, which—for lack of obvious safeguards—can lead to the erosion of the avowed political purposes that give meaning as well as cohesion to the events of history. It may seem paradoxical, but it can be true, that there is danger in an attempt to write history merely from the kind of documentation that might be called "bed-rock". A man who wished to write the history of my College, and tried to confine himself to the documents in the College Treasury, might too easily imagine that we were a body concerned only with the administration of money, buildings and other property. If he would go outside and consult some forms of evidence that he might regard as inferior—discussions in the *University Reporter* and the *Cambridge Review*, for example, or the essays of Sir Adolphus William Ward—he would discover that men in Cambridge have a real interest in education too. And this analogy illustrates another of the errors of the Namier school.

5. The Occupational Disease of the Research Student

IN ONE of the most interesting and brilliant and important passages in his *England in the Age of the American Revolution* (pp. 147–149) Sir Lewis Namier attacks the tendency to overrate "the importance of the conscious will and purpose in individuals". He asks us "to ascertain and recognise the deeper irrelevancies and incoherence of human actions, which are not so much directed by reason, as invested by it *ex post facto* with the appearances of logic and rationality". He insists that "when watched at close quarters, the actions of men are in no way correlated in weight and value to the results they produce". We must see history, therefore, as a thing which "started in ridiculous beginnings, while small men did things both infinitely smaller and infinitely greater than they knew". All this doctrine is particularly applied to those events immediately after the accession of George III which for nearly two centuries now have been the object of so much discussion and political controversy. In a sentence that is meant to carry particular significance, we are therefore told that "History of infinite weight was to be made in the absurd beginnings of this reign".

Certainly there is an important truth in all this exposition; and a realisation of the importance of the truth is possibly an essential step towards the achievement of historical understanding. The truth has genuine relevance, moreover, for the student of these early years of the reign of George III. Historians once imagined that Pitt fell in 1761 because the King and his favourite, Bute, had determined to drive him out of office. It is easy to imagine in this way that the things which happened were things which George III and Bute had resolved to bring about. Even from the earliest times, there had been men, however, who were not deceived by the optical illusion; and from the closing decades of the nineteenth century it was being shown once again that Bute had not in fact conspired to bring about the resignation of Pitt. When Winstanley, nearly fifty years ago, explained that this resignation had not been "part of the original programme of the court", he, too, had called attention to the paradox in the historical process. He, too, had written with some justification: "Events had shaped themselves in a way that had not been foreseen".

There is truth in the view, then; but we must remember that if we carry the idea of Sir Lewis Namier to an extreme, it is difficult to see why the study of history—a history so woven out of chances and ironies of circumstance—should be considered an important matter for anybody. Like Professor Isaiah Berlin, one may see history as only a succession of chances or conjunctures—but, if so, there is nothing to study, there are no correlations to be made between events, and in fact there is only a rope of sand, a series of non-sequiturs which one can do nothing but narrate. Just as one can be too doctrinaire even in one's anti-doctrinairism, one may be too wilful in one's emphasis on the wilfulness of history and the caprice of time.

All political narrative becomes more complicated—more trickily entangled with chance and change—when seen under the microscope. Young research students are even apt to be disillusioned with their work, and too contemptuous of the subject of it, when they study the policy of even a first-class statesman at close quarters, and see the untidiness of the result. The thing which, when telescoped into abridged history, appears as a mighty act of volition, may be broken by research into a multitude of little pieces, the statesman appearing not to know what he wants, and showing an apparent readiness to drift with wind and tide. In spite of all this, the political practitioner, even if he is only a George III, does possess a framework of ideas and purposes which affect his actions and modify the course of things. They may seem to be checked or side-tracked, they may even seem to be contradicted entirely, as one watches the man in his day-to-day conduct of business. But it is the optical illusion or the occupational disease of the research student to imagine that only the details matter, and that the details are all of equal value—that the statesman has no cohesive purpose but is merely a bundle of contradictions—and that everything is under the rule of chance, under the play of absurdly little chances—history reducing itself at the finish to an irony of circumstance.

George III himself is the first to suffer from the new method and from the theory that history issues from absurdly small and irrelevant beginnings. But all parties—the court, the Rockinghamites and the followers of John Wilkes—can be reduced to the same uninspiring level if this method and this view of history are pressed too far. A century ago Ranke dealt with the question of the uniqueness of each event, each conjuncture in history, and the way the historian must take pleasure in detail as such. But he saw that history also was not without its "inner connectedness"; and, indeed, that one could not write history if one did not see the possibility of grouping the details into coherent shapes, and if one did not possess also an eye for generalities.

6. The Framework of George III's Ideas and Purposes

THE MOST important, perhaps, of all the issues presented to us, and all the topics of controversy ever provoked, by the reign of George III, is the question of the framework of ideas and purposes which shaped the attitude and conditioned the conduct of that King at the beginning of the reign.

It is hardly denied that George longed to get rid of the Duke of Newcastle and place the Earl of Bute at the head of the government. It seems clear that this affected the way in which the King and the Favourite treated the Duke, the way in which they talked about him, and the figure that he made in the gossip of the court. In the precarious waters of politics, however, it would be necessary for the King to take account of winds and currents, to tack and trim, and to steer for a moment at times towards a point very far from the one it was intended to reach.

We all know that when abridged history finds a formula for the policy or the intention of a ruler this must be taken with a certain flexibility. We realise that the research student will uncover many complications, and is likely to find even many apparent contradictions in detail. We are hardly surprised, therefore, if we learn that at one moment George III may be asking Newcastle to stay in office, and at another moment—when the change of ministry has actually been effected—may anxiously desire that Newcastle should return into service (lest worse befall). And we should not feel that all such actions and intentions on the part of the King are of equal weight, and that all such details of his mind and conduct (as they are uncovered by the research student) deserve to be told in a level accent—all of them reproduced with the same emphasis. If we imagine that each decision taken has

216

only its immediate spring, its purely momentary origin, we can reduce everything to flux, and make it appear that George III had no policy in respect of the Duke of Newcastle, no idea even of what he wanted. George III then emerges as moving indifferently to one point of the compass and then another—moving purposelessly, in fact, and with no guiding aim that governs his detailed decisions, no deeper spring of action to give him a long-term purpose. And this is how it can be made to appear that George III did not know his own mind—could not decide, for example, whether to work with Newcastle or not.

We know from George III's own words that, till he felt compelled to accept Henry Fox as his political manager, he cherished the dream of destroying corruption—"then" as he wrote later to Bute, "when we were both dead our memories would have been respected and esteemed till the end of time". Some years later, he put it on to paper that, when he came to the throne, he set out to destroy the "unhappy distinctions" of Whig and Tory, and that he regarded this as a new departure. It has been known for at least a century that the elder Pitt claimed the priority in this policy, and indeed from the time of Robert Bisset in 1803 there have been occasional historians who regarded Pitt as either the precursor or the original stimulus behind this part of George III's programme. But if it could be proved that Pitt promoted more Tories before 1760 than George III himself in the subsequent years, this touches on just the kind of issue that we must never try to settle by the mere counting of heads. A piece of policy that is unimportant when measured in material terms may gain great significance through the context in which it occurs, the ideas with which it has been associated, the kind of pronouncements made about it to the public, and the political controversy that it may have provoked on some particular occasion. Horace Walpole made the point that the elder Pitt's policy of abolishing party distinctions meant something different in the hands of George III, and was in any case turned into something different by the conduct of the Tories themselves in the new situation. He pointed out in this connexion that, before Bute ever dared to make a change in the ministry, there had been an alarming alteration in the language of the court.

It might seem that George III, with his talk of destroying "corruption" and annihilating the distinction between "Whig" and "Tory", had not sufficiently soaked himself in Namier. If he was wrong, perhaps he erred along with some of that Leicester House circle whose influence upon his mind Sir Lewis Namier at times seems to assume but at times seems strenuously to deny. Passages which Sir Lewis Namier himself reproduces would appear to suggest that George was infected with more of the ideas of the same circle. Bute tells Newcastle, for example, "That the King had a notion of not being governed . . . by his Minister or Ministers, as the late King had been". There is even evidence that the alleged resentment of the court against the might of the magnates is not really to be regarded as the fiction of the imagination of later historians. Bute writes to Newcastle: "No, my Lord, I know your power, you have all the great men of the kingdom [on your side]". George, when he talks of the succession to Newcastle, discloses a further bitterness of feeling which confirms the general picture. He is determined that Bute shall succeed Newcastle at the Treasury, for, he says, Bute "thinks of mine and his country's good, not of jobs".

In all this, surely, we have the outer framework of George III's ideas and purposes; and it is one which in the correspondence of later years was to give proof of extraordinary fixity. And what is all this but the framework provided by Adolphus a hundred and fifty years ago—the very system that has dominated the serious historiography of the subject during most of the intervening period? Without such notions, George III and Bute would have treated Newcastle very differently.

7. Party as a Mental as well as a
Material Phenomenon

AND IF George III was wrong in his talk of "Whig" and "Tory", of "corruption" and of ministers who tried to govern the king, we must remember that what men imagine the situation to be— what they dream or feel that they are out to do—is an actual dimension of the political events that are the object of study. The modern school are too neglectful of this dimension which political conduct possesses—too neglectful even of those glimpses or leakages of purposeful policy which occur in the documents they are actually using. At a different level, they are over-contemptuous about the writers on politics—too supercilious in their treatment of Bolingbroke and Burke, for example—too blind to the part which such literature may play in actual life and in the political development of society. Here is an interpretation of history which, through an anxiety to avoid being hoaxed—through an understandable desire to avoid the mistakes of the doctrinaire— is in danger of refusing to realise the operative force of ideas.

At a time when political parties have come to assume new shapes it is wonderful to see how the politicians may still go on thinking about them in the traditional way. In the reign of George III men might at one moment conceive of the factions somewhat in the manner of Sir Lewis Namier; but at a different level of their thinking—or when they approach the question from a different angle—the same men might discuss parties in categories that have long ago become antiquated, the Whigs being set against the Tories still. It is possible that the future historian, when he has to write about the Liberals of our own recent decades, will be similarly puzzled by the way in which two planes of existence manage to intersect. "Whiggism" in George III's reign may denote a particular set of people, even though there is a sense in which all—including George III and Lord North—must be regarded as Whigs. Alternatively, Whiggism may represent a point of view—a hostility to what are regarded as Tory doctrines of the prerogative—or even only a shadow cast by the battles of long ago. The writings of Bolingbroke, David Hume and Edmund Burke show how difficult it was for the minds of the eighteenth century to produce a coherent, consistent and practicable idea of party. A purely positivist attempt to describe party in the nude—to anatomise the material thing—is bound to have its pitfalls for the historian; for a great proportion of the existence of party lies in the realm of human thought.

The recent addition to "England in the Age of the American Revolution"—namely Mr. Brooke's volume on *The Chatham Administration 1766-68*—illustrates the dangers of a point of view which, because it is too materialistic, dissolves away too much of the continuity of history and produces excessive atomisation. His work calls attention to the way in which the new historical method opens the door to possible fallacies; and his conclusions at this point (which he does not establish by evidence and which are rather the result of his own kind of approach) are worth examination, because they represent the most serious novelty that his book has to offer, and they affect the shape that we give to our general history. Because changes of personnel had taken place, and because the factions or political connexions of the time were always more fluid than modern parties—because, also, Lord Rockingham himself was "the youngest of the party leaders" in 1766—Mr. Brooke insists that the Rockingham connexion was a party not brought to birth until just after the middle of the 1760's.

⌡ In the eighteenth century a party rarely created an Administration; an Administration always created a party. Grenville and [in 1765] Rockingham were not appointed to the head of the Treasury because they were party leaders; but they were party leaders when they were dismissed, and they were able to take some of their followers into opposition. [p. 234]

In half a dozen incidental ways, at various points in his book, Mr. Brooke indirectly attacks the traditional view that the Rockinghamites were anything more than an ordinary faction, like that of the Duke of Bedford—he regards them as a body newly created by Lord Rockingham in a political world in which (p. 236) "no leader could bequeath his followers to a successor". Mr. Brooke is able to condemn Macaulay, therefore, for believing that "the Rockinghams were *sui generis* among eighteenth-century parties" (p. 276); and he has a full-dress attack (p. 218) on the nineteenth-century historians who provided parties with "mythical pedigrees", tracing the "apostolic succession" of Whiggism in a continuity which (amongst other things) linked the party of Walpole and the Pelhams with that of Rockingham and Fox.

Changes of personnel had indeed occurred, and the entry of a new generation upon the political scene is particularly remarkable in the middle of the 1760's. It had been recognised for over a century before Mr. Brooke produced his work that a spurious and excessive continuity had been given to the history of party and the genealogy of Whig and Tory—that, as Mr. Brooke asserts (p. 284) the Rockinghamite opposition in George III's reign even "inherited a great deal" from the Tory opposition of the first half of the eighteenth century. Yet Mr. Brooke himself repeats some of the data which have always given decisive support to the very view he sets out to condemn. He does in fact admit that the Bedford party was "a family group", and that the peers who belonged to it were "connected by marriage with the Duke". The Rockinghamites were different in structure, not like a single clan but rather an alliance of clans, or (as was realised over a century ago) a confederacy of heads of clans; and the papers published by Mr. Brooke and others draw attention to the remarkable size of the combined body. Rockingham himself followed his father in support of Walpole and Pelham, and Mr. Brooke, in spite of his denial that leadership could be transmitted, describes Rockingham as "naturally" transferring his support to "Pelham's brother and successor, the Duke of Newcastle". When the Duke of Cumberland was opening a negotiation for a new ministry on 7th May, 1765, he reported that he "spoke to the Duke of Newcastle and the Marquis of Rockingham". On 30th June it was a meeting of lords and gentlemen, including Rockingham, which met at the Duke of Newcastle's and decided by a substantial majority in favour of the formation of a ministry. Certainly there was much fluidity, but when Mr. Brooke mentions the Dukes of Newcastle, Portland and Richmond, and the families of the Yorkes and Cavendishes we can hardly fail to be reminded of the earlier decades of the eighteenth century, even of the alliance of "the great Revolution families". And Mr. Brooke himself describes how, even after 1766, the Duke of Newcastle still tries to have a hand in the leadership of the party, showing jealousy because, in his opinion, Rockingham gives too little weight to his advice. The Duke of Cumberland, speaking of the opposition in 1765 [*Rockingham Memoirs*, I, 191] separates Mr. Pitt and Lord Temple from the party of Newcastle and Rockingham, which he describes as "great Whig families". Horace Walpole, whose evidence in this period must not be despised, says that the Duke of Cumberland "pressed the Whigs to undertake the Administration, and proposed Lord Rockingham for head of the Treasury". Indeed he perpetually refers to the Newcastle-Rockingham confederacy as either "the Whigs" or the "Opposition", and Mr. Brooke himself (pp. 241–2) shows that, in lists of parties, Rockingham classed his own supporters as "Whigs". The Duke of Cumberland tells us that in May 1765 (*Rockingham Memoirs*, I, 195) he told Lord Temple that, besides negotiating with Temple and Pitt, he had been ordered to treat "with those Lords that formed the head of the Whig party". Here he certainly meant the Newcastle-Rockingham connexion. The same idiom—the same use of the unqualified term "the Whigs"—can be seen amongst the followers of Newcastle at the very beginning of the reign. The problem of identity and the metaphysics of continuity are not so mysterious, or so beset with paradox, that the party of Rockingham and Newcastle from 1766 must be separated from the party of Newcastle and Rockingham in 1765, or from that of Newcastle in 1760, or from the Whigs of the time of Walpole and Pelham. Indeed, if it were granted that the material or tangible connexion were more tenuous and remote than it really is, one must still not overlook the continuity that comes in the realm of ideas or in the consciousness of men. In the last resort we need not deny all importance even to the continuity that may be fabricated retrospectively when a body which is unquestionably new seeks to create its own link with tradition. As in the case of the relationship between the Church of England and the earliest centuries of Christianity, continuity may be conceded if only because men have forged it afterwards—if only because thinking made it so. Burke operated to this purpose and his idea of an alliance of great Whig families carries us back not merely to Rockingham in 1766, but to the age of the earlier Hanoverians.

Over a century ago both Mahon and Croker led the campaign against that kind of historical reconstruction which tried to see in eighteenth-century politics the traditional form of the conflict between Whigs and Tories. Croker pointed out that when there are not great political issues to divide public life party is turned into "faction"; and we must not imagine that this aspect of the teaching of the Namier school is new. If I may quote what I said in *George III, Lord North and the People*, however, "Ages of history . . . overlap, and curious throw-backs occur, or it will happen that, as the world changes, men are slow in making their mental adjustments. . . . Like one film superimposed upon the pattern of another . . . there still survived till it was almost anachronistic . . . a vague cross-division based on old ideas of whig and tory". The *Annual Register* for 1762 described how Newcastle had come to be "considered as the head of the whigs" and how Bute felt it necessary to call on "the tories, or country gentlemen". And similarly there survived the impression or the assumption that the Rockinghamites were the main body of "the Whigs".

8. George III's Programme as presented to the Public

WHEN GEORGE III commended Adolphus's account of the early years of his reign, he praised its accuracy particularly in so far as it concerned himself. We need not presume on this piece of testimony over-much; and we might admit that the historian may easily (and perhaps not always illegitimately) transfer to the person of the King the ideas which are put forward by the men around him. Such ideas may in fact be put forward in the King's name or may come to be attached to him merely because they are so closely associated with his reign. The things which are declared by the men who enjoy the royal favour may in any case be more significant historically than the things which the King himself is meditating in the privacy of his soul. Even politically they may be significant at the time when they occur, and in the case of George III's reign we repeatedly meet the opposition charge that a disturbing factor from the very beginning was the change in what was called "the language of the court".

The men in the neighbourhood of Bute certainly seem to have imagined themselves to be collaborating in a new system, a comprehensive change of policy. In 1762, Gilbert Elliot, "one of the closest associates of Bute", wrote: "Nor is it to be expected that in critical times ancient systems of power will fall to the ground without a struggle". And if 1762 seems too late to throw light on the original intentions of the reign, it is interesting that Bubb Dodington should have used language so similar to this when writing to Bute in the earliest weeks of the reign. His words were: "Remember that to recover monarchy from the inveterate usurpation of oligarchy is a point too arduous and important to be achieved without much difficulty and some degree of danger". Here, from the very bosom of the age itself, and from the very

P   225

brink of the new era, is the converse of Sir Lewis Namier's view that ridiculously small purposes led to a paradoxically great commotion. And here—before the Duke of Newcastle had come out into opposition to the King—are men who are in a position to make mischief, men who clearly do consider that a change of system, an attack on the Whig oligarchy, is in question. If many of the writers of the past can be alleged to have gone wrong on this initial issue, they followed the testimony of witnesses who might well have seemed close to the heart of things.

Let us change, however, the angle of our vision once again; for the thing which most concerns the ordinary student of history is the issue as it divided the public in the earliest years of the reign of George III. And this again is possibly calculated to be more important for the shaping of our narrative framework—more relevant to the way in which we formulate our general history— than the secrets of George III's inner mind. Here, too, we find the attacks on corruption, on party distinctions, on the Whig oligarchy, on the system that had put the royal authority under eclipse. We see all this brought out in the propaganda that is produced on behalf of the court; but it appears over again in the replies of the opposition, who pick out the successive points, now for taunt and now for attack. Polemical writings may be an inferior form of evidence in some respects, but they do show what public opinion is being asked to decide, even if that question has been provoked hypocritically in the first place in order to cover something else. The *Annual Register* did not say that the court of George III had attempted nothing new or that the alleged attack on "the Whig oligarchy" was merely a hoax. It even admitted (see p. 49 above) that in the political conflict a genuine constitutional issue had been raised—an issue which, at the end of the argument, the *Annual Register* decided in favour of the King. Supposing it could be proved that no "Whig" party existed and that there never had been an "oligarchy" the question of the

existence of this overt issue would be unaffected. It was sufficient if people *believed* in the existence of a Whig oligarchy and
imagined that this was what they were fighting against. Concerning the Duke of Newcastle, the *Annual Register* for 1762 tells us
that "during a great part of the late King's reign his family had
directed all things without controul". The view may have been
wrong, or it may have been an exaggeration; but the point is
that it represented an opinion obviously prevalent at the time.

And so, though we may take our cross-section at different
levels we find that, at each of those levels, we meet the same set of
political issues. Whether we look at George III, or the circle
around Bute, or the case as it was presented to the public, it is the
same framework of narrative that seems to emerge. The framework in question—both in its general shape and in its specific
elements—is the very one within which the prevailing historiographical tradition, from Adolphus to Winstanley, construed the
early years of George III's reign. If the framework is correct, it is
an ancient one; but if so imposing a tradition is to be overthrown
we must be clear about the evidence on which we are acting,
clearer still about the process of inference to which the evidence
is subjected. And we must be clear that we are prepared to apply
the same principles and modes of interpretation to other areas and
periods of history.

9. *The Patriot King*

THE NEW school becomes particularly intolerant when the name of Bolingbroke and *The Idea of the Patriot King* are mentioned. It is assumed that, when associated with the policies and purposes of George III, these must be employed to introduce a hostile innuendo. Bringing them into the picture at all is regarded as a device of the Whig historians, anxious to double the unpleasantness of the charge of personal despotism. In any case there is no patience for Bolingbroke as a political writer, if indeed the new school will have any truck with the producers of political doctrine, whatever the colour. It has evidently been forgotten that, as we have seen, the association of George III with "Patriot" ideas, and indeed with the theory of the "Patriot King", was first conceived by his supporters, who imagined that they were complimenting him.

We must be prepared to consider the possibility that George III was not less benevolent than his friends have maintained, but that the world has been wrong in imagining Bolingbroke to have been the patron of tyranny. Historians of recent generations came to be more hostile to George III, and the Whigs naturally read back into the ideal of the *Patriot King* the evils that they had come to associate with that monarch. As a result of this, the Bolingbroke that many people have in mind at the present day is far removed from the Bolingbroke of earlier historiography, far removed from the Bolingbroke whom the radicals of the 1770's were ready to claim as a precursor. The modern view seems to have a certain plausibility because it was easy to remember Bolingbroke as a man who at one time had actually been a Jacobite. It was only too easy to overlook the fact that when he wrote the *Patriot King* the situation was different, for this was a period when mere Toryism and Jacobitism could not have served his purposes. At this stage in the story, he had to be somewhat radical in order to trump the Whig aces of Sir Robert Walpole.

The positivistic method, though it is so plausible in appearance, can be used to afford admirable cover for a piece of evasive action. On this system the whole discussion of the question now at issue can be eluded—there is no evidence, we are told, that George III had even read Bolingbroke. Yet the ideas of the "Patriot" faction were in the air, and they burst out again in a new crop of "Patriot" literature after the accession of George III. In 1760 the writer of *A Letter addressed to two great men on the prospect of peace* resurrected the ideas and the very terminology of Bolingbroke. He called on ministers themselves "to undertake the work of reviving the constitution" and to secure the "independence of Parliament" by preventing bribery and eliminating place-holders in the House of Commons. The author of *Reasons why the approaching Treaty of Peace should be debated in Parliament* took up the precise form of Bolingbroke's own demand for a House of Commons which should vote under free conditions and even be competent to issue instructions to ministers. We have already seen that in *The Auditor* the propaganda of the new régime claimed that George III was the "Patriot King", while the opposition repeatedly mocked this precise suggestion. That the tradition did not quickly disappear is evident from what happened at the meeting which inaugurated the famous Yorkshire Association at the very end of the year 1779. Leonard Smelt, who spoke at this meeting, had been sub-governor of George III as Prince of Wales, and it was a matter of common knowledge that he was intimate with the circle around the King. He offended most of his hearers because, at an unseasonable moment, he spoke what it was customary to describe in those days as "the language of the court". If one reads the reports of his speech one can easily see that in reality he brought out the catchwords of the "Patriot" party, including the suggestion that

George III was the "Patriot King". We have even seen how the "Patriot" ideals could persist irrespective of any special regard for George III, and how, as late as the year 1795, the historian, Belsham, could advertise them still, while complaining that they had not been the ideals of George III.

And what are the "Patriot" ideas? They are the attack on corruption, the demand for the abolition of party, the call for the abandonment of proscription, the plea that the Crown should not be the slave of a faction. They include the view that only a virtuous monarch can rescue the country from the demoralisation into which it has fallen. The ideas that we have found expressed in George III, and still more in Bute himself and the men around him, conform in a remarkable way to the pattern of the "Patriot" programme in general. The enemies of George III were the men who said that the proclamation of these ideas was hypocritical—those who, like Belsham, said that this King had in reality deserted the "Patriot" policy of his father, and sought merely to magnify his own prerogative.

In the last chapter of my *Statecraft of Machiavelli*, I have tried to show how avowedly (and yet also how much more greatly than he even avowed) Bolingbroke was attracted and influenced by the Italian writer, interesting himself particularly in the most crucial of Machiavelli's problems—the question of how to restore virtue in a state that had become corrupt. If in one sense he was a political propagandist, addressing himself to the situation in England in his time, there was another sense in which he was interested also in producing what might be called an exercise in political philosophy—consciously writing, in fact, for posterity. He had come to the conclusion that England could not be saved by a party, and that even the members of his own party were ready to take advantage of corruption if they saw the opportunity. He realised that the situation gave him an opening for the discussion of Machiavelli's extreme case—the case of a country which had become *totally* corrupt. In the *Patriot King*, which follows both the formal pattern and the essential idea of Machiavelli, he imitates *The Prince* but at the same time we find him reacting against it. He sets out in fact to re-examine Machiavelli's famous thesis, that a totally corrupt society cannot raise itself above its own level, and must be disciplined into virtue by the authority of a powerful ruler. Bolingbroke believes that a prince who has gained power on the methods recommended by Machiavelli is likely to have become corrupted himself before he has reached the end of the process. Salvation is a more difficult matter than Machiavelli had imagined, therefore; for it depends on the prince having genuine virtue—on his being a "Patriot" in more than name. By the definition of the case, a prince who has every opportunity to corrupt his people and establish a tyranny, must take a self-denying ordinance, choosing not to use corruption at all, and making parliament totally free, while giving it all the reality of power. And this, says Bolingbroke, is the unfailing "panacea"—nothing but this one act of self-limitation is necessary for the salvation of the state. For its achievement it is only required that the virtue of the prince shall be genuine. The *Idea of the Patriot King* is, therefore, a carefully contrived "Anti-Machiavel".

Down to the time of Macaulay, historians seemed willing to respect the intentions of the "Patriot" programme, if not to commit themselves to any particular faith in its possible political effectiveness. And we have seen that even Macaulay in 1844 describes the ideal of the "Patriot King" as one which was understandably popular in the eighteenth century, though he had no faith for his own part in the political regeneration which it was supposed to promise. Bolingbroke himself had admitted that the virtue which he required from the King could hardly be expected —if it existed, he said, it would be "a standing miracle". And it was the whole point of his argument to insist that if the virtue were not genuine, there was no remedy for the evils of the body politic. The supporters of the ideal were dazzled furthermore by a kind of mystique; for the whole theory took it for granted that a truly "patriot" king would find that an absolutely free and independent parliament would be entirely at one with him, so that, like Queen Elizabeth, he would be in mysterious harmony with the will of the entire people. Macaulay himself, and later critics of George III, saw the fallacy here, and recognised the degree to which the doctrines of the *Patriot King* would serve the purposes of an ambitious tyrant, whose pretended virtues were merely a cloak for despotic designs. Some writers in the nineteenth century were prepared to ignore the central argument of Bolingbroke's book and overlooked its most essential dialectical exercise. They quoted rather the incidental passages in which it was said that a "Patriot King" would begin to govern as soon as he began to reign.

If George III received some infection not only from the "Patriot" programme, but from those ideas of a "Patriot King" which were in the air at the time (and it would appear that he did) he was influenced by the notion that corruption needed to be checked and that only a king in a position to use it could ever secure its abolition—only a king making a self-denying ordinance could rescue the situation. If on the other hand George III merely sought to magnify the prerogative and increase his personal power, he needed no literary source for a policy that must have been as old as kingship itself, and as old as human nature. *The Idea of the Patriot King* certainly does not concern the student of George III unless George was moved at any point in the story by a desire to check corruption; and a king might deplore corruption without necessarily being influenced by the work of Bolingbroke. In the last resort, the issue depends on whether one finds in the ideas of George III in 1760 something which is reminiscent of the pattern of the "Patriot" programme; though it should be recalled that even in the propaganda of the court it is asserted that George III is the "Patriot King".

Let us make a supposition. We have seen what was said in the circle of Bute and in the propaganda of the court about the "enslavement" of the monarchy. The fact that this was the language of the new régime is confirmed by the reports in the *Annual Register* as well as by the slogans which the opposition thought it necessary to attack. We have even seen Bute telling Newcastle that George III "had a notion of not being governed . . . by his Minister or Ministers, as the late King had been"— the new monarch certainly wanted to escape what he regarded as the fate of his grandfather. Let us assume, however, that Temperley was right in 1909 and Dr. Owen is correct in 1957 on the point that the so-called "imprisonment" of George II by Walpole and the Pelhams comprises a considerable element of myth. We are then reduced to the position which Donne adopted in the Introduction to the *Correspondence of George III and Lord North* in 1867, when he said that George III had been more or less deluded into thinking that the monarchy had been enslaved by the Whigs. The delusion must have been fairly widespread, and it does not necessarily cease to stand as an error because George II (who certainly felt the pinch somewhere) seems at least on occasion to have shared it himself. But who generated this myth, and who gave George III this impression, before his accession to the throne? Who communicated it to men like Dodington? If it was a myth, it was the very one which it was necessary to invent before the "Patriot" programme and the argument of *The Patriot King* could be set on foot at all. I think that to a considerable degree, though not entirely, the notion of "the King in bondage" was a matter of legend; and I imagine that I am in agreement with Dr. Owen when I say that, in so far as it was not a legend, it was inherent in the nature of the case—it represented something which George II (and, indeed, possibly, George III) was wrong to resent. But the more one presses the argument that George III and Bute, Dodington and *The Auditor*, were merely fighting a myth in the years immediately after 1760, the more important becomes the source of that myth—the "Patriot" literature, and the "Patriot" ideas that were so much in the air. I am not sure that the recent developments in historiography do not make these "Patriot" ideas—when they are properly understood—more important than they seemed before. And in a similar way, I am not sure that the new teaching about the state of politics in 1760 is not going to increase the importance of the Rockingham party, and of men like Burke, as the reign proceeds.

10. Corruption

IN SPITE of the places where Sir Lewis Namier has given some credit to Adolphus, there can hardly ever have been another school of history so severe on its predecessors as the one we are considering. They possibly hold that little trouble needs to be taken over the previous historiography of the subject. It seems to be the habit of the school to recognise no debt to any forerunners, and to make acknowledgments only to one another. Even the militant criticisms which are issued against unnamed offenders seem really to be directed against types of popular error that have a way of hanging in the air long after they have disappeared from genuine scholarship. And perhaps for the same reason a number of things are put forward as though they were novelties, when in reality they entered the literature of our subject long ago. One example would be the repeated insistence (in terms which might suggest that it was a new thing) on the fact that eighteenth-century politics are not to be understood if they are construed in terms of the nineteenth-century party-system. Another is the discussion of the political importance of the presence or the absence of a Prince of Wales capable of standing as something of a rival to the King. Another is the well-known explanation of the King's Friends by use of the analogy of the modern "civil servant".

From this point of view some interest attaches to the work on *The Rise of the Pelhams* by Dr. J. B. Owen—a book which has many beauties and excellences, and which at many points carries research to a further stage. If we examine some of the main strategic lines of his picture—including some of those picked out by Sir Lewis Namier in his review in *The Spectator* for 15th February, 1957—it is curious to see how the general shape of the political world corresponds with a pattern we have already

235

examined. "The Court and Treasury Party", says this author, in almost the very words that Temperley used, numbered "at the time of Walpole's fall only slightly over 100." He talks of the role and the importance of the independent members of parliament; insists that direct corruption has only a small part to play in the story; and holds that corruption was not in itself sufficient to save a government. He draws attention to the necessity and the effectiveness in George II's reign of those methods of managing and persuading the House of Commons which the leaders of a government still have to employ. He deprecates any attempt to interpret the politics of Walpole's time on the principles of the modern party-system. He does not agree with the ancient and traditional view which regarded George II as having been held in bondage by the oligarchical Whigs. In all the points that have been mentioned this stratification of the epoch is very much the same as that which Temperley had put forward in his article in the *Cambridge Modern History* in 1909. And Temperley follows an analogous course, if not quite the same course, when he reduces the constitutional significance which had been traditionally imputed to the political crisis of 1746. If it is important for the student of the politics of a period to grasp what might be called the strategic situation of the time, we may wonder a little that, practically fifty years ago—and decades before the Namier technique had been elaborated—an historian by virtue not merely of industry but also of insight, should have delineated so much of the character of an age in a way that has now received interesting vindication. And still it is open to us to ask ourselves whether, in judging the present day, we would rely on a research student who goes around counting heads rather than upon the statesman who has a grasp of the strategic situation—whether indeed the Namier method will not have its dangers for those who lack the insight of a Temperley, the intellectual grasp of Dr. Owen.

The world did not have to wait until the arrival of the new

school of historiography for the application of severe criticism to the extravagant legends concerning eighteenth-century corruption. In his *Cambridge Modern History* article Harold Temperley declared that "the scale on which it prevailed was far too large, but the influence of the Crown had been regularly employed by the Minister since the days of William III". He referred to Onslow (who, he said, "had every reason for knowing") as the authority for the view that "it was Sunderland who extended and systematised corruption". And he told how a Secret Committee of Enquiry, "which consisted, with two exceptions, of political opponents", failed to produce evidence "of an impressive character" against Sir Robert Walpole after his fall in 1742. Temperley notes that "the officials of the Secret Service Fund (out of which direct bribes would be paid) refused to give evidence to the Committee"; but he gives it as his opinion that "there is not much reason to suppose that an unusual amount of money went in this way". Direct bribery, he says, has been proved against Walpole in a few cases, "but the evidence suggests that it was not common, and most of Walpole's 'corruption' consisted in the use of indirect means of securing party allegiance which every parliamentary leader employs". He adds that "in the imperfect state of parliamentary discipline it would seem that indirect bribery at any rate was a necessity". On the other hand, Temperley points out that the men who enjoyed the favours of government were liable to be a weakness, and not a strength, to a declining or unpopular ministry—they would be "anxious to make terms with a possible successor". In his view, corruption increased under Wilmington and Pelham, and came to its maximum under Lord North; but in an article on "Chatham, North and America" in the *Quarterly Review* for October 1914, he discusses North's long tenure of office, and even here he insists that "royal influence and parliamentary corruption" are "explanations which satisfied the Whigs but must not deceive the historian".

In fact, he says, North "knew better than Walpole how to 'smile without art and win without a bribe'; and the independent members often followed the easy genial Premier where they might have deserted the cold Grenville or the haughty Pitt". Even North, then, owed much to what we should regard as the orthodox way of securing parliamentary support; and "if he could not inspire or control he could certainly debate". Temperley is insistent: he tells us that "no eighteenth-century government lasted long without popular support"; that "the mob had caused the withdrawal of bills and the fall or elevation of ministers, in 1720, 1733, 1754, 1756"; and that in 1768–9 "popular hostility" did real injury to the administration, while in the following decade it seriously endangered the ministry of North.

In the Introduction to his *Parliamentary Papers of John Robinson, 1774–84*, W. T. Laprade pointed out that, in the world which had developed since 1832, the parliaments of George III's reign had come to be regarded as having been "corrupt", when in reality a mental transposition was required—those parliaments ought rather to be envisaged as machines which worked to a different purpose. In any case, he said, the new documents chiefly impressed one by "the moderateness of the sums involved".

> These papers by no means give evidence that George III and his ministers indulged in the practice of bribery and corruption in the degree that has sometimes been alleged. Probably few members of parliament would have tolerated anything as crude as open bribery even in that time. In any case, bribery would have been a much more costly method of obtaining a majority than that actually used.

Money, he says, was "essential for election purposes, and that in sums of considerable size, but the purposes for which it was used were, for the most part, conventional at the time and were not regarded by members of the ruling class as corrupt practices". The funds provided "were used for purposes differing little from those regularly practised by all parties"; and there was "not much to show" that George III resorted to "more corrupt practices than were used by the Whig magnates". Laprade's documents and Introduction, however, do draw attention to the kind of point which posterity is always likely to overlook—namely the dangerous potentialities of the eighteenth-century system, supposing it were allowed to evolve in a certain way, or to develop unopposed. He shows how even that hardened and experienced parliamentary manager, John Robinson, was uneasy at the way in which "the new power of organized wealth" revealed its possibilities as the reign proceeded.

The forces that began to be potent in the general election of 1784 were destined ultimately to make the sums used by both George III and the Whigs seem paltry and almost insignificant in comparison with their lavish expenditure.

It is curious that George III, who had been taunted at the beginning of his reign because of the claim to special purity which had been made on his behalf, and who had entered serious historiography as the enemy of political jobbery, should have come to be pilloried by a series of historians as the master-mind in a system of political corruption. Neither Sir George Otto Trevelyan nor Edward Porritt, who held extreme views on this subject, regarded him as the originator of corruption; but they described him as more than ready to put the existing system to his own use. When the word had gone round that George III was an arch-trafficker in corruption, historical students were quick to mimic one another, to adopt the last thing that had been said, and to project unduly the significance of the supposed discovery, or exaggerate its implications. In a similar way I once heard in a University lecture-hall a discourse from a man who had caught at second-hand some of the ideas which had been put forward in the earlier decades of this century about the connexion between the Calvinistic faith and the rise of modern capitalism. This lecturer made short work with the subtleties of what in any case had always been a somewhat dubious form of argument. According to his account, Calvin, in Geneva, had actually set out to devise a form of Christianity which would be more acceptable to the rising *bourgeoisie*. Now, however, one historian treading on the heels of another since 1909 if not earlier, has been impressing upon us a more historical point of view, a more structural kind of analysis, and a greater scepticism on the subject of eighteenth-century corruption. Most of this is admirable, but we must be careful not to allow the usual historiographical tendencies to build the subject up into another superstitious myth. Some of Professor Namier's work is not easy to understand or to set squarely in order; but I was surprised some time ago when an historian of considerable learning in other fields told me (whether as a result of reading or not-reading, I cannot tell) that Professor Namier had disposed of the whole view that corruption had existed in the eighteenth century. And the trouble is that some of these points can be harped upon so repetitively as to create a new type of legend and make the situation less satisfactory than it was when Laprade wrote in 1922.

Yet one of the people who recorded in a signal manner his belief that corruption did exist and ought to be abolished is George III, well after the date of his accession to the throne; and if he could talk as he did about his dream of getting rid of the evil (and about the collapse of this dream) he may well have written as a partisan or based his remarks on a much too limited experience; but we need not be too hard on historians who over a century later registered their own protests, not yet knowing that George III had once written so clearly against it. We may recall, furthermore, that when Newcastle (after his downfall) deplored the corruption in the political life of the time, Hardwicke did not contradict him—he merely said that Newcastle, after all his experience, must not pretend to be surprised at the fact. (See p. 101, above). In any case, we must be on our guard against the puritanical literalness and dogmatic insistence of historians who are too hard in the faith that they put in the counting of heads or the amassing of figures. Given the number of placemen in the eighteenth century and the normal reasons why many people would be inclined to the support of government, as well as the number of people who had no places but were only hoping to get a reward sometime, it would be a small margin that would need to be provided for from the Secret Service Fund, just as a very small factor may decide the turn of the balance in various kinds of committees at the present day. In fairly recent years I have heard people argue that a proportion of thirty-five per cent of communists in a country was not a very significant matter since thirty-five per cent is so far from representing a majority; but those who use figures must carry their mathematics further and reckon on the amount of leverage which a small quantity might have in a certain situation of things. And that is why one must take the figures relating to corruption with flexibility and a sense of humour—if corruption had been the worst that the needs of government could have called for, there would only have been a comparatively small margin required for ordinary purposes; and in any case it was unsafe to rely on corruption or influence when a great crisis had arisen or high passions had been aroused. The Rockingham ministry in 1782–83 only clipped away a marginal fraction of the patronage at the disposal of the Crown; but Burke, in the French Revolutionary period, held that this had been sufficient to tip the balance, so that henceforward the danger did not come from the side of the King. On the other hand one must consider corruption not merely as it existed in hard reality, but as it existed in the thought of the time—the thought of even a man like George III.

In general it would be the enemies of the existing administration who cried out against corruption, and we must make allowance for their partisanship; though we must not forget the place which the problem did come to hold in the literature and talk of the time, and we may have to recognise the fact that at least there was an issue for the opponents of government to raise. The promoters of parliamentary reform and a more democratic system of government would be hostile to the administration of the day; but this does not mean that they were necessarily in the wrong, or that they were not serving the future, even in the very fact of their opposition, the very form of their partisanship. It is also true that the conduct of various ministers or the practices of various periods would not be always the same, so far as the problem of corruption is concerned. And this point applies to the general problem of political jobbery, which also provoked the hostility of George III at the beginning of his reign. George III himself in later years expressed the view that at least a headmaster of Eton might be appointed on his merits; and, in spite of the truth of Temperley's remarks, it was a supporter of government who once said that Lord North sometimes trusted too directly to corruption when it was rather a little "seasoning"—a little geniality or, perhaps, a little nursing—that was required. Dr. Owen suggests in one place that the favours distributed by government were rather rewards for past services—not bribes intended to affect future conduct. I dealt with this matter many years ago and showed how the rewards might be particularly appropriate if a man had for a long time been at considerable expense in local elections which he had conducted in support of government. But I tried to draw the distinction—and Dr. Owen's own treatment of the matter shows that he ought to recognise the difference which may arise—when favours are actually offered in return for future support, and when indeed the point is reached at which legitimate influence does seem to turn into corruption. In *George III, Lord North and the People*, I examined the case of

William Eden, who had begun to pretend that in conscience he did not feel that he could go on supporting a government as disastrous as that of Lord North. And Lord North instantly and rightly assumed that in reality Eden was rattling the sword in order to gain money—was putting up the price of his support. When rewards and punishments were too directly connected with votes in parliament, men were sometimes a little shocked; and it is not merely the actual number of the occasions but also the effect on ideas and on the language of political intercourse which may prove to be the relevant aspect of the matter. If we analyse the affair down to its fundamental principle, it would sometimes appear that some of its aspects would not be without their analogies at the present day; but it was sometimes the case that an abrupt change of sides or a latent menace in a House of Commons speech was too directly connected with the distribution of favours and offices, and was recognised to be so connected. The very language of political discussion was affected by this, so that it sometimes seemed to be too easy, too much the natural thing, to translate the events of the day into terms of what was called jobbery. Granted that the situation of those days makes the whole affair historically explicable, it is not clear that the particular order of things was the best that could be imagined for the promotion of public spirit and political morality, or that the system as generally accepted was not subject to recognisable abuses. And, granted that the politics which Sir Lewis Namier describes had so intimate an association with the character of the existing order, we must not rule out the possible value of a change in the order itself. We must not assume that if corruption and jobbery have been made historically understandable, the opposition to them is not also historically understandable, and that the demand for a new system of things was unreasonable and wrong.

11. The Duke of Newcastle

THE MATERIALS which are supplied by Sir Lewis Namier suggest a portrait of the Duke of Newcastle not essentially different from what had been familiar to students of history for a considerable time. The ridiculous side of his character had been exposed by practically every historian who had discussed the man; though some, like Winstanley, had introduced reservations on the ground that a person in the position of Newcastle could not have been without some respectable qualities. If Sir Lewis Namier makes him appear even more ridiculous than usual this is because we now see the man in greater detail, so that sometimes we seem to be following his career day by day. He seems more fussy than ever as he jealously watches the political barometer; though it is possible that he was right to be jealous about little things at this moment, right to imagine that after the accession of George III every little thing was to be regarded as a "symptom". His hesitations and self-contradictions are not incomprehensible to us; and on the large issue that was presented to him surely he was correct in seeing that the "symptoms" pointed to a court design which was distinctly unfriendly to himself. He talked about his indifference to power and he would moan on occasion about his wish to retire from politics. It must not be pretended that there is anything strange in these self-contradictions; for, in such cases as this, we take the insincerity of the protestations almost as a matter of course. This kind of thing is only too familiar not only in the political world but also in other realms.

When some of us were young—and before the books of Sir Lewis Namier had appeared—we were already taught that in the eighteenth century the accession of a new king was likely to mean the installation of a new ministry. We were also taught, however, that those who had been dispossessed would be likely to go over to the opposition; nor is it easy to see why Sir Lewis Namier should appear to be surprised at such a thing. We were even taught that the Duke of Newcastle denied the intention of going into regular opposition in 1762. But we were also told that retiring politicians generally talked in this manner—that they regularly deprecated such a policy of opposition even though they were on the point of taking it up. Indeed, if they did otherwise in those days they would be making a gratuitous avowal of the purest factiousness, and condemning themselves in advance. And Professor Namier, who makes much of Newcastle's contradictory statements, and draws a brilliant but cruel picture in his *England in the Age of the American Revolution*, may be allowing his method to trip him into a piece of unimaginativeness. Newcastle made it clear that he did in fact mean to oppose the government if there should be reason for this; and he made it fairly plain that there were indeed going to be reasonable grounds for embarking on a policy of opposition on this particular occasion. This was the only way in which he could have formulated his attitude without making a confession of factiousness. It is difficult to believe that his meaning could have been misunderstood at the time.

On pp. 13–15 of his *Lord Chatham and the Whig Opposition*, D. A. Winstanley complained in 1912 that "Newcastle has suffered from being judged by Whig historians who have chosen to consider him a disgrace to their party". Newcastle's name, he said, had in fact "become a byword for inefficient administration and wholesale corruption".

> Historians have depicted him in graphic language as little better than a dotard who, by dint of a certain low cunning and great wealth, rose to political eminence; and his contemporaries never wearied of enlarging upon his lack of dignity, his childish inconsequence, his colossal ignorance, and his absurd jealousies.

Winstanley thought that Newcastle's incapacity as an adminis-trator had probably been exaggerated. He, for his part, was ready to concede that the man had some political insight—that, for ex-ample, he excelled his contemporaries (and was correct) in his belief that ministers should concentrate their attention on the power which it was possible to establish in parliament. "Long before Burke had preached the necessity of a party system, New-castle had practised the same doctrine, devoting all his energy to the formation of a strong personal following in both houses." As a result, Newcastle had had a contribution to make; and some part of his work was actually inherited by the Rockingham Whigs. He was the real founder of that connexion, though he did not in fact work out an adequate idea of party—did not realise, for example, how his own following was doomed to be reduced as soon as he came into conflict with George III.

The most vivid comments on Newcastle, however, are those of Sir Lewis Namier in *The Age of the American Revolution* (pp. 77 *et seq.*, 400–1 and *passim*) where there are certain points at which description and analysis seem to be fused together at a high temperature. In works that are sometimes too untidy—with the materials on occasion shovelled too carelessly into the text—this author can sprinkle patches of very beautiful writing which leave the impression of great imaginative power, though the pen still seems to be playing at ease. Of Newcastle Namier writes:

His nature and mind were warped, twisted, and stunted, and his life must have been agony, though perhaps he himself did not clearly realise how much he suffered. He was haunted by fears; every small incident was the portent of terrible things to come; every molehill a volcano. With an abundant substratum of intelligence and common sense, he looked a fool, and with an inexhaustible fund of warm human kindness and sincere goodwill, he acquired a reputation for dishonesty. His thinking was sound, but it was paralysed by fears;

unable to stand up to anyone or to refuse a pressing request, he could not keep honest, and the weak resentments of an exasperated coward, who felt constantly bullied and browbeaten, were bound to create the appearances of treachery.

In politics, Newcastle made "disconnected detail his chosen province"; and "even into foreign politics he managed to infuse his habits or obsessions".

We may suspect that historical personages are like icebergs and though certain protruding parts of them are visible to posterity, the greater proportion of them is always submerged. The written evidence is inadequate, and if we take each piece of testimony, and draw a line from one point to another, we may produce a system or a picture, but the result is liable to be caricature. That considerable portion of a man which is average human nature is just the thing that tends to be left out. One is reminded of the portrait which one makes for oneself when one has heard at Oxford high tables discussion and gossip about a man whom one has never met. When ultimately one meets the man himself, one discovers how accurate the conversation has been—all that one has heard turns out to be even more true than one expected. Yet there is disappointment, because the person in question appears at the same time to be a more ordinary human being than one imagined to be possible—it is not the great bulk of normality in a man that manages to get itself reported in high-table conversation. One of the things which seem to be established in history is the extraordinary charm which Charles James Fox was able to exert on both political friends and political enemies. It is difficult to discover exactly where this power really lay; but in his youth Fox could behave in a disgraceful manner, and men who said "We have forgiven him before, because of his charm, but we cannot possibly forgive him this time", would succumb to the spell again within six months. And in spite of the warm humanity which reveals itself in some of his letters, history—including even the art of the painter—fails to provide evidence which is quite commensurate with the power and charm that must have been there. Some months before the Suez crisis, a great concerted attack was made on Sir Anthony Eden in important sections of the press. When it was over, one newspaper remarked that it might have occurred to people to ask how, if he was as foolish as had been alleged, he could ever have become Prime Minister. In the case of the Duke of Newcastle—who certainly cuts a poor figure in the evidence—one wonders sometimes whether all the relevant factors have been considered.

At any rate, Dr. Owen, in *The Rise of the Pelhams*, seems to revert rather to the position of Winstanley, and (on pp. 127-8) condemns "the picture of the Duke as a faithless driveller; a picture which Macaulay immortalised". Writing, apparently, in 1955, he complains further that "posterity has not yet restored the balance". He emphasises Newcastle's "comprehensive knowledge of foreign politics, his cogent and consistently-held principles, and his ample fund of shrewd common sense". What is important is the feeling that he shares with Winstanley—the general impression that somewhere or other Newcastle has been unfairly treated and that the errors of the past have not been sufficiently rectified.

And here, in a very small matter, we have a pointer to what seems to be happening in many small things and even some large ones: namely, a tendency for the historiography of this whole field to reverse direction and swing back, nearer to the position which it held just before the Namier school emerged.

12. The Nature of the Constitution

It is extremely important that—no matter what amount of scientific apparatus one may have at one's disposal—one should not be too dogmatic about the state of the British constitution at any moment in history. At any moment it is extremely likely, in point of fact, that more than one view of constitutional principle and more than one diagnosis of the state of government itself will be in existence. Professor Laski after the crisis of 1931 made it apparent that even in our own contemporary world, where many things have been cleared up and many practices have hardened into custom, there is still an area in which people may differ in regard to the constitutionality of an action or the interpretation of a measure. Professor Laski on this occasion illustrated also the fact that a man's interpretation of the constitution is liable to be affected by his idea of what he wants the constitution to become.

The associates of Newcastle in 1760 did not deny the fact that the king had the constitutional right to choose his own ministers. Their predecessors in the days of Pelham had not denied it; on the contrary they had asserted the king's right at a time when it was almost like taunting him to assert it, since they were defying him to exercise the right and making it impossible for him to do so. George III must have had a fair idea that, if Newcastle and his associates were removed, they were likely to oppose any minister who supplanted them—to behave as such men had done under the first two Hanoverians—however much they declared their abhorrence of mere faction. Hence the caution with which this King and Bute were compelled to move, and the apparent hesitations and contradictions in their conduct as well as that of Newcastle. Hence also the predictions of Bubb Dodington and Gilbert Elliot about the risk and magnitude of the attempt to overturn "ancient systems of power". If regular opposition was unpopular in the country, this might make it one degree more difficult for those who resorted to it; and they would know that they must acquire strength and popularity somewhere—they must base their opposition on a public cause. Such an opposition party would have to discover or create a public issue if there was no such thing actually at hand. The position is somewhat different, but not absolutely different, in the twentieth century.

If there could exist differences of opinion about the state of the British constitution at any period, we must remember that at a given date—at the year 1760, for example—the constitution is not to be regarded as a rigid and static thing. And certainly we today, who can see how it developed through the centuries, must not imagine it in 1760 as finished and fully formed, with no openings for new conflict, no occasion for further quarrel about the direction in which it ought to be moving. Nor should one be rigid and academic about the kind of conduct which could be regarded as unconstitutional. Then, as indeed at any other time, some things might be prohibited by law and some might have been rendered impracticable by convention. But, for both the king and the opposition, many things would be possible in the sense that they would secure acceptance (and would help therefore to condition future development) if it proved possible to "pull them off". We must not rule out the possibility that either the ministry or the opposition would raise indeed a new constitutional issue or set out to establish a new constitutional principle.

Even if all this were not true—and true in fact of any and every period of English constitutional history—there are particular reasons why it must be doubly true in the middle of the eighteenth century. The same reasons would appear to justify the assertion that the Namier school ought in reality to be the first to recognise the truth. The view of the eighteenth-century government which that school now present to us is one which calls not for rigid dogmatism on the subject of the constitution but for the highest degree of flexibility. Their teaching is best illustrated, perhaps, in Sir Lewis Namier's Romanes Lecture, entitled "Monarchy and the Party System"—one of the most attractive pieces of work which that school has produced, printed in *Personalities and Powers* (1955).

It is not always realised, that, apart from the pleasure which can be added to history by verbal skill and by the imagination of the literary man, there is an exquisite loveliness that can arise within the realm of historical technique itself. The peak is reached when it is out of the actual scientific procedures of the authentic student that we gain our æsthetic moments, so that the artistry is not an additional adornment but lies in the historical thought itself, like the beauty which a piece of mathematics can possess. Perhaps only the historical technician can appreciate some of the felicities of the essay on "Monarchy and the Party System", just as only the skill of a practised eye can find the highest pleasure in some masterly stroke on the cricket-field. The basic idea of this Romanes Lecture is not a new one—it is the notion of the eighteenth-century constitution as a "mixed form of government", a system in which the ministers of the Crown held a curiously ambiguous position. In a sense ministers were the servants of the king, chosen and appointed by him, and responsible to him. Yet, since they depended on their power to win or hold the support of parliament, there was a sense in which it was necessary for them to have a footing also in the House of Lords and House of Commons. In his *Robert Walpole et la Politique de Fleury* (1924, p. 366), Professor Paul Vaucher long ago provided an excellent formulation of the whole system. Walpole, he said,

> remained the servant of his Master [the King] and it was the confidence of the latter which put him in a position to govern the realm. This confidence, however, was not to be conferred on any favourite who happened to be clever enough to prevail at court; it could

only be justified if it was bestowed on a minister capable of rallying the majority in parliament behind him, and relying upon it for the conduct of his government.

If the general strategic situation, as described in "Monarchy and the Party System" (and, to a certain degree, in *England in the Age of the American Revolution*, pp. 58 *et seq.*) is not new, Professor Namier shows something of his personality in the way in which he illustrates the case and draws out the implications of the system. Fundamentally, however, to him, as to some previous historians, the organisation of political parties, affords the real clue to the modern developments of the constitution. Only with the rise of more modern parties could the king himself, on the one hand, and the civil service on the other hand, be elbowed out of the political arena.

Now it seems to be the fact that the Namier school are capable of being unfair to George III, and ignoring systems of ideas which help to put him in a better light. They have been tempted on occasion to say more cruel things about him than some of their immediate predecessors or those earlier historians who followed Adolphus. At the same time the school have shown a certain inclination to set themselves up as the professional defenders of George III. This feature is most apparent, perhaps, in their more popular writings, and may really represent something of a reaction against the Whig historians and the popularisers who came in their wake. The reaction against the Whig historians has gone so far that an article in *History Today* has purported to provide a justification of the conduct of Lord George Germain as Secretary of State. In reality it offered no concrete evidence in the man's favour, and it is perhaps significant that it made no mention of George III's own verdict: that Germain had "not been of use in his department". George III in fact had taken the line that only through most meritorious services could Germain have induced the world to overlook his former "misfortunes". The anti-Whig bias encourages the Namier school to direct against the Rockingham party the very kind of malice which George III himself at one time had to suffer; and the criticism sometimes reduces itself to carping on minor points, while it never seems to be accompanied by any apparent effort to see that the Rockinghamites shall share with George III or the King's Friends the benefits of historical understanding. It is difficult, therefore, to escape the view that we are still somewhat in the realm of historical partisanship.

The same bias would seem to have been responsible—at least in the earlier days of the Namier school—for a tendency to lay a hard stress on the formal constitutional rights of the king; though, once we squarely accept the fact that in the eighteenth century Britain was under a "mixed form of government", these formal rights must call for subtle kinds of qualification. In *England in the Age of the American Revolution* (p. 58), we read:

> It was the King's business to see the government of the nation carried on, and for that purpose he had a right to choose his "instruments"; and "support of Government" was considered "a duty, while an honest man could support it". To try to impose oneself on the King by means of a systematic opposition . . . was considered by them factious and dishonest . . . all "formed opposition" was in some measure tainted with disloyalty.

Similarly Mr. Romney Sedgwick, in the Introduction to *Letters from George III to Lord Bute* (1939, p. xvii), writes:

> In the eighteenth century it was established constitutional doctrine that the King had a right to choose his own ministers and that any organised attempt to prescribe to him on the point was a wicked, factious and almost unconstitutional combination.

These things were certainly said and believed in the eighteenth century; and it must be conceded that at least they represented one view of the constitution at that time. We must not merely make them our own, however, and adopt them as our absolute verdicts on the constitution, especially as the men who expressed these views at one period might even contradict them (at least by their actions) in another period. Indeed some men would appear to have been capable of belying them in their actual conduct at the very time at which they were giving utterance to them. Some things may be formally true and yet it may be wrong to insist upon them in too literalistic a manner in the real world of politics. Professor Richard Pares, in his interesting Ford Lectures on *King George III and the Politicians* (p. 100) sums up the true state of affairs:

> Bute, claiming to prevail by court favour alone, slighted not only the so-called "Revolution families" and their cliques but also the House of Commons and the broader public. . . . It was one thing to defend the king's liberty of choice; quite another thing, to acquiesce in a choice which meant that court favour alone was enough to make a minister. For that is what the new king and his new minister believed, and some others with them. Bute himself said that it was a question whether His Majesty was to exercise "the liberty that his poorest subject enjoys of choosing his own menial servants." That was no longer a sensible thing to say about a ministerial appointment.

The "mixed form of government", with the ministers dependent on the king, yet dependent also on their ability to manage parliament, represents an essentially unstable equilibrium. It would be difficult to think of a situation which could have been more burdened with tensions, more clouded with ambiguities, more pregnant with varied possibilities of development. Once we squarely face the fact that the British constitution stood during the eighteenth century in this somewhat equivocal and indeterminate state, we can hardly escape the necessity for flexibility as we handle the relationships of the ministers with both king and parliament. If there were no other constitutional issue under the early Hanoverians here was one which was ready-made or at least latent in the actual situation of things; and signs of it do in fact appear at an early date. For ministers are not mere counters, mere passive subjects of a prescribed set of relationships. Even when government is completely despotic or theoretically democratic, ministers—by the very nature of things—are almost bound to be playing for power.

There is considerable evidence in favour of the view that the fall of Townshend and Walpole in 1717 was connected with disputes with the king about actual policy. At an early stage in the crisis these men were prepared to base their argument on the difficulty they would have in winning the support of parliament for the measures they disliked. According to Coxe, Walpole complained to George I that if he continued in office he would have to answer to King and Country for policies of which he might not be the author and might not personally approve. His colleagues, he said, would propose to him "such things that if I agree to support them my credit and reputation will be lost and if I disapprove or oppose them I must forfeit Your Majesty's favour". In the House of Commons he claimed that, "for his own part, if he would have complied with some measures, it had not been in the power of any one of the present ministers to remove him". It was Stanhope who in this period insisted rather on the voice that the king must have in matters of policy, and, at the close of 1716, declared that he could not, like Walpole, think of resigning in order to compel George I to have Townshend as Secretary of State.

Owing to the dynastic combinations and complexities of Europe it was often in diplomacy—though diplomacy was so regal a function—that the tension between Court and Country, Closet and Ministry, occurred in the period after 1714. And, curiously enough, it occurred amongst governments not even hampered by the British parliamentary system; for, within France and even Spain, there were conflicts of policy—leading to "secret diplomacy" or the "double diplomatic system"—the interests of the dynasty being so clearly separable from those of the state as such. Under the first two Georges, Englishmen showed themselves jealous of Hanoverian policy and Hanoverian advisers, or they would resent the influence which at one moment a Stanhope, at another moment a Carteret, might possess at the side of the king. Even amongst the people who were sharing in the government of the country the distinction between the Hanoverian and the British, the dynastic policy and the national policy, the Closet and the Ministry, was familiar before 1760. Since the issue occurred, though perhaps in a peculiar form, in a monarchical country like France, where a king could differ from his ministers and even set out to cheat them, we must not allow any literalistic interpretation of the theory of monarchy to seduce us into believing that the constitutional difficulty was not a real one. Here was an issue that might well have arisen in one form or another if there had never been a revolution of 1688.

A British monarch might have an undoubted constitutional right to adopt a certain course of action—to choose his own ministers, for example, or even to listen to the advice of men who would not be responsible for that advice to the House of Commons. We are still not allowed to assume that it was unconstitutional for men to oppose him politically in any particular exercise that he might make of such a right. A man could of course reject ministerial office for no other reason than that an enemy of his was granted (or a friend of his was refused) a place in the same administration. Similarly, there was nothing to prevent ministers from combining to secure that a king himself should not be allowed to have his way, or that the man whose recommendations found favour in the Closet should be forced to come forward and face the music, making himself responsible for the placating of parliament too. It is almost impossible to imagine that the men who had the duty of rendering policy palatable to the House of Commons should have failed to exploit the potentialities of the interesting dual situation in which they stood. They were servants of the king, but it was possible that much of their strength, much of their influence with the king himself, would be due to their weight in the country or their management and debating-skill in the House of Commons. Here was one of those regions where a living and developing constitution must not be regarded as being closed—where indeed room was left for what the political historian must accept as a legitimate competition for power. To suggest that ministers ought to have been too loyal to play such a political game with their king would be tantamount to the thesis that the eighteenth-century constitution ought to have remained frozen in its strongly monarchical form. The opposition "Whigs" and the Whig historians were wrong if they asserted that the Hanoverian kings were trying to be "unconstitutional". But let us keep our flexibility of mind—Walpole in 1717 and Pelham in 1746 are not to be condemned as "unconstitutional" either. The British political system tended to develop partly through the agency of people who insisted that the king was breaking rules now recognised by the historian not to have been established rules at the time—things which were rules only for a section of the country who interpreted the existing situation in the light of the system they wanted to achieve. We must not dismiss from our mind the possibility that in certain fields (in respect of certain aspects of the responsibility of ministers, for example) men might raise as a constitutional issue something which had never been a constitutional issue before. The future might decide whether the raising of such an issue were a justifiable thing, and in rare cases of this kind (though perhaps not usually) the future may fairly have its part in the judgment that we make of the past. And though the people concerned might have been moved by private aggressiveness or by vested interests, some merit may attach to a political party which manages to link its private purposes with what may prove in the long run to have been a public cause.

If we recognise that in 1760 "the mixed form of government" already provided a constitutional issue which—to say the least—was latent in the situation itself, it is easy to understand how the early conduct of George III would tend to bring that issue out into the open. A controversy soon came to be centred upon the question of the way in which the king should choose his ministers, and, though many things were said on both sides of the question—though also the controversy itself may have been fed by the spirit of faction—it is important that we should not dismiss the issue as an illegitimate one, or even pretend that if it was illegitimate it was non-existent. Even the outcry against the Favourite involves certain issues which make it part of the same essential controversy. When the Duke of Newcastle opposed the peace-treaty with France in 1762, the *Annual Register* regarded his conduct as open to criticism because it was so clear that he himself, when in power, had been anxious for a treaty of the same kind. But the *Annual Register* (see p. 49 above) did not say that it was illegitimate to question George III's use of his prerogative in the appointment of Bute as the head of the ministry. It was prepared to discuss the claim that the prerogatives of the Crown were too dangerous unless they could be rescued from possible abuse and brought to operate through constitutional channels. It gave its verdict in favour of the king, as we have seen, but it did not argue that the issue itself was one which ought not to have been raised. Indeed, in the reign of George III—and even amongst those people who were on his side against the Whigs—there were some who regarded the appointment of Bute as questionable. They argued that the king should have chosen his minister from amongst those who had qualified for his confidence by public service—he should not have promoted a man merely out of private favour.

It may be true that, at the time, each of the parties to such political conflicts would charge the other with a breach of constitutional principles. The fluidities and the ambiguities were such, however, that we need not follow either of them, though it is necessary that we should concede to both of them the effort of historical understanding. It may even be true that one of the parties was formally right—right on a legalistic view of the question—and yet that to leave the matter here would be to assume that neither party had the right to try to carry the constitution one way rather than another.

It is not clear that the Namier school are willing to recognise the fact that the early policy of George III—even if it involved nothing more than the appointment of Bute—brought to the surface a constitutional issue of the greatest importance. And if it is asserted that the constitutional issue was not a genuine one, because it was in a certain sense a novel one, the argument appears to overlook the fact that our constitution could only progress through the emergence at successive stages of novel issues. The ultimate decision of the point of constitutional principle would simply depend on whether George III succeeded in what he was attempting—whether he "pulled it off"—or the views of his enemies prevailed in the long run. There is a sense in which it does not matter if the opposition tended to assert that the king was behaving unconstitutionally, when in reality he was doing nothing of the kind. The opposition were in fact following the customary technique, though it might be true that they would have expressed the case more accurately if they had avowed it as their determination rather to secure that such conduct should be regarded as unconstitutional in future. All this is liable to happen in any period of English history. And it is perhaps this which helps to decide the direction in which the constitution will in fact move at the next stage in the story.

In his *England in the Age of the American Revolution* (p. 63), Professor Namier wrote that "the situation of George III on his accession differed from that of his predecessors in that he was young and had no competing heir". As we have seen (pp. 174–5 above), von Ruville in 1905 had stated the unobjectionable thesis that George III's "chief advantage . . . over his immediate predecessors" was this absence of a competing heir. Mr. Romney Sedgwick in his *Letters from George III to Lord Bute* (p. xvi) quotes the words of Hardwicke in 1761: "There is now no *reversionary* resource . . . a healthy young King and no successor in view". He boldly carries the argument a stage further and says of Hardwicke's remark:

> There is nothing to add to this explanation of that so-called "break in the smooth development of our constitutional history" which, according to the familiar legend was due to "the able attempt of George III to recover the powers of the Crown".

In other words we are asked to ignore the fact that the appointment of Bute and "the language of the court" had provoked the kind of constitutional issue that is described in the *Annual Register*. We are asked to accept the absence of a "reversionary interest" as the sole and sufficient cause of the political turmoils in Great Britain after the accession of George III. Even if there were no evidence for the alternative view, it is difficult to see any scientific basis for the exaggeration and the twist which Mr. Sedgwick has given to a thesis hitherto stated in unobjectionable terms.

13. The Rockingham Party and the Position of Ministers

WE MIGHT expect that Horace Walpole, in his *Memoirs of the Reign of George III*, would deal with the politics of the time at the level of mere narration, providing anecdote and gossip, but, where more serious issues are concerned, adding only partisan comment or records of his personal reactions. Precisely because it is natural to regard him as a light-weight, and as a sort of bantam-cock in an era of important history-making, Walpole has a way of surprising us to attention at times, however; and there are moments when he seems to take a look at the structure of things, and to write as a more serious historian. When his *Memoirs* reach the spring of 1765 (Vol. II, p. 66) he gives us an account of what was happening to political parties in that period, and comes nearer to the kind of analysis that we require than Adolphus or Croker, or any historian before the beginning of the twentieth century. The passage appears to be so important that one who has done no particular research at this point in the story must feel hesitant about giving an opinion upon it until no less a person than Sir Lewis Namier himself—for possibly not even a disciple would serve in such a case—has given us his final analysis and commentary. For, those of us who will not undertake always to agree with Sir Lewis Namier at the end of the argument will recognise the value not only of the materials but also of the diagnosis which he can provide on such occasions as this.

Horace Walpole begins by telling us that, after the recess of April 1765, "a very new scene opened to the public, though unfolded by degrees, and of which all the springs were not at first discovered". The mutual jealousy of Bute and Grenville

gave birth to the various and fluctuating exhibition[s] of politics that took place and succeeded one another from this period. In truth this was the era of faction, though it did not immediately predominate. Hitherto it might be said that the two parties of Whig and Tory still subsisted, though Jacobitism, the concealed mother of the latter was extinct.

The court, he says, had "admitted few Tories into place, from their total want of abilities". Bute, however, "had left the standard of prerogative in the Court, and his successors had relaxed none of those high-flown doctrines". So far as the existing government was concerned, it was true that George Grenville and the Duke of Bedford "had always called themselves Whigs", but "nothing could be more despotic than Grenville's nature" and Bedford was ready to betray his principles in order to pander to the Duchess's love of power. The cabinet was "so framed to embrace boldly any arbitrary measures", and Lord Mansfield, who was "always ready to suggest" them, retained great weight in the government. Here, as on so many occasions, Horace Walpole makes the excessive attachment to the prerogative and the love of "arbitrary measures" the essential political test. These things were clearly to him the negation of Whiggism, even if he found them in men who retained the conventional name of "Whig". He is explaining in fact, that, though so few of the Tories had been admitted into place, men who still called themselves Whigs had gone over to what he regarded as Tory ideas of government. In this sense he tells us (p. 67 n.) that Lord North, from 1770, was a Tory, following "the Court's system of prerogative". A Whig, in other words, was not merely a supporter of the Revolution of 1688—in which sense George III and Lord North were undoubtedly "Whigs". A Whig, to Horace Walpole, was the enemy of prerogative doctrine and governmental high-handedness. He tells us, further, at this point in the story, that henceforward, the term Whig was an appellation not exactly "disclaimed", but "rather dropped" (i.e. abandoned) by the court.

Although one must never make an easy surrender to Horace Walpole, especially as some of his angers and indignations were retrospective in the way that has already been discussed, I am not convinced that he is entirely wrong in his assertions about the prevalence of prerogative prejudices, or his repeated reference to "a change in the language of the court" after the accession of George III. I am ready to be converted on this subject, but in some of the letters and some of the propaganda of these years (leaving aside the evidence to be found in the replies of the opposition) there are points of language and tone which seem to me not to have been explained away. And the analyses of the Namier school do not really go to the point that is at issue in a subject of this kind. Authoritative assertion is not enough; and Walpole's accounts are not to be dismissed until the evidence has been marshalled, and the answer worked out, in a scientific manner.

What Walpole has to say about the opposition at this point of the story is, however, the topic that concerns us here. Newcastle, he says, "had sailed with every current", and his party was "composed of great and proud families". All the same, he says:

the Opposition . . . dated from the stand they had made, or by resentment had been forced to make, to the Favourite's plan of extending the prerogative.

Lord Temple, on the other hand, depended on popularity; "and the cast of Mr. Pitt's life, contrary to his temper, had thrown him too on the affections of the people". Concerning these opposition parties, Walpole says, however:

The crisis I am going to describe [the crisis over the Regency Bill and the subsequent fate of the Grenville ministry] broke these ill-consolidated connections into factions. . . . The subsequent contests were rather a struggle for power than the settled animosity of the two parties, though the body of Opposition [and here, perhaps, he may mean, as he certainly means sometimes, the party of Newcastle and Rockingham] still called itself Whig.

Even in the epoch of pure faction, however, he says that "one of those factions adhered more steadily to their professions than the rest". And here he is certainly referring to the party under the leadership of Newcastle and Rockingham.

In spite of the great defeat which the Duke of Newcastle had suffered at the hands of Bute, and in spite of losses sustained when members of the party adhered to the Chatham ministry of 1766, it must be remembered that the connexion which still arrogated to itself the name of "Whig" retained in the days of Rockingham a considerable weight and an imposing appearance. Even in the mere point of numbers it stands by itself amongst the political factions; and if in 1767 more than 200 members of the House of Commons were attached to the administration as such, the Rockinghams could claim 100 or 120, while the Bedfords might be numbered at 35 and the Grenvilles at 17. If the Bedfords and the Grenvilles were in one sense somewhat like a clan or a dynastic system, the Rockinghams would have to be regarded as rather a league between the heads of clans—still a confederacy of great families. Even at the time of the French Revolution they continue to be conscious of their political weight as an aristocracy; Burke reminds them that he had always regarded them as an aristocratic party, "connected with the permanent, long-possessed property of the country". When Horace Walpole tells us that the Rockinghams "adhered more steadily to their professions than the rest", we must not be too contemptuous of his judgment, in spite of the anomalies and inconsistencies which always characterised the politics of those days. There may be a sense in which, if we examine events at a certain level, everything may seem capable of reduction to the phenomena of purely factional politics. We may take this as our basis, but still another film superimposes itself upon the old one; the Rockinghams remember that they are "the Whigs", and the traditions of the older kind of party-politics still hang over the story and have their effect on men's minds. It is not even quite true to say that the world had to wait until the American controversy before these "Whigs" could find a cause of any consistency to sustain. In his *England in the Age of the American Revolution* (p. 401) Professor Namier, after describing the failure of Bute's attempt to bring Newcastle back into the ministry, says that "popular passion and prejudice were threatening to overwhelm the King's favourite", and that Newcastle "talked about the need to free the nation of 'the Scotch Minister'". Professor Namier complains that the Duke had previously "recognised the King's right to choose his own advisers and condemned all attempts to force 'the closet'". But the later works of even the Namier school seem to recognise that the conventional nature of this language—and the political inconsistency here in question—are evidenced in many politicians throughout a considerable period. The Rockingham ministry of 1765–6 was condemned at the time, and is reproached by the Namier School, because, in its refusal to make any compromise with the party of Bute, it rejected the opportunity to strengthen itself, and so justified its dismissal. Its conduct may have been unwise, in a sense, but this repeated intransigeance on the subject of Bute enabled the party of Newcastle, and then of Rockingham, to build up a certain consistency of attitude. As Walpole said (p. 263, above), "the Opposition . . . dated from the stand they had made . . . to the Favourite". That "Opposition" recognised, as congenial to Whiggism, the very issue presented by what Professor Namier called the king's "right to choose" his ministers, as his "instruments".

There can hardly be any doubt that one of the factors which most decisively influenced the historiography of George III's reign—and particularly the development of a hostile interpretation of that King's policy—was the evidence which accumulated in the 1840's and 1850's on the subject of the downfall of the Rockingham ministry in 1766. This is one of the topics on which the account in Horace Walpole's *Memoirs* was particularly detailed and impressive, and was supported at critical points by documents in the *Rockingham Memoirs*. Mr. Brooke, at the opening of *The Chatham Administration*, does nothing to undo the effect of this evidence; for, if he attributes the fall of Rockingham to his weakness, he does not in any way confront the argument that the King and the court party were responsible for a good deal of that weakness. Adolphus wrote in 1802 that "it ill became the Rockingham administration to attribute their loss of power to a cabal, a double cabinet, or a closet junto". He quotes General Conway —who served in the Rockingham ministry and then stayed on in the next one—as having declared that "he neither knew, saw or felt a secret influence". Adolphus admits, however, that the "expulsion" of the Rockinghamites was an act "no less ungracious than sudden". And it might be argued that the Rockinghamites would have had to be extraordinarily stupid if they had learned no political lesson—extraordinarily charitable if they had not set out to make political capital for themselves—from the treatment they received on this occasion.

Lord Brougham, amongst others, inferred from the correspondence of George III that this King could show an extraordinary fidelity to the ministry of the day. Many years ago, I personally recorded my impression that George particularly needed what he called a "Confidential Minister" in whom he could repose his trust; and that even if, for some special reason, such a minister might fail him, he was the kind of person who still constantly felt himself to be in need of political advice. It has sometimes been the custom to assert that he favoured a kind of "departmental" system of government—each of the ministers reporting personally to him, so that he would be his own Prime Minister—himself the only coordinating authority. But in 1766 he set his hopes on an administration in which Chatham was to have been the superintending leader, virtually without the burden of departmental duties. The most interesting experiment he ever made—and the one to which he seems to have been most greatly attached in this part of his reign—was the one in which it would appear that Chatham was to have had a particularly presidential position as Prime Minister. There is much to be said for the view that if the "departmental" system existed in the 1770's this was not by the wish of George III but was rather due to a certain indolence or weakness in Lord North. North, indeed, would say on occasion that he accepted responsibility only for his own department, and he once made it a virtue not to have interfered in the departments of his colleagues. Grafton, however, had accepted the Treasury in 1766 on the condition that he should treat the office as a purely departmental one, and that Chatham should be the effective leader of the ministry. When Chatham proved to be almost totally inactive Grafton made no serious attempt to take over the role of chief. A "departmental" system would appear to have been simply the automatic result of this defect in the supreme authority; and North had not the energy, the ambition or the confidence quite to rectify the system that he inherited on Grafton's fall. In fact, North's colleagues, and even the King's Friends, as well as the King himself, desired to see North exercising a more effective authority in the administration.

The fate of the Rockingham ministry of 1765–6 is a very different matter, however. Mr. Brooke's argument that this administration fell as a result of its own weakness contains a truth that has often been ignored; but the story is a remarkable one, and requires that we keep our critical faculties awake. On 22nd April, 1766, Horace Walpole (as he tells us in his *Memoirs*) returned from abroad to find that "Mr. Pitt was grown impatient for power". Two days later, Pitt, just before leaving for the west country, made in the House of Commons a statement which George III, in the subsequent period, seemed determined not to allow him to forsake or to forget. He gave it to be understood that, if he was ever called upon to form an administration, he would construct it without reference to the political connexions of its members. He refused to negotiate with the existing ministry of the Rockinghamites, and Walpole tells us that George III was unwilling to see him allied with the ministers because he did not wish the latter to have the merit or the advantage of his return to office. Whether Walpole is right or not, it is necessary to apply criticism to those letters in which George III expresses his anxiety that Lord Rockingham shall continue in his service; for, in some of those very letters, he shows his hostility to the ministry; he explicitly says that it is his purpose to gain time; he realises that if he acts over-hastily he may become the prisoner of another political group, or may have to submit to the continuance of the Rockinghamites on terms less satisfactory than the existing ones. He is also anxious to make sure that the elevation of Pitt shall not commit him to the admission of the hated Grenville to office.

The crux of the whole problem is really the question of the relations of the ministry and the King, respectively, with the party which in those days was regarded as belonging to Bute. Horace Walpole, who was capable of asserting a true thing and then adding a malicious innuendo, talked of "Lord Bute's faction giving no support (to the ministry); and the court discouraging all men from joining the administration". And on this subject he writes further:

> The King was not only in opposition to himself, [but] had connived at Lord Bute's seducing such of his servants as were connected with that Favourite to vote against the measures of Government, and, in truth, those servants were some of the ablest men in the House of Commons, as Elliot, Dyson, Martin and Jenkinson, besides Sir Fletcher Norton.

According to Walpole, the Duke of Grafton once quoted a promise by George III to the effect that Bute's faction, though it would not co-operate in the repeal of the Stamp Act, would "support the administration" after that business had been settled.

If this was the case, the promise was not kept, and it is not clear that it was quite out of the power of the King to secure its fulfilment. When the Rockinghamites desired that some members of the Bute faction should lose their places because of their opposition to government, George III refused to comply with their request, partly perhaps because the ministry was so weak and partly because there was a hope of replacing it. Walpole tells us further that men were unwilling to accept office under Lord Rockingham, "being discouraged by the discountenance with which the King treated his ministers". The *Rockingham Memoirs* make the same point, and print a curious refusal by Lord North to take an office which he had apparently been disposed on the previous day to accept.

That is only one side of the question, however; for even the friends of the Rockingham ministry had complained of its inability to secure an alliance with one group or another. Horace Walpole himself criticises the Rockinghamites for being so intransigeant in respect of the Bute faction—he manages in fact to blame the latter party for the way they demanded places, and the ministry for the way they refused them. Even Lord Hardwicke expressed the view that "by his want of management for Lord Bute, he (Lord Rockingham) had lost his interest at court". Pitt was to be wiser in regard to this matter for, according to Walpole, he took the line that "Lord Bute had been too much proscribed". It would appear that this was at least one of the crucial issues; and it became notorious that on this point Pitt's policy differed from Rockingham's—Adolphus says that he came to be "decried for crouching to Lord Bute". Lord Chesterfield, in his *Letters to his Son*, says of Pitt, "qu'il aura mis de l'eau dans son vin par rapport à my Lord Bute". He thinks that the result of this compliance will mean a loss of popularity for Pitt.

Unless the narrative is altered more radically than it has been altered in the brief sketch by Mr. Brooke, here is an issue posed and poised about as beautifully and delicately as any problem in modern constitutional history. The detailed story would provide us with an admirable critique of Horace Walpole, who sometimes shows correct knowledge of the contents of letters that passed between other people. Whatever changes modern research may bring to the narrative, nothing can alter the importance of this episode in the subsequent story, the significance of this experience in the future thinking of the Rockinghamites. Nothing can alter the part which the fate of the Rockinghamite ministry has played in the development of the historiography of the reign. On the one side we can sympathise with George III, confronted by a ministry distasteful and weak—criticised by its friends for being unwise even in respect of its own interests. From the Rockinghamite point of view, here were the King, the Earl of Bute and a court party who, to all appearances, set out to thwart and then to destroy the ministry of the day. We today would not say that George III behaved in an unconstitutional manner; but first the Whig historians and then their enemies have been too concerned with what is constitutional in this sense, when we ought rather to be considering what is politic. If the Rockinghamites were worth their salt as politicians they were bound to exploit the anomalies that the story of their downfall made so patent. Only the fact that they were succeeded by a Chatham, who desired to break political connexions and began by attracting some of the members of the Rockinghamite government, was needed to complete the main ingredients of Burke's *Thoughts on the Cause of the Present Discontents*. And the memory of this episode clearly affected the future attitude of the party to the question of the relations between ministry and king. Whatever the rights and the wrongs of the case, here was an issue to be raised.

*   *   *

Since the time of Croker at least, it has been argued that the absence of great political issues during much of the eighteenth century caused parties to degenerate into mere factions. It is a question whether we ought not to consider the inversion of this and entertain the possibility that the prevalence of faction prevented politics from being envisaged in a broader manner, and helped to conceal the constitutional issue that was there all the time. I do not know whether it is by accident—or whether, perhaps, it is not an optical illusion—that the Namier school, in "Monarchy and the Party System" (as well as in more recent works) has been returning to a more central tradition. There now appears to be a greater readiness to discount the formal doctrine which suggested that it was illegitimate to attempt to force the hands of the king. In any case, once it is admitted that the achievement of the modern party system had the effect of edging the king out of the political arena and producing the modern form of constitutional monarchy, we must recognise the fact that in the eighteenth century the production of more inadequate forms of political combination—imperfect forms of party—was calculated to operate at least somewhat in the same direction. Furthermore, we must not accept too easily the view that the history of party only begins in the reign of George III, especially as there existed before 1760 the complaint that party had been allowed to degenerate into faction. It would be better to say that both theorists and practical politicians—both Bolingbroke and Walpole, both Newcastle and Burke—were seeking their way to something which should at least be the equivalent to the modern idea of party. Sometimes even the men who were crying out against party were groping rather towards a more rational idea of party. Bolingbroke himself—who wrote so much in his capacity as the builder of an opposition party—would seem to have been doing this on occasion.

Sir Lewis Namier tells us, in "Monarchy and the Party System" (p. 12), that "in the earlier stages the growth of constitutional monarchy was impeded rather than aided by conscious political thought", which, he says, resisted the idea of prime ministers and parties. His suggestion is both striking and novel, and it is important that one should recognise its validity; though it still remains true that thought must be introduced to undermine the conservatism of men's thinking—the enemies of both prime ministers and parties would open their eyes when events gave them something new to think about. Sir Lewis Namier makes a point equally interesting when he goes on to say (p. 37) that "parliamentary government based on the party system is not an ingenious device, the product of creative thought, for which credit is due to one set of men". This further thesis certainly embodies an interesting truth; but it would be a mistake to allow it to blind us to the great amount of thought and experiment which the eighteenth century gave to the problem of party. Since Sir Lewis Namier recognises how far the requisite conditions for the emergence of the modern form of party were absent during this period of our history, we must marvel to discover to what a degree the eighteenth century is found repeatedly aspiring to an adequate idea of party. George III on the one hand was hostile to such forms of political combination, while the Rockinghamites on the other hand quickly advanced to the recognition of party as a matter of principle. Those historians who have said that the rise of party is the key to the emergence of modern constitutionalism must make it clear why they pay so little attention to the avowed principles of the connexion associated with Newcastle and Rockingham.

If a constitutional issue existed, or if it were only latent in the structure of "the mixed form of government", there is something to be said for those followers of Newcastle and then of Rockingham who, so early in the day, succeeded in seizing upon what were to be the essential aspects of it. These men may have been factious; they may have been desirous of a return to power—though clearly they had no intention of merely returning at any price. This kind of motive can always be imputed to an opposition; for those in opposition will undoubtedly be seeking to lay hold on power. But we must ask whether the Rockinghamites found a public cause with which to cover and excuse their desire for power, a cause by means of which they might further hope to achieve a primary object, namely, the capture of independent votes. In seizing upon the appointment of Bute, the question of closet influence and the whole problem of the relations between party, ministry and king, these men would seem to have put their fingers on the strategic issue. They showed a sense—though perhaps an imperfect sense—of the long-term needs of the country, the needs that the future was going to make plain. It is not clear that our constitution would have developed quite so satisfactorily as it has done if George III had been allowed simply to proceed unopposed. Those of us who have been enemies of the Whig interpretation all our lives, and have deplored the injustice done to George III, will not necessarily follow a form of historiography which lacks the breadth to comprise the higher purposes of the Rockinghamites—an historiography which seems to reduce the programme of this party to a mere device of eighteenth-century faction.

By 1770 Edmund Burke had set out the essential principle in his *Thoughts on the Cause of the Present Discontents*:

> The discretionary powers which are necessarily vested in the monarch, whether for the execution of the laws, or for the nomination to magistracy and office, or for conducting the affairs of peace and war, or for ordering the revenue, should all be exercised upon publick principles and national grounds, and not on the likings or prejudices, the intrigues or policies, of a court. [*Works* (1803) Vol. II, p. 260].

This was the answer to the appointment of Bute and the conduct of Bute's friends during the Rockingham ministry of 1765–6. These men suffered some injustice no doubt; but if they have a

S   273

place in our general history it is because they produced this reaction. In *George III and the Politicians*, p. 109, Professor Pares shows that, in the period 1765–6, "Rockingham was already claiming, by implication, that the King was to put his personal influence and connexions unreservedly at the disposal of his official servants". He talks of "the conception of ministerial responsibility which Newcastle and Rockingham were trying to build up", and suggests that this helps to explain "the disproportionate attention which the politicians and the public paid to Bute for nearly a decade". In his *Thoughts on the Cause of the Present Discontents* (pp. 259–60) Burke already gives his answer to the mere legalism which insisted on the King's right to appoint anybody he liked as minister. He writes:

> The discretionary power of the crown in the formation of ministry, abused by bad or weak men, has given rise to a system, which, *without violating any law* [my italics], operates against the spirit of the whole constitution.

If some men had not been prepared to argue in this way (even though it might have meant stretching a point) we must wonder what the future of the constitution would have been. And, this being the case, even a Whig historiography in decline will hardly allow itself to be knocked off its perch by Presbyterian literalists and counters of heads who talk about the king's right to choose his own ministers, and the "almost unconstitutional" crime of resisting the king's choice. It is not proper for anybody to stress these latter points unless he balances them with their significant counter-weight—namely, the fact that throughout the eighteenth century the right to oppose the king's choice of ministers was incessantly exercised by members of parliament, ex-ministers and political groups.

14. Closet Activity

IN THE earliest months of George III's reign it might be the most natural thing in the world for the King to place special reliance on the advice of the Earl of Bute. It would be the most natural thing in the world for the leading ministers to resent this, however; and their attitude to the whole affair would no doubt depend to a considerable degree on their mutual confidence, their relations with one another. A Scotsman might even seem only less objectionable than a Hanoverian; and in any case the opening had long ago been given for making a distinction between the Closet and the Ministry. It is not surprising that, after the fall of the actual ministry of Bute, both George Grenville and the Marquis of Rockingham—however unskilful they may have been on this subject—should have shown considerable jealousy of the influence which Bute might still go on possessing in the Closet. What is surprising is the fact that, from the time of Adolphus, so much of the more serious historiography of the subject denied that Bute continued to have any influence at all after his resignation. In fact, it should be noted that the writers who adopted this view of the matter turned out to be wrong, and Bute did continue to have political relations with George III until the year 1765. Indeed, in spite of the promise which the King had made to Lord Rockingham, some significant exchanges occurred even in 1766. In the intermediate stage at which the government of this country stood in this period, it should not be assumed that there was anything unconstitutional in the contacts that took place, any more than there was anything unconstitutional in the attempt to put a stop to them. But, given the difficulty of learning the truth about such a matter, the fact that the contacts did continue at all after 1763 will surely excuse a little those historians who went on refusing to believe that they ceased on the resignation of Bute. It must excuse even those historians who suspected that the political contacts went on longer than they actually did. When they denied that Bute had exercised influence in the Closet for any considerable period after his resignation, historians like Adolphus did not say that such a thing would have been "unconstitutional"; but they wrote as though they knew that it would have been felt to be offensive if it had actually occurred.

Granted the intermediate state in which the constitution stood in the eighteenth century, the question of "Closet influence" was bound to produce difficulties and tensions like those which arose from the dual position of ministers. It was legitimate to stress the monarchical aspect of government; but it could be argued that the men who enjoyed the ear of the king should be responsible to parliament for the advice they submitted to him. And the men who tried to develop the implications of this latter principle were not unconstitutional in their attempt to limit the king, though everything might depend on whether they could "pull the thing off". They were interpreting the compound system, "the mixed form of government"—or perhaps they were trying to develop it—in an understandable way. The problem had arisen before George III came to the throne, though the position of Bute, both before and after 1763, was calculated to make the issue more pointed, and events made the conflict more bitter. Historiography during the last fifty years has been trying to do justice to the monarchical character of the eighteenth-century constitution, and we should no longer accept the testimony and the verdict of the Whigs on the subject of George III. The modern teaching, however, ought not to make us lose sight of the fact that some emphasis might legitimately be placed on the implications of the other aspect of the "mixed form of government". The men who opposed George III—like the men who at times had similarly opposed George II—must at least not be regarded as entirely devoid of intellectual system. The question of "Closet influence" is closely related to the question of the king's prerogative in the choice of his servants, and to the question of the position and role of ministers, so that men's ideas on these topics tended to form a consistent whole. Sometimes the opposition anticipated the language of modern constitutional government to such a degree that historians were once tempted to ante-date the rise of the modern form of constitutionalism. Historians have had to learn that the language of some of the eighteenth-century Whigs requires to be interpreted in the context of the *ancien régime*.

George III would choose certain people in his confidence, and would ask their advice about the state of the government, the possibilities of change, or the way in which the Prime Minister ought to be treated. In the closing months of Lord Rockingham's administration, for example, we find him consulting Lord Egmont, who was in office, the Earl of Bute, who was out of office, and Lord Northington, who held the Great Seal. He would use Lord Egmont to negotiate on behalf of the Closet with Rockingham; he would ask Lord Northington whether he ought to grant Rockingham's request for the dismissal of the recalcitrant followers of Bute. At the end of the year 1779 his communications with Charles Jenkinson on the subject of the ministry of Lord North are very remarkable indeed, since the intimacy and confidence appear more close than that which he had with Lord North himself. These communications, however, were conducted primarily for the purpose of saving the administration.

In the year 1777 George III began a regular secret correspondence with John Robinson, who was Secretary to the Treasury and Lord North's right-hand man. The real intention was to assist the Chief Minister, but considerable nervousness was shown if Lord North stumbled upon evidence of these communications. The two correspondents were clearly aware of the displeasure it would give him. Robinson was commissioned, furthermore, to write secretly to Charles Jenkinson, whose influence with the King was out of all relation to his official position. In the time of Lord North, therefore, one is struck by the amount of underground activity that was taking place; though the intention was benevolent enough, and the processes which produced this result are understandable ones. Much of the underground activity was intended to rescue North from intriguers at times when he himself was weak, or when he found the situation over-facing. The King would use Robinson in order to bring the Chief Minister to a decision which all the world was waiting for, or to press upon him a policy that had been initially his own. Alternatively, it would be Robinson who would send to George III a cry of alarm —would declare that the ministry was in danger and that all would be lost unless the King intervened. The emergency interventions easily turned into a regular and continuous system, however, particularly at the time when the Chief Minister was weak and depressed. The attempt to save Lord North was of the kind which could slide imperceptibly into an attempt to save him from himself. It could be argued that his "weak Mind requires Support", and this might mean that he would be pressed to take a kind of action to which he was not quite reconciled. Trouble would occur on occasion when North suspected that Robinson might be speaking to him under instructions from the Closet. At times the King would have to be told that North suspected "some Trick in the Closet". Robinson even reports to George III that his chief had been concealing things from the Closet. And on one occasion the discovery of this underground activity drove North to a bitter complaint about "the disgraceful footing" on which he stood. The Rockinghamites, therefore, were not the only people who complained about these secret communications and this Closet activity. The intention here was to strengthen an administration in which the King was presumed to be more than a sleeping partner. But "the mixed form of government" had its strains and tensions; North felt them; and North was held to be a man who would air his little grievances in private conversation.

It is not surprising that a great parliamentary attack on this system should have occurred towards the end of the year 1779—a time when the secret activity of Robinson, Jenkinson and others had been multiplied because of the distresses and the paralysis of North. More surprising, perhaps, is the fact that a further secret correspondence of a somewhat parallel kind was taking place at this very time between Dublin and Westminster. Once again, John Robinson in London was the principal agent, and once again the communications were brought, at least on occasion, under the eye of the King. This time it was the Lord Lieutenant, the Earl of Buckinghamshire, who bitterly complained of what he knew was going on behind his back. Curiously enough there occurred a third form of secret activity in this period, and from the debates at the close of the year 1779 one may even wonder whether it had not come to the knowledge of the opposition leaders. As a great crisis was developing in Ireland, Charles Jenkinson—though the matter was not by any means in his department—had undertaken the task of studying the critical problem of Irish trade and examining some important materials that had been sent from Dublin. We know that he had accepted the work most unwillingly and purely in order to make good the terrible defects in the ministry itself. We know also that he had insisted on strict secrecy because he was aware that his intervention in the Irish business would be calculated to raise an outcry against him. Indeed, there was a moment in August when he withdrew his undertaking to carry out the task, because the secret had not been kept; and only when disaster seemed actually imminent in the following October did he consent to intervene again. In November the opposition were crying out that "ministers were no longer responsible", that they were "under the guidance of secret advice . . . of the most hateful and pernicious kind". So far as the Irish question was concerned, the intervention of Jenkinson occurred in a manner that makes it easily understandable; though it involved anomalies that make it not quite comparable to the activity of a civil service official.

This is not the end of the matter, however. It is not clear that Lord North, if left to himself, would not have been more generous in his policies than the influences around him actually permitted him to be. In regard to the Irish question in the autumn of 1779, for example, it was suspected that he wished to be more liberal but was restrained by the influence of men like Robinson and Jenkinson. At the end of the year, when the Irish upheaval had had the effect of breaking down the barriers in Great Britain, Lord North seemed to show a curious exhilaration, and his spirit seemed to expand as he announced generous concessions to Irish trade. Even George III wrote a famous letter to North which seems to confirm the view that the Chief Minister did not really put his heart into the American War. On this issue it was sometimes alleged that North's private utterances were at variance with his public policy. And if all this is true, the point is not to be overlooked in any discussion of the role of the Chief Minister or the operation of the monarchy itself in the reign of George III. George's requirement that any man who was appointed to the ministry must be resolved to "keep the Empire entire" may be understandable, but once again it must not be dismissed as insignificant. Lord North's long retention of office is a more difficult matter still, particularly in the light of the things he said and the unwillingness he showed.

When the policy of George III's reign is clearly open to criticism, the Namier school, like Croker, take refuge in the doctrine of constitutionalism and the responsibility of ministers, and in this they may be sometimes right. But they are the people who have set out to remind us of the monarchical character which eighteenth-century government still maintained, and to show that the King was not intended to be merely a sleeping-partner. It is admitted that at a much later stage in our history the monarch retained a considerable influence, which could be exerted in genuine discussions of policy. It requires to be proved that George III had no partnership, for example, in such errors as those which were involved in the handling of Wilkes. Decades later he had his own policy in regard to Roman Catholics and was able to hold his ground on this issue against Pitt. It is not at all clear that North would not have shown a higher statesmanship but for the fact that he was constricted by the influence of men like Robinson, Jenkinson and George III. The Whig historians were prepared to concede George's merits in respect of the routine of kingship and the more mechanical side of public business. They denied that he possessed the qualities of a states-man; and the Namier school are in entire agreement with this.

Finally we must not forget that, if George III behaved in a constitutional manner, he showed signs of a certain recalcitrancy. On occasion he looked back with nostalgia to an earlier period in the history of the monarchy. In February 1779 we find him writing: "I am convinced this Country will never regain a proper tone unless Ministers as in the reign of King William will not mind being now and then in a Minority, particularly on subjects that have always carried some weight with popular Opinions". In March 1782 he seems to have shown an unwillingness to submit to the verdict of the House of Commons; and perhaps it is not without significance that Lord North should have thought it necessary to write to him in the following terms:

> Your Majesty is well apprized that, in this country, the Prince on the Throne, cannot, with prudence, oppose the deliberate resolution of the House of Commons: Your Royal Predecessors (particularly King William the Third and his late Majesty) were obliged to yield to it much against their wish in more instances than one: They

consented to changes in their Ministry which they disapproved because they found it necessary to sacrifice their private wishes. . . . The concessions they made were never deemed dishonourable, but were considered as marks of their wisdom, and of their parental affection for their people. . . . The Parliament have altered their sentiments, and as their sentiments whether just or erroneous, must ultimately prevail, Your Majesty having persevered, as long as possible, in what You thought right, can lose no honour if you yield at length, as some of the most renowned and most glorious of your Predecessors have done, to the opinions and wishes of the House of Commons.

If it is argued that, in their attitude to the royal prerogative, to the king's choice of ministers and to the influence of the Closet, the Rockinghamites and Edmund Burke were less virtuous than they might appear to have been, since they were devising constitutional doctrine that would serve the purposes of an aristocracy, the answer is, of course, that the Rockinghamites lived in a society and a period which were still thoroughly aristocratic in structure. This represented the intermediate stage during which the country gained against the king many of the constitutional benefits which were to be the indispensable preliminaries to a more democratic form of government. If the Namier school require us to make transpositions in our minds, so that George III shall be interpreted in his proper eighteenth-century context, the same historians must not refuse to the Rockinghamites the benefit of similar transpositions and a similar effort of understanding. And, if the total victory of the Rockinghamites might have imprisoned the country in an oligarchical system, there were parallel monarchical dangers to be apprehended if George III had not been confronted by an imposing opposition. Both parties to the conflict were necessary for the production of the constitution that actually developed; and we must not write our history as though the conflict ought not to have taken place.

15. The Chatham Administration

THE CHATHAM administration was one which, in the country at large, was delineated in strong lines at the time of its formation. A few years later it received memorable characterisation in the famous speech by Edmund Burke on *American Taxation*. In the historiography of the succeeding generations it has stood out as a ministry which possessed a personality and a structure of its own. It is possible that in English history it stands unique—that no other administration has had anything like the same fame because of the peculiarity of its essential idea, its underlying purpose and its avowed structural shape.

The occasion of its establishment was an important one; for the ideas of George III and the elder Pitt had been brought together at last. Both of them hated the evils of connexion—the practice of jobbery, the formation of combines to force the hands of the king, and the idea that one should select a minister for anything save personal merit. The whole point of the plan was to choose men irrespective of their aristocratic alliances and to establish an administration on a non-party basis. Pitt himself was to be freed from departmental duties, and even from the burden of leading the House of Commons in what was expected to be a purer régime. But these burdens were to be taken away from him so that he should be able to devote himself to the higher strategies, the superintending duties—so that he should save his energies for effective leadership. He was to reign over a body of extraordinarily young men, some of whom were genuinely devoted to him, and had been longing to see him at the head of affairs. He was to be the bond of union between men who had been hand-picked, plucked out of their different parties, and chosen without regard to their political connexions. He was caricatured at the time as a monarch who towered above the ministers around him, unleashing once again the forces of his dominating personality. Lord Egmont retired, saying that "he could submit to be over-ruled by a majority in Council and hoped he was open to con-viction, but could not bear to be *dictated* to". Pitt, in fact, was to possess a superintending authority which his predecessors had never thought of—was to stand as Prime Minister *par excellence*.

One simple idea might lie at the basis of the Chatham ad-ministration; but in politics one simple idea may produce a multitude of important displacements—even George III's original idea of abolishing the distinction between Whig and Tory was one which was bound to have a host of unexpected implications in practice. And in the case of the Chatham ministry we can de-tect even a desire to exploit the implications of the original idea. A ministry formed from so many parties could be presented as a great instrument of political reconciliation, for example. We find it described as a ministry based on "a great and conciliating plan".

If the Namier school depict the Chatham administration with-out any strongly-marked character—without giving it a form which distinguishes it from its predecessors—we should have to ask ourselves in the first place whether the tradition of our his-toriography has imposed upon us a picturesque legend. In any case we must always accept the fact that in politics men's ideas become entangled in time and circumstance, so that it becomes impossible to give effect to them in their pure and unmixed form. And certainly the Chatham administration wheeled into an unex-pected course—even achieving the actual reverse of its intended character—when its leader was incapacitated and became an absentee, so that the most essential part of the machine was taken away. If, however, the work of the Namier school actually adds to the evidence previously possessed about the distinctive character of the ministry, and if that character is not merely left blurred and unportrayed but actually denied, we can hardly blind ourselves to the danger of the modern methods which produce such an atomisation of history, such a failure to see the wood for the trees. And the defect is a strategic one in the present instance, for the Namier school are concerned—only too concerned—to deny that George III had his own ideas about the government of the country. In a sense it is true to say that they answer the Whigs who charge George with prerogative doctrines, and they answer the school of Adolphus who excuse him as the would-be reformer —but they do this by what amounts to an insistence that he had no ideas at all. Yet, whatever the complications that might occur when it was put into execution, there can be no doubt that the formation and the conduct of the ministry of the elder Pitt was governed by a superintending idea. And the evidence shows beyond doubt that the idea was one that was cherished by George III—indeed it was George's rather than Pitt's and George was the one who insisted that it should be kept in mind. It is even difficult to believe that George III, who showed so much anti-pathy to political connexions, failed to realise the way in which a non-party ministry, such as the one he envisaged at this time, would be calculated to add to the power of a monarch. The opposition quickly realised the implications of the system. And Sir Lewis Namier himself has shown the importance which party was to have in the development of our modern form of constitutional government.

One of the more recent works of the Namier school is the volume by Mr. John Brooke on *The Chatham Administration 1766–68*. It is part of the series which is being produced under the title "England in the Age of the American Revolution", and which, according to Sir Lewis Namier, is, in one aspect at least, "a co-operative undertaking" so that "the individuality of the col-laborators merges into that of the team".

It is not too much to say that Mr. Brooke falls into the trap which he has laid for himself. Catching the contemptuous attitude which seems to be characteristic of the school, he seeks to take a rise out of Edmund Burke. The latter, in his speech on American Taxation (*Works*, Vol. II, p. 420), had called attention to the peculiar character of the Chatham administration, and had written the following famous lines about its creator:

> He made an administration, so checkered and speckled; he put together a piece of joinery, so crossly indented and whimsically dovetailed; a cabinet so variously inlaid; such a piece of diversified mosaick . . . that it was, indeed, a very curious show; but utterly unsafe to touch, and unsure to stand on.

It is hardly possible to believe one's own eyes when one reads in the pages of Mr. Brooke that "Burke's description fits every Administration of the period". If it were possible to entertain the idea that Mr. Brooke is correct in so far as he is talking about the Chatham administration itself—which he is not—it would still be of the utmost relevance to say that he has at least misunderstood Burke himself. All the other administrations of the time were "checkered and speckled", says Mr. Brooke; but he means that all the other administrations were combinations of groups, unions of political parties. Burke was referring to the fact that Chatham's whole design was to extract individuals from their groups and combine them into a new kind of confederacy. If there were any doubt about this being the case Burke would have been guilty of wild absurdity in singling out the Chatham administration as a peculiar body. Mr. Brooke thinks that the Coalition of Fox and North in 1783 was a more "diversified piece of mosaic" than the Chatham administration. He plunges only the more deeply into error, for the Fox-North coalition may have been a more fantastic alliance between groups, but still it was a coalition of parties—it was not diversified in the particular way that Edmund Burke has in mind. And this means that Mr. Brooke has missed the structural character of that very Administration which it is primarily his purpose to study. It means that, when he uses the word "non-party", he merely thinks of it as meaning "all-party". It is rare to find an historian guilty of so great a structural error in regard to a topic on which he has conducted a detailed research—rare to find so great an incapacity to see the wood for the trees—especially where the earlier historiography of the subject had provided so many clues. Mr. Brooke illustrates to a supreme degree the tendency of the new methods to take the character, the contours, and the substantial shape out of history. We have seen the same fault in respect of his treatment of the Rockingham party—and these two large issues represent the main points of novelty in his book. Where his main picture is true it is not new. Where he chiefly differs from his predecessors, he is fundamentally wrong. And, sometimes, where he has learned from the texts to use the proper form of words, it is clear that he has taken the words too conventionally and failed to see the meaning they had at the time.

The point is one of a number on which an over-all decision will provide the means of deciding whether the Namier interpretation of narrative history (where it is a novel one) is true. It is worthy of note, therefore, that Mr. Brooke slides over three of the most important documents relative to the origin of the Chatham administration—he withholds altogether the strategic quotations which show the character of the ministry, and the policy of its founders. The documents in question exactly illustrate the point that ideas do have their place in politics—that men's notions and purposes in the establishment of a ministry are part of the complex of things which give that ministry its character. They are documents in which George III is explicitly insisting upon the distinctiveness of the principle on which the ministry is based.

When the King summoned Pitt on 7th July, 1766, he specifically expressed his attachment to the basic idea on which Pitt in the previous April had said that he would build an administration if ever he were called to the task. Pitt's declaration, which is not mentioned by Mr. Brooke, envisages a ministry which should be "independent of any personal connections whatsoever". In other words, both the King and Pitt agree with Burke that the ministry represents a special example of political combination—a collection of individuals and not an alliance of groups such as that which Mr. Brooke has in mind. And if it is argued that the words of George III and Pitt are on this occasion of no significance since they refer merely to ideas—here is the very point that is at issue in our discussion of the whole Namier method. Here lies the point of the criticism that the Namier school either omit or tend to slur over just those sections of the very documents they use which refer to ideas and purposes and conscious policy. If it is argued that ideas cannot be carried out in their absolute purity—that Pitt himself had to make his start with the remnants of the Rockinghamite ministry, and that even where he intended to negotiate with individuals he could not help negotiating in part also with groups—we must still beware of the temptation to imagine that the ideas have been lost or even that they have ceased to have any practical effect. It is George III himself who supplies the answer to the objection and who is determined not to let the basic idea of the Chatham administration drop out of sight. When, in December 1766, Chatham was negotiating for the accession of the Bedford Whigs, the King saw that this faction were stipulating rather for their accession as a party, and he objected to this procedure in terms which are unmistakable. He reminded Chatham that this "would at once overturn the very end proposed at the formation of the present administration". He described this end without the slightest ambiguity: "to rout out the present way of parties banding together".

There is more remarkable evidence than even this, however, and it is surprising to find that it is supplied by the Namier school itself—but the Namier school flogging dead horses like men in a day-dream, and again able to repeat the form of words without showing any realisation of their paradoxical significance. Pitt, when he was forming his administration, went further than Rockingham in accommodating the party of Lord Bute, but did not go far enough to satisfy Bute himself. Mr. Romney Sedgwick in the Introduction to *Letters from George III to Lord Bute* (p. lxvii) tells us that "when Bute complained that he and his party had been ignored by Pitt in forming the new government, George III apparently retorted by quoting Pitt to the effect that it was undesirable to form a government on a party basis". In fact, as we have seen, the idea of the non-party government was dearer to George than to Pitt himself, and was to be pressed by George even against Pitt at a later time. But that George should have pressed the idea against Bute himself, and that this very fact should have ended their relationship, as Mr. Sedgwick tells us on the next page, is a matter of perhaps even greater surprise. In a bitter letter of August 1766 (*ibid.*, p. 257), Bute writes to the King:

> I protest I could scarcely believe my eyes when I read this; is it possible you should not see the total difference between men setting up to be leaders of a party, for seditious or ambitious purposes, and me. . . . Now then what is Pitt's language[?] [He says] I will not take men that look up to the King himself, they must be mine and come as individuals; the Kings friends are Lord Bute's. . . . Poor Norton now feels the effects of it; he [said] he would serve the Minister [but that] his attachment was to the King and Lord Bute. . . . This gallant answer did his business before Your Majesty saw Mr. Pitt.

Even though Bute insisted that his party was no faction, but was merely the King's party, George III was prepared to see that it was made no exception to the rule. The King's Friends, when it came to the point, were not treated as civil servants; and perhaps George III had found in a non-party ideal a broader basis for a monarchy than any party, even a King's party. At any rate, Mr. Sedgwick tells us, this was the very issue which "ended the relationship".

The distinctive character of the Chatham administration affected its internal relations, as the earlier historiography of the subject has shown. Mr. Brooke's evidence does in fact confirm the earlier ideas about those relations; but once again he is not concerned to recover them and reconstruct the system. He has not followed those previous historians who rightly used contemporary satire, cartoons, propaganda and gossip, as well as the reports of foreign diplomats, to show how the ministry was regarded at the time. Neither has he brought evidence to correct the inferences which had been made from such sources by earlier historians. His evidence in fact confirms the former picture and fills it in, though he fails to reproduce the picture himself. If ideas and purposes had no part in politics one could certainly atomise everything and take the very shape out of history. But one must not marvel if the result is to reduce everybody— George III, the Rockinghamites and the Wilkites—to one dull level, in the manner that has already been noted.

Mr. Brooke is ready to tell us that when a political group has formed part of a ministry, and then that ministry has fallen, the group finds itself depleted and makes its exit in a maimed condition. The solidarity of the connexion is broken; for some of its members will remain behind to support the King and take part in the next administration. It is curious that, while he emphasises this point, he does not realise the tremendous relevance it has to Burke's *Thoughts on the Cause of the Present Discontents*. Apart from his attack on the very form of the Chatham administration (which, as the Duke of Richmond said, was based on the desire "to pick and cull from all quarters, and break all parties as much as possible"), Edmund Burke complained of the whole tendency of the new régime, which had had the effect of disintegrating political connexions. Mr. Brooke is in reality confirming the factual basis on which rested this important argument of the *Thoughts on the Cause of the Present Discontents*. The Chatham administration represented only the climax of a policy which had the effect of seducing men from their party allegiance. And George III shows that the effect was deliberately intended, and that the purpose of the Chatham administration lay precisely here. Hence the formula in which that king defined the stipulated objective: "to rout out the present way of parties banding together". The evidence of Burke combines with that of George III to show that Mr. Brooke is wrong—and is in fact too materialistic in his mode of judgment, too indifferent to the force of ideas—when he describes the Chatham ministry as only like the rest.

There is a further sense in which Mr. Brooke's narrative gives a remarkable revelation of the defects of the Namier method— the defects of a technique in which the historian so loses himself that he forgets things that exceed the realm of mere technique— he fails to achieve the comprehensiveness of a genuine historical vision. The Namier school have been curiously neglectful of London; yet London ought to occupy an important place in such a study as theirs. In 1741 there had already been published *An Historical Essay wherein the Example, Influence and Authority of Londoners in Publick Affairs are occasionally considered and compared*. That great population almost stood as a separate power in politics, almost ranked as a separate estate of the realm in itself. In its midst there had developed a political consciousness far ahead of anything that existed elsewhere in the country at that time. Mr. Brooke is deceived in his assumption that the politics of George III's reign can be studied without reference to the public opinion of the period. Whatever might be the condition of the rest of the country—which was awake by 1780—London had significance in this respect, and precisely because it was more advanced than other regions it had a disproportionate influence on events at Westminster. Sir Lewis Namier, as we have seen (p. 265 above) describes how the Duke of Newcastle followed the voice of public opinion when it was demonstrating against Bute. Mr. Brooke is prepared to make an oblique reference to the rise of radical politics in the capital; but it is curious that he should fail to examine this phenomenon. The political propaganda that was published, the power of Pitt over public opinion, and the vastly disproportionate importance of London, ought to have been sufficient to induce him to widen his whole view.

But this is not all. On the top of all this, Mr. Brooke has to deal with the return of John Wilkes, and with his activities in Middlesex, and his election to the House of Commons in the year 1768. Here is something like the introductory chapter to what we might call an epic of British politics—a subject which ought to stimulate the student of factions and groups, and ought to give pause to those who study "the structure of politics". When one reaches this point in the narrative, at least, it is important to widen one's grasp and see the political history in a comprehensive way. And at this point every student of history should be provided with a clue to the fact that a political movement of portentous significance has begun to show itself. Here politics must call for a different kind of analysis; there ought to be an imaginative apprehension of the great forces that were beginning to be manifest in the world. In this way the whole narrative requires to be raised to a level far above that of faction-fights and intrigues—ought to move more weightily like a writer who is embarking on a great theme. Here, where the research student is at his deadliest, we discover the limitations of any mere schooling in technique. And we see to perfection the way in which the Namier method can communicate to its practitioners something like an occupational disease. Dr. Owen in *The Rise of the Pelhams* (p. 34), is aware that he has been explaining the downfall of Walpole "from a purely mechanical point of view". This sense of limitation is the gateway to knowledge. But the historian is the last person in the world who should rest satisfied with the "purely mechanical point of view".

16. The King's Friends

THOSE OF us who have spent our lives in combat against "the Whig interpretation of history" may still be a little perturbed by the way in which the new school are treating their predecessors. Even in all this, they are setting their own work against that of defunct popularisers and text-book writers, with hardly a reference to the things that held the field in higher regions of scholarship till *The Structure of Politics* appeared. Yet, in a generation that is supposed to be scientific, they themselves resort to the very pattern of "Whig" device and fallacy, presenting the formula only in reverse. Over fifty years ago von Ruville suggested that the men who deserted their parties to follow the cause of the King might be regarded as "government servants". He made no more of this point, which is interesting in itself, but the Namier school have transformed the term a little, and prefer to say "civil servants". This latter designation is perhaps a less fortunate one, in that it carries more distinctively modern connotations into the eighteenth century. And here the disciples are not always as careful as their master who, in his most central work on "Monarchy and the Party System", refrains from using the term as a kind of nickname and makes all the distinctions that the case requires. In nothing is the new school more persistent than in its use of the term for polemical purposes—the exploitation of precisely the modern flavour that it carries. The King's Friends were not in fact "civil servants", though we may accept the view that they were like them in certain respects. There is a point at which the analogy is being over-pressed, and this is exactly the point at which it happens to serve a polemical intent. If these men had really been modern "civil servants" they would not have been in the House of Commons, and then the problem would not have arisen. They did in fact present an issue—one which it was easy to resolve as soon as they were excluded from the House of Commons. The Whigs were wrong in imagining that these men were an unconstitutional phenomenon in those days, in the way that they would be if they existed at the present time. But it is not permissible to short-circuit the question by giving the King's Friends a nickname less appropriate and more anachronistic than the one which they had in their own generation. And we are the victims of a conjuring-trick if, just because an anachronism has been waved in our faces, we allow ourselves to be persuaded that the Whigs had no right to oppose these men in their political role—no right to try to push the constitution in one direction rather than another for the future. This—the most famous of the formulations of the Namier school and the most reiterated of their clichés—is simply the Whig fallacy turned inside out.

17. Can History be too Mechanically Scientific?

SO FAR as the narrative history of George III's reign is concerned, Sir Lewis Namier, in his *England in the Age of the American Revolution*, and Mr. John Brooke, in its successor, *The Chatham Administration*, may be said to have added to the density of the evidence in favour of the older framework of narrative, the prevailing tradition of what might be called Tory interpretation. In respect of those mental transpositions which are regarded as necessary for the student of eighteenth-century politics—and which appear in the form of structural commentary in the two above-mentioned works and in Dr. Owen's book on *The Rise of the Pelhams*—we can say that some of the most strategic things are set out in beautiful formulas on pp. ix–x of Laprade's *Parliamentary Papers of John Robinson* (1922) and even to a considerable degree in the articles by Harold Temperley in 1909 and 1914. The work of Mr. Brooke and Dr. Owen confirms the suspicion that the Namier school are over-contemptuous in regard to their predecessors; and that, though they may be right in reacting against the earlier Whig historians, they have overlooked some excellent work that has intervened. Dr. Owen, dealing with the parliament of 1741–1747, gives an account of the general election of 1741 but this does not supersede the section on the same subject in Professor Vaucher's *Robert Walpole et la Politique de Fleury*, which appeared in 1924. He does not examine the strategic features and factors in the way that Vaucher did; though he is himself a wise historian in his admission that he is explaining things "from a purely mechanical point of view". Again, his analysis of the political role of Sir Robert Walpole follows the formula provided by Vaucher, though his expansion of the formula is a beautiful piece of exposition. He is unaware of the fact that Vaucher tracked down a mis-dating of a letter from Chesterfield to Dodington which he quotes. It is to be inferred, perhaps, therefore, that the withholding by members of this school of practically any acknowledgments to preceding historians is due to neglect rather than deliberation. Dr. Owen's book, especially when taken along with the treatise by Mr. Brooke, seems to confirm the view that, so far as political history is concerned, the work of the Namier school is shaking down into something less novel than was at one time claimed. Lord Waldegrave's portrait of George III, which, as we have seen, was so important in nineteenth-century historiography, is regarded by Sir Lewis Namier himself as "so penetrating and just that it deserves quoting almost in full". The effects of "structural analysis" on our interpretation of the actual narrative is in any case much less revolutionary if one sets it, not against the writings of the Whig historians, but against the scholarship of the period 1909 to 1924.

The new school may have been justified in reacting against a too ideological treatment of political history, as indeed of politics itself—an issue on which Sir Lewis Namier has had wiser things to say than perhaps any other historian of our time. But men like Adolphus, Croker, von Ruville, and—in some parts of his work—Winstanley, have managed to avoid much of the doctrinairism of the Whigs. The Whig interpretation, already declining before the beginning of the First World War, can hardly be revived again in its conventional form, unless it is produced with an unprecedented subtlety and originality of exposition. If there is to be a Whig interpretation in the future it is likely that it will possess a new shape, a new framework, altogether. And, in a sense, the Namier school may have provided the starting-point for this.

But the reaction against ideas—the reaction against the kind of history which is woven at least in part out of men's conscious aims and purposes—is a thing that may be carried too far. If we see in George III at the beginning of his reign only a bundle of contradictions, a restless succession of changing ends, all of them on the same level—and without any priorities amongst them— it is not the framework of the narrative that is being changed; we are merely asserting that the narrative possesses no framework at all. We are denying that amongst the data before us there is anything that gives shape and cohesion to the story, any sign that in George III and in other people there are profounder purposes, deeper continuities of aim and endeavour. If we do this in the case of the early years of George III's reign, there is no reason why we should not do it throughout history, turning the whole into "a tale told by an idiot". Historical research always uncovers a multiplicity of complications, a forest of intricate details, a host of qualifying facts and factors; but amongst these we must keep our heads, and over them it is necessary to exercise a presiding mind. Historical research may lead us to a scientific discovery when it forces us to see that some apparently unimportant event is the tiny pivot on which the larger course of history turns. It should not leave us desolate and bewildered in a land entirely without shapes and contours—leave us with the feeling that in fact there is no larger course of history, no theme that can turn one way or another. We exaggerate the role in human destiny of freakish chance and we make too much of the ironies of circumstance if we insist on the atomisation of the narrative, as though reason and purpose had no effect in the world. By having regard for the framework of ideas and conscious purposes which George III and everybody else possesses, the narrative acquires shape, acquires continuities. The historian is at least left with something meaningful to interpret.

It is even true that, in History if not in Nature, one can be too scientific, or rather one can be so mechanically scientific as to defeat the purposes of science itself. That is why sometimes the smell of a contemporary statesman who possesses a good nose may give the later historian something more significant than he will gain by the counting of heads. Finally, the nineteenth-century historians worked too exclusively on certain types of evidence—the type which turned one's attention perhaps too much to avowed political ideas and overt political controversies—but they did so out of necessity. We must not throw that kind of evidence overboard, and we must not lightly throw overboard all that earlier historiography of George III's reign which in Adolphus, Croker, Mahon and perhaps partly in Winstanley was dominated, save for a comparatively short period, by a Tory view, and again in von Ruville was at least anti-Whig.

INDEX

New Edinburgh Review, 80, 123, 125
North Briton, 44
North, Lord; administration of, 87,
97, 116–17, 198, 220, 237–8, 242–3,
262, 267, 277–81; and C. J. Fox,
286; and George III, 158, 267;
and the Rockinghamites, 269;
papers of, 87, 97, 134, 155–8

Oldfield, T. H. B., *History of
Boroughs*, 196
Opposition, before 1760, 53, 79;
under George III, 47, 53–4, 56, 64,
96, 102, 116–17, 245, 250, 257,
262–3; and the heir apparent, 53,
132, 174–5, 259–60
Owen, J. B., *The Rise of the Pelhams*,
205, 233, 235–6, 242, 248, 293, 296–7

Pares, Professor Richard, *George III
and the Politicians*, 254, 274
Paris, Treaty of, 47, 68, 103, 105, 113,
128, 138, 148, 171, 182, 186, 258
Parliament, 17, 26, 31, 52, 56, 79,
85–7, 113, 116–17, 144–5, 147, 149,
154, 173, 181–2, 189, 196–202,
204–5, 231–2, 238–9; *see also* Corruption *and* Elections
Parties, 54, 81, 85, 93, 96, 131–3, 168,
181, 185–6, 201, 219–21, 223–4,
235–6, 246, 257, 259–63, 270–2,
274; abolition of, 48, 52–6, 59, 67,
84, 92, 95–6, 105, 107, 110–11,
146–8, 150, 154, 157, 161–5, 173–4,
176–8, 217–18, 226, 230, 283–90;
see also under George III
"Patriot" Ideas, 52–3, 58–9, 67, 92,
190, 228–30, 234
"Patriot King", The, 58, 91, 106, 140,
154, 175, 228, 231–3
Pelham, Henry, 221–2, 233, 237, 249,
257
Phillimore, John George, *George III*,
155
Pitt, William, 1st Earl of Chatham;
personality, 100, 141–2, 174, 238,
263; and the Seven Years' War,

66, 142, 171, 177, 182, 207; resignation of, 42, 47, 50–1, 66, 68, 102,
148, 168, 182, 213–14; in opposition, 51, 54, 110–11, 156, 222–3,
237; his administration (1766–8),
142, 157, 264, 266–70, 283–91; and
party, 66–7, 95–6, 110–11, 164–5,
171, 177, 217, 270, 283–91; and
George II, 70, 80, 92, 95–6; and
Bute, 42, 51, 68, 102, 148, 171,
182–3, 186, 190, 213–14; *see also
under Chatham Correspondence, and*
George III
Pitt, William, the Younger, 166
Porritt, Edward, *The Unreformed
House of Commons*, 181, 197, 239
Prerogative, Royal, 64, 80–1, 83–5,
87–8, 92, 109–11, 114–16, 138, 141,
144–5, 148–9, 153, 165, 167, 173,
177–8, 232, 262–3

Quarterly Review, 77, 79, 97, 119, 122,
126, 129, 132–40, 142–3, 237

Ranke, L. von, 8, 215
Reform Bill, 91, 93, 120
Representation, Parliamentary, 85–6,
90–1, 137, 196–9, 201
Rigg, J. M., on "The King's Friends",
185–6, 190
Robinson, John, 198–200, 238–9,
277–281
Rockingham, 2nd Marquis of, 54, 98,
140, 220–3, 241, 268–9, 274–5
Rockingham Memoirs, 97–8, 100, 105–
106, 136, 140–1, 152, 179
Rockingham ministry (1765–6), 265–
270, 273, 288
Rockingham party, 54, 133, 168, 179,
185, 190, 220–4, 234, 246, 253,
263–6, 268–70, 272–4, 278, 287–8,
290
Rose, George, Rt. Hon., *Diaries and
Correspondence*, 64
Russell, Lord John, 98, 103–4, 136, 151
Ruville, Albert von, 171–7, 182, 190,
260, 294, 297, 299

St. Bartholomew, Massacre of, 21–2

Sandwich, 4th Earl of, 156–7

Sedgwick, Romney, *Letters from George III to Lord Bute*, 202, 253, 260, 289–90

Seven Years' War, 27, 47, 58, 66, 171, 182, 207

Smelt, Leonard, 229–30

Smyth, William, 69–72, 183

Stanhope, James, 1st Earl, 255–6

Stanhope, Philip Henry, 5th Earl, *see under* Mahon, Lord

Stone, Andrew, 74, 78, 125

Structural Analysis, History as, 79–82, 85–6, 131–3, 195–202, 204–9, 212, 261–4, 297

Temperley, Professor Harold, 182–5, 189, 236–8, 242, 296

Temple, 2nd Earl, 54, 182, 222, 263

Tilsit, 31–2, 35

Tories, 44, 52, 59, 79–80, 85, 96, 98, 110–12, 132, 141, 146, 150, 156–7, 163, 165, 178, 217–18, 262

Tory Interpretation, 61 ff., 83, 119 ff., 138, 161, 164, 184, 296, 299

Toryism, 92, 106, 109, 111, 114, 120, 131–133, 163

Trevelyan, Sir George Otto, 73, 166–168, 181, 239

Twiss, Horace, *The Public and Private Life of Lord Eldon*, 121

Vaucher, Paul, 251–2, 296–7

Waldegrave, 2nd Earl, 75–7, 80–1, 110, 122, 165, 188, 297

Wales, Dowager Princess of, 74, 76–8, 102, 109–10, 116, 140, 144, 167, 177

Walpole, Sir Robert, 66, 70, 90, 97, 123, 138, 140, 148, 150, 163, 183–5, 189, 221, 229, 232, 236–8, 251, 255, 257, 271, 293, 296

Walpole, Horace, 1st Baron, 124

Walpole, Horace, 90, 109, 122, 142, 210–11; letters, 22–3, 86, 97–8, 115–118, 131; *Memoirs of George II*, 75–76, 78, 122–6; *Memoirs of George III*, 22–3, 91, 97, 99, 106, 108–18, 124–131, 134–5, 144, 152–3, 165, 178, 217, 261–70

Whig ascendancy, 43, 45–8, 53, 56–9, 66–7, 84, 89, 92, 106–7, 137–8, 144–6, 150, 152, 154, 156–8, 173, 178, 180, 183, 188–90, 193–4, 233

Whiggism, 69, 70, 72, 99, 106, 109, 111, 131, 186, 210, 219–21, 262, 265

Whig historians, 7, 54, 73, 98, 133, 139–40, 143, 167, 193, 196, 205, 209, 228, 245, 252, 257, 270, 276, 297

Whig interpretation, 22, 69, 93, 98, 106, 119, 140, 150–1, 155, 160, 166, 169–72, 180–2, 195–6, 273–4, 294, 297

Whigs, 45, 53, 58–9, 79–80, 85, 96, 98, 109, 111–13, 116, 132, 141, 156, 165–6, 175, 185–7, 221–4, 239, 257–8, 262–4, 276–7; *see also under* Newcastle as party-leader, *and* Rockingham party

Whigs, alleged oligarchy of the, 43, 45, 49, 53, 56–7, 63–4, 66–7, 70, 72, 75, 83, 89, 90, 96, 103–5, 136–7, 139, 150, 156–8, 161–2, 176–7, 180, 184–5, 225–7, 236

Wilkes, John, 54, 100, 116, 141, 168, 215, 281, 290, 292

William III, 31, 74, 153, 237, 281

Williams, Professor Basil, 197

Winstanley, D. A., 182, 186–90, 193–4, 211, 214, 227, 244–6, 248, 297, 299

Wraxall, Sir Nathan, *Memoirs*, 121–2